BOOKS BY KEVIN STEIN

Private Poets, Worldly Acts

PUBLIC AND PRIVATE HISTORY
IN CONTEMPORARY
AMERICAN
POETRY

Kevin Stein

OHIO UNIVERSITY PRESS

ATHENS

01 00 99 98 97 96   5 4 3 2 1

Ohio University Press books are printed
on acid-free paper ∞

Library of Congress Cataloging-in-Publication Data

Stein, Kevin, 1954-
    Private poets, worldly acts : public and private history in
contemporary American poetry / Kevin Stein.
        p.   cm.
    Includes index.
    ISBN 0-8214-1163-2 (hardcover : alk. paper)
    1. American poetry—20th century—History and criticism.
    2. Literature and history—United States—History—20th century.
    3. Literature and society—United States—History—20th century.
    4. Modernism (Literature)—United States. 5. Group identity in
literature. 6. Community in literature. 7. Self in literature.
    I. Title.
PS310.H57S74   1996
811'.509358—dc20   96-13263
                                                            CIP

Designed by Laury A. Egan
Type composed in Berner Book by Professional Book Compositors

For Deb, again

CONTENTS

Acknowledgments

When curiosity led me down yet another promising but briared path—and simple stubbornness proved to be insufficient to the task—I was fortunate to have a score of friends kind enough to consider my dilemma. More than once, their suggestions offered direction toward some necessary destination. If I failed to arrive, the fault is all mine. Chief among those who helped is Roger Mitchell, whose advice deepened my understanding of the issue. Michael Greene was as generous with his insight as with his books, and James Ballowe aided me by questioning easy assumptions. I'm grateful to poets Dean Young, Keith Ratzlaff, and Tony Hoagland, whose remarks often instigated and encouraged my study. Thanks are also due Bradley University, especially Margaret Carter and Claire Etaugh who gave me time to pursue this book. Lastly, I'm thankful for the unwavering support of my wife, Deb, without whom this project would have been impossibly ponderous.

Some of these chapters, in various disguises, originally appeared elsewhere. Thus several editors are due thanks for their interest in these essays. Jim Elledge included, "'Everything the Opposite': A Literary Basis for the Anti-literary in Frank O'Hara's *Lunch Poems*," in the *Under Discussion* series anthology, *Frank O'Hara: To Be True to a City* (Ann Arbor: University of Michigan Press, 1990). Arthur Vogelsang printed "'A Dark River of Labor': Work and Workers in James Wright's Poetry," in *The American Poetry Review* 22 (November/December 1993). Richard Burgin published "Why 'Nothing is Past': Philip Levine's Conversation with History," in *Boulevard* 25 and 26 (Spring 1994). Rie Fortenberry sought out "Lives in Motion: Multiple Perspectives in Rita Dove's Poetry" for *Mississippi Review* 23, Number 3 (1995). Finally, Mary Heath accepted "Vietnam and the 'Voice Within': Yusef Komunyakaa's *Dien Cai Dau*" for *Massachusetts Review* (Winter 1995) and Kostas Myrsiades published "Manipulating Cultural Assumptions: Transgression and Obedience in David Wojahn's Rock 'n' Roll Sonnets" in the June 1996 issue of *College Literature*.

The following authors and publishers have granted permission to reprint selections which appear in this book:

Reprinted by permission of Farrar, Straus, & Giroux, Inc. Selections from *History* by Robert Lowell. Copyright © 1973 by Robert Lowell. Selections from *Selected Poems* by Robert Lowell. Copyright © 1977 by Robert Lowell. Selection from *To a Blossoming Pear Tree* by James Wright. Copyright © 1977 by James Wright.

Reprinted by permission of Faber and Faber Ltd. Selections from *Life Studies* by Robert Lowell. Copyright © 1959 by Robert Lowell. Selections from *For the Union Dead* by Robert Lowell. Copyright © 1964 by Robert Lowell. Selections from *History* by Robert Lowell. Copyright © 1973 by Robert Lowell.

Reprinted from *The Fact of a Door Frame: Poems Selected and New, 1950–1984,* by Adrienne Rich, by permission of the author and W. W. Norton & Company, Inc. Copyright © 1984 by Adrienne Rich. Copyright © 1975, 1978, by W. W. Norton & Company, Inc. Copyright © 1981 by Adrienne Rich.

Selections reprinted from *Lunch Poems* by Frank O'Hara, by permission of City Lights Books. Copyright © 1964 by Frank O'Hara.

"Whose Language" by Charles Bernstein from *Rough Trades* (Sun & Moon), used by permission of the author.

"The Continental Can Company at Six O'Clock," excerpts from "People are Sick of Pretending that They Love the Boss" and "On the Foreclosure of a Mortgage in the Suburbs" by James Wright. Reprinted by permission of Anne Wright.

"Autumn Begins in Martins Ferry, Ohio," from *The Branch Will Not Break,* © 1963 by James Wright. "Willy Lyons," "The Minneapolis Poem," "Two Postures Beside a Fire" from *Shall We Gather at the River* © 1968 by James Wright, Wesleyan University Press by permission of University Press of New England.

Excerpts from *Two Citizens* by James Wright. Copyright © 1970, 1971, 1972, by James Wright, © 1986 by Anne Wright, executrix of the Estate of James Wright. Reprinted by permission of Anne Wright.

"Honey," "A Finch Sitting Out a Wind Storm," and "The Sumac in Ohio" from *This Journey* by James Wright. Copyright © 1977, 1978, 1979, 1980, 1981, 1982 by Anne Wright, executrix of the Estate of James Wright. Reprinted by permission of Random House, Inc.

Excerpt from "Bells for John Whiteside's Daughter," from *Selected Poems* by John Crowe Ransom. Copyright © 1924 by Alfred A. Knopf, Inc. and renewed 1952 by John Crowe Ransom. Reprinted by permission of the publisher.

Excerpt from "The Present," from *Sweet Will* by Philip Levine, published by Atheneum. Copyright © 1985 by Philip Levine. Used by permission of the author.

Excerpt reprinted from *A Walk with Tom Jefferson* by Philip Levine, by permission of author and Alfred A. Knopf, Inc. Copyright © 1980, 1983, 1984, 1986, 1987, 1988 by Philip Levine.

Selections reprinted from *What Work Is* by Philip Levine, by permission of author and Alfred A. Knopf, Inc. Copyright © 1991 by Philip Levine.

Selection reprinted from *The Simple Truth,* by Philip Levine, by permission of the author and Alfred A. Knopf, Inc. Copyright © 1994 by Philip Levine.

Yusef Komunyakaa excerpts from "The Dead at Quang Tri," "Starlight Scope Myopia," "Re-creating the Scene," "Tu Do Street," "The One-legged Stool," "Report from the Skull's Diorama," "Communique," "Eyeball Television," "Seeing in the Dark," "Jungle Surrender," "Facing It" from *Dien Cai Dau,* copyright © 1988 by Yusef Komunyakaa, by permission of Wesleyan University Press and University Press of New England.

Selections reprinted from *Selected Poems* (Pantheon/Vintage) by Rita Dove, copyright © 1993 by Rita Dove, and *Grace Notes* (W. W. Norton) by Rita Dove, copyright © 1989 by Rita Dove. Quotes from Rita Dove's poems by permission of the author.

"Matins: James Brown and His Fabulous Flames Tour the South, 1958," "The Assassination of Robert Goulet as Performed by Elvis Presley: Memphis, 1968," "Photographer at Altamont: The Morning After, 1969," and excerpts from "W. C. W. Watching Presley's Second Performance on 'The Ed Sullivan Show,' Mercy Hospital, Newark, 1956," "Necromancy: The Last Days of Brian Jones, 1968," "At Graceland with a Six Year Old, 1985" "Homage: Light from the Hall," "Malcolm McClaren Signs the Sex Pistols, London, 1976," and "'It's Only Rock and Roll But I Like It': The Fall of Saigon, 1975" from *Mystery Train* by David Wojahn, copyright © 1990. Reprinted by permission of the University of Pittsburgh Press.

Selections from *The Angel of History* by Carolyn Forché, copyright © 1994 Carolyn Forché. Reprinted by permission of HarperCollins Publishers, Inc. Excerpt from "Return," from *The Country Between Us* by Carolyn Forché. Copyright © 1980 by Carolyn Forché. Reprinted by permission of HarperCollins Publishers, Inc. Excerpt from "San Onofre, California," from *The Country Between Us* by Carolyn Forché. Copyright © 1978 by Carolyn Forché.

Reprinted by permission of HarperCollins Publishers, Inc. "The Colonel," from *The Country Between Us* by Carolyn Forché. Copyright © 1981 by Carolyn Forché. Reprinted by permission Harper-Collins Publishers, Inc. Excerpt from "The Memory of Elena," from *The Country Between Us* by Carolyn Forché. Copyright © 1977 by Carolyn Forché. Reprinted by permission of HarperCollins Publishers, Inc.

Excerpt from "Fractal Diffusion" by Christopher Dewdney, from *The L-A-N-G-U-A-G-E Book* (Southern Illinois University Press), used by permission of the author.

Preface

This book examines a diverse group of American poets who have labored under the remnants of a Modernist tradition that encouraged them to turn their backs on larger historical forces—poets who struggled, some over decades, others more recently, to reconnect themselves and their work to those same forces. As a result, the book focuses on poets who have located the intersection of private and public history in their lives and art, and thus on the aesthetic and social dynamics operating there. It is my contention that these poets have, by emphasizing the communal responsibilities of a deeply personal art, demonstrated an awareness of poetry's social and public functions ignored by much of twentieth-century American poetry. Doing so, they have engaged in the kind of worldly acts for which this book is named. Their work promises not only to enliven the art form but also to broaden poetry's supposedly dwindling audience.

It seems sensible, early on, to indicate what I mean by history. I have in mind something like Martin Heidegger's "Historie"—so-called objective history, what is "recorded" and thus chronicles the rise and fall of nations and peoples, the history of their wars and governments, the largescale workings of civilization and culture. This is what Heidegger referred to roughly as a "science" of history. Admittedly, I have expanded the definition to include subjects as various as rock 'n' roll's popular culture and issues of class and race. Against that background, I have implicitly, and occasionally explicitly, juxtaposed Heidegger's "Geschichte," an individual's inward and "authentic" sense of history, the immediate experience of being-in-the-world. Working from these definitions, this book's introduction argues that history and poetry are complementary forms of art, owing in actuality more to interpretation and intuition than to elusive notions of objectivity. There I also trace twentieth-century American poetry's general avoidance of public history as chosen subject matter.

My decision to focus the book's first half primarily on those poets coming of age in the early 1960s has, I realize, both merit and limitation outside the fundamental reality that space is simply not available to discuss every poet I'd like to. First the limitation. It means the necessary exclusion of a number of poets whose work bears to some degree on my subject, particularly William Carlos Williams. Now the merits. Starting at that point enables me to look closely at poets intoxicated by the heady influence of both High Modernism and its heir, the New Criticism, and yet poets on the cusp of something new and rebellious. Encountering at once Modernism's doctrine of Impersonalism and New Criticism's dogma of intellectual rigor slammed these poets with the proverbial aesthetic double whammy. That is to say, these poets were acutely aware of another kind of history, *literary* history, and their varied reactions to its pressures prove enlightening. This study begins with two poets confronting the vestiges of Modernism and New Criticism, poets who sought in different ways to bring historical matters to bear in their writing. Looking at the work of one poet older than Frank O'Hara—Robert Lowell—and one roughly his age—Adrienne Rich —establishes an aesthetic context for O'Hara's 1964 publication of *Lunch Poems* and also reveals how poets with quite different aesthetics deal with the convergence of the personal and communal. Despite the ostensibly disparate nature of their work, Lowell and Rich share a fundamentally active conception of poets' private relationship to the larger forces of public history and culture. Both believe history inscripts our lives in subtle and manifest ways. Both recognize the necessity of understanding history—the need, as Lowell suggests, to "live with what was here" and the obligation to speak of it.

One response to the pressures of living with history is, as Frank O'Hara's work demonstrates, to celebrate the Self as subject and the minutiae of one's daily life—in essence, to esteem individual experience. But, as Chapter Two indicates, O'Hara understood the literary basis for doing "everything the opposite," and his use of the era's collective history ("Khrushchev is coming on the right day!") only serves to underscore the nature of his aesthetic and personal rebellion.

James Wright provides another case, one made more poignant by the fact that, of all so-called Deep Image poets, Wright most notably displays a social consciousness. Born and raised in the factory town of Martins Ferry, Ohio, Wright works tenaciously to establish meaningful communion between himself and that region and those industrial workers he left behind. Philip Levine, on the other hand, quickly developed a "conversation," as Hans-Georg Gadamer would suggest, with history's vanquished or forgotten. The continuity of that conversation throughout Levine's career attests to the political and social contexts of his poetry, as Chapter Four makes evident.

The last half of the book is devoted to four poets who came of age in the 1980s, twenty years after O'Hara, Rich, Wright, and Levine, and thus twenty years further distant from Modernism, New Criticism, and the Deep Image. Certainly, they represent a group more diverse in race and gender than the first gathering, a fact which reflects the increasingly pluralistic nature of American poetry. Likewise, their poetry's relationship with history is equally varied. Yusef Komunyakaa offers an African-American perspective on the Vietnam War through his own experiences as a soldier, speaking from the margins of both race and official history. David Wojahn's series of rock 'n' roll sonnets evokes the pathos and self-destructiveness of the rock era, all the while playing upon the perceived tension between his sleazy subject matter and the sonnet's heightened form. Through her use of multiple perspectives, Rita Dove reveals the unreliability of history, whether social or familial, answering history's indeterminacy with poetic imagination. The book's final chapter closes this dialogue: If O'Hara represents the full expression of personal and apolitical poetry, Carolyn Forché embodies its diametric opposite—a poet for whom private acts, and thus poems, are ultimately communal and ethical.

My critical approach to these writers is admittedly eclectic, drawing from sources as various as *Sports Illustrated* and Wittgenstein's *Tractatus*. It reflects, perhaps, for good or ill, a poet's manner of reading other poets. What remains constant is an insistence on using sensible critical, theoretical, and cultural sources to illuminate a poet's work, on asking why and how to situate the poetry in the vital intersection of private and public history. In short, I have sought a humane practical criticism. If I believe that words matter in a poem, that they mean things, I also believe asking how and why words obtain those meanings—and for whom—offers an immensely compelling area of study. That process is inextricably social and aesthetic.

Finally, because the book's purpose is more to be suggestive rather than exhaustive of the subject, no doubt I have omitted a number of poets whose work would be appropriate for this study. A partial list would surely include Charles Olson, W. S. Merwin, and Elizabeth Bishop of the older generation, and William Matthews, Andrew Hudgins, and Lynn Emanuel of the younger crowd. My point is that the subject—a big one, casting an even bigger shadow—has been sorely neglected. Which means, of course, that there's much left for others to say, a dialogue this book is meant to welcome and encourage.

Private Poets, Worldly Acts

Introduction

Worldly Acts

History and Twentieth-Century American Poetry

> Historical sense and poetic sense should not, in the end, be contradictory, for if poetry is the little myth we make, history is the big myth we live, and in our living, constantly remake.
> —Robert Penn Warren
> *Brother to Dragons* (1979)

It is easy to overlook the radical nature of Robert Penn Warren's above remark, if only because Warren has come to be seen as a genteel and reasonable man, not the likely advocate of wild poetic feastings, a stirrer of the great black pot of aesthetic debate. Still, Warren's subtle equating of poetry and history would strike many twentieth-century American poets as foolish or naive, especially if the "History" he refers to comes with a capital "H" and thus implies the larger workings of culture beyond the hermetic impulse of poets to express their peculiar personal history, as we shall see later in this chapter. Warren's remark reveals that he's willing to dispute the apparently "contradictory" nature of historical and poetic writing, at least as viewed by some theorists and practitioners of both forms. The distinction is an ancient one, traceable to the work of Herodotus, the "father of history." It goes like this: on one hand, history is regarded as a science in which the historian discovers "facts" (about an historical personage or event) en route to "objective" truth. On the other, poetry is considered an art in which the poet, no matter the subject, intuits, imagines, and creates "subjective" truth. Warren will have none of it. Implicitly, he equates these forms of "truth," suggesting that both share myth's power to inform and invigorate our lives, and suggesting as well that both are susceptible to the human will to "remake" or alter them.

Warren's conjoining of the aesthetics of history and poetry flies in the face of the dominant western notion of history. Since the time of Herodotus and Thucydides, the west has been heir to the conviction that historical study can—and must—be scientific. As R. G. Collingwood argues in his landmark study, *The Idea of History* (1956), Herodotus first moved Greek history away from a mixture of legend and theocracy toward a "scientific" history.[1] He did so by asking questions of those who witnessed or participated in memorable events of the recent past, his only viable source for historical accounts. Herodotus rejected hearsay or legend, and critically challenged his eyewitnesses' recollections. To this insistence on asking questions, rather than accepting legend, Collingwood ascribes the beginnings of historical study that is "scientific," "humanistic," "rational," and "self-revelatory."[2] To Herodotus goes the honor, or the blame, depending on one's camp, of initiating historical study as a science producing supposedly objective results.

Against such fastidious distinctions, Warren's poetic work manifests his belief in the complementary rather than contradictory nature of the two forms. His poetry collections *Brother to Dragons* (1953 and 1979), *Audubon: A Vision* (1969), and *Chief Joseph of the Nez Perce* (1982) (not to mention his historically based novels such as *All the King's Men*) demonstrate that he understands quite well the symbiotic relationship between history and poetry. *Brother to Dragons,* for example, traces the new life of Colonel Charles Lewis and his family, including slaves, after their move from Virginia to set up residence in western Kentucky. Colonel Lewis had married Lucy Jefferson, the sister of Virginia statesman and United States President Thomas Jefferson, and the book-length poem details the family's tribulations as they encounter what Warren calls "evil days." Though Warren freely admits to "tampering with non-essential facts," he steadfastly maintains: "poetry is more than fantasy and is committed to the obligation of trying to say something, however obliquely, about the human condition. Therefore, a poem dealing with history is no more at liberty to violate what the writer takes to be the spirit of his history than it is at liberty to violate what he takes to be the nature of the human heart. What he takes those things to be is, of course, his ultimate gamble."[3] Warren's comments are curious for reasons which bear largely upon our discussion. While he suggests the need for the poet's keeping to the facts of an historical incident and the nature of the human heart, he also acknowledges how such a gesture amounts to a fundamental act of interpretation. Through the interpretive discerning of "what he takes to be" the "spirit" of history and the "nature" of the human heart, the poet as well as the historian reaches toward "truth." It is precisely this "gamble" which both share—and the "gamble" historiographers have made much of.

Recent Theories of History As Art

Warren's work exemplifies Benedetto Croce's attitude toward the issue of historicity. Historicity, Croce argues, is not a matter of "form but content: as form it is nothing but intuition or aesthetic fact."[4] Croce believes history and literary art operate according to similar principles. Each "posits intuitions" instead of objective truths, each rejects induction and deduction in favor of narrative, and each functions in the "domain of art" Croce describes as the "this and here," what he calls the *individuum omninode determinatum.*"[5]

In a nutshell, I suggest history, like art, is a *made* thing. That making lies not so much in a person's actions or an event's details but in the *interpretation* of the same. Though perhaps troubling to fervent believers in objectivity, the commentator's perspective, selection, ordering, and presentation of these events contribute as much (if not more) to the making of history as do the actions of those involved—which, of course, puts new spin on our culture's casual reference to someone's achievements as "history making." This realization has disabused many historiographers of Leopold Ranke's conception of the historian's "objective eye" which carefully records a chronicle of "what actually happened." Most agree with Hayden White that an "irreducible and inexpungeable element of interpretation" marks every historical account we had previously been prone, perhaps blithely, to consider stolidly scientific and thus objective.[6] In *Tropics of Discourse,* White forcefully debunks the notion that only in history do "art and science meet in harmonious synthesis," arguing instead that history has earned its "expulsion" from the "first rank of the sciences" because of its absolute dependence on interpretation.[7]

History's loss of status as science is no cause to mourn, however. White asserts that historians' use of the "trope" and narrative strategies common to literary art makes history living and valuable, capable of speaking of the past in meaningful ways to the present and future. It is, in fact, this emphasis on narrative and storytelling that predicates history's role in our culture. History is mostly narrative, mostly story, and thus, to reduce the issue to its simplest terms, history is literature. White postulates that historians rely heavily on forms germane to literature—not only the conception of a story to be told but also the manner of its telling, its "plot": "just as there can be no explanation in history without a story, so too there can be no story without a plot by which to make of it a story of a particular kind."[8] Historians interpret in this fashion by choosing an overall plot strategy by which to order their accounts—common literary narrative forms such as tragedy, farce, comedy, satire, etc. This act of interpretation offers historians, much as it does writers, a structured form to work within as well as a form recognizable to their readers.

What I am getting at is this. Historical accounts, though bound in time by a chronology of dates—perhaps their sole objective aspect— owe much to matters of intuition and interpretation which we normally associate with literature. What differentiates, then, a poem about an event and an historical account of the same event? Objectivity, perhaps? Not if the very issue of objectivity lies in dispute. Moreover, if each merely "posits intuitions" about the causes and repercussions of a particular historical incident, what makes one more reliable than the other? In this regard, Roland Barthes launches his own attack on the vaunted objectivity of traditional historiography, asking: "Does the narration of past events, which, in our culture from the time of the Greeks onwards, has generally been subject to the sanction of historical 'science,' bound to the underlying standard of the 'real,' and justified by the principles of 'rational' exposition—does this form of narration really differ, in some specific trait, in some indubitably distinctive feature, from imaginary narration, as we find it in the epic, the novel, and the drama?"[9]

Barthes suggests that historical accounts are, like literary works, constructed from fragments of experience, bits and pieces cobbled together to make a "unified" whole. Much like poets who must deal with the multiplicity of ideas, emotions, and details inhering within a specific event, historians "choose, sever, and carve them up," as Claude Lévi-Strauss puts it, in order to overcome the "chaos" which a "truly total history" would present to author and reader alike.[10] Looping together a series of such historical accounts, as, for example, a poet writing of his experiences in the Vietnam War might do, makes the historian's task something approaching myth. The will to be inclusive, mitigated by the necessity to "carve" and "sever," gives historical writing the elliptical quality of poetry, where what is left out looms as large as what remains. In addition, the architecture of myth, where one spoken thing speaks for multitudes left silent, offers the work an aesthetic scaffolding which grows more ponderous with each decision to include or omit. Northrup Frye sums up the situation quite nicely: "We notice that when an historian's scheme gets to a certain point of comprehensiveness it becomes mythical in shape and so approaches the poetic in its structure."[11]

This muting of the distinction between historical writings and literary art forms (particularly poetry) led several others before Croce to similar conclusions regarding the aesthetic basis of history. Hegel, for instance, regards history-writing as a version of prose poetry, a task sharing poetry's aim and form and differing mainly in its emphasis on the "prosaic" events of day to day living. Although history is not "free"—bound as it is to "facts" and events related in documents—Hegel believes the writing of history to have much in common with principles governing the writing of drama, especially tragedy.[12] Likewise, Nietzsche in *The Use and Abuse of History* (1874) treats history as the proper domain of the artist, ideally the dramatist, who is able "to think one thing with another, and weave the elements into a single whole, with the presumption that the unity of plan must be put into the objects if it be not already there."[13] This is the artist's "objectivity," his "powerful and spontaneous creation," which amounts to "'composition' in its highest form."[14] Far from devaluing historical writing by its refusal of what we usually conceive of as objectivity, such artistic "objectivity" grants the author the "internal flame" necessary to turn cold facts into the kind of history that arouses its readers to action instead of passivity in the face of the great deeds of the past.[15] Nietzsche thus questions not only the possibility but also the value of traditional notions of objectivity in historical writing. Requiring a bland objectivity of the history writer presumes a lack of personality that, if attained, thoroughly invalidates his account. Nietzsche proposes, on the contrary, "a kind of historical writing that had no drop of common fact in it and yet could claim to be called in the highest degree objective."[16]

Nietzsche viewed history as something to be "seriously hated" if it merely paraded the accomplishments of the past before the eyes of stunned readers and left them with a feeling of having been born too late, well after the store of splendid human acts had been sorely depleted.[17] Such belief would leave readers averse to or incapable of the heroic action Nietzsche so highly valued. Worse yet, such behavior, carried out under the scurrilous guise of "objectivity," makes historians "a race of eunuchs" assigned to "guard the historical harem of the world."[18] Thus, historical writing, written in vain search for objectivity, creates in its readers a state of stunned passivity and isolation from the vitality of their own lives.

One sure source of that feeling can be found in the common mode of conventional histories, which, as Fernand Braudel contends, often focus on the "intercrossing of . . . exceptional destinies," the great acts of heroes who seem very much unlike the rest of us, the common herd. Confronted by the deeds of these "exceptional beings," we are made to feel ineffectual, left to swoon at our own inadequacy in the face of those who seem the "masters of their fate and even more of ours."[19]

The idea that history might be a debilitating burden rather than a generative force has occurred to modern critics of literary history as well. Harold Bloom and Walter Jackson Bate argue that poets are particularly susceptible to such feelings of inadequacy when comparing their own work to that of noted precursors. Bate reduces to simplest form the question facing poets building what he calls, after Dryden, the Second Temple: "What is there left to do?" Bloom believes poets are often struck dumb by the notion that they might be—in Nietzsche's term—a "latecomer" in the world, courting a Muse whose affections (and whose gifts) have been passed to scores of others before them.[20] Their words are thus not their words only, but merely the echoes of those who spoke before, or the bitter, unwanted leftovers of a feast long since devolved to the murmurings of the sated.

There is, however, a lively alternative, a means by which to reconnect both writer and reader to the currents of public history that surge through their personal lives. That lively and redemptive alternative, I contend, can be found in recent American poetry, much of it the subject of this study, poetry which operates in the intersection of private and public history, poetry that welcomes its social function.

This poetry serves to amend the ranklings of history Michel Foucault describes in unsettling terms: "The history that bears and determines us has the form of a war rather than that of a language; relations of power, not relations of history."[21] For Foucault, what is left out of history through the feverish workings of power, what is either thoughtlessly omitted or purposely eviscerated, provides the most meaningful area of historical study.[22] As his *The Archaeology of Knowledge* attests, Foucault frequently shuns the conventional interests of traditional history, its emphasis on sources, influences, and continuities. Foucault is often much more devoted to history's "discontinuities," its "ruptures," and "disjunctions." Recognizing these ruptures, several American poets have labored to fill these gaps with accounts of those people and events omitted from the "official" history. This book's table of contents provides a list of recent poets who do just that, someone like James Wright, for example, who carves a history of work and workers in the Ohio River Valley in the tough bark of a native sumac tree.

This poetry connects both poet and reader more intimately to the flow of historical events that would otherwise seem to be the workings of an exclusive band of "exceptional" heroes. If this is indeed the case, why have so many twentieth-century American writers largely segregated their work from historical concerns? Hayden White remarks that twentieth-century literature has manifested a "hostility toward the historical consciousness even more marked than anything found in the scientific thought of our time."[23] He cites the work of Gide, Ibsen, Thomas Mann, Camus, Sartre, and Albee—novelists and playwrights—who have used their characters as means of castigating or poking fun at historians and theories of history. The case is somewhat different for much of twentieth-century American poetry. Many of our poets have shown their disregard for historical matters simply by their silence, as if ignoring history were the sharpest insult.

History and Twentieth-Century American Poetry

Twentieth-century American poets have generally run in fear of history. After all, the century's poetry has been influenced in succession by groups of poets whose aesthetics urged them to turn their backs on historical realities. Notable exceptions include Langston Hughes' poems of racial identity and politics, W. C. Williams' *Paterson,* much of Charles Olson's and Robert Lowell's work, the social consciousness of the Beats, and the recent work of a number of Feminist poets, Adrienne Rich in particular. Still, the shifting course of this century's poetic mainstream has remained fairly static in one regard: its careful avoidance of public history. What brought American poetry to this curious state in the first place?

At the turn of the century, Modernist poets, confronted with both the shock of World War I and the insufficiency of Victorian moral order as means to deal with such horror, abandoned the collapsing social order and replaced it with their own aestheticized version. T. S. Eliot's "Tradition and the Individual Talent," in fact, argued that the proper basis for understanding poets and poems resided not within the context of historical or social forces but within the insular realm of poetry. A poem gained context and meaning solely through its relationship to other poems. The work of most Moderns became, at best, a private code that simply would not admit world or reader. No matter. Ezra Pound announced with aplomb that "the public is stupid," and thus began the elitism that segregated poetry from its communal functions. "Make it new," Pound urged, implying in that well chosen "it," that if one could not remake the self one could at least reinvent one's mode of self-expression. Pound spoke with brutal frankness for a generation of poets for whom ours was a "botched civilization," a hopeless "old bitch gone in the teeth," as he declared in "Hugh Selwyn Mauberly." Given that, it's no surprise that Modernists charted another course, one gesturing off the then-current page of social and literary history, mapping a different if not antagonistic relationship to present realities, as Graham Hough argues: "For the most part . . . the poets have refused the great public mythologies of our time, and have evolved rival myths of their own, some grandiose and comprehensive, some esoteric and private, but none with any status in the world of organized scientific and historical knowledge by which the world conducts its business."[24]

Which is just the point, as Roger Mitchell suggests in "Modernism Comes to American Poetry," asserting that the "pressure under which the Modernists wrote would have made any thinking person question" the current realm of "scientific and historical knowledge."[25] This is, of course, the same knowledge base by which the world had found its way to the machine gun, mustard gas, and the tank—thus to a frightening perfection in forms of mass and anonymous destruction. While Mitchell argues persuasively that Modernists "gave us strategies of perception and criticism which continue to be valid" and generally "lit up the body of the world in ways we are still learning from," he also offers this cogent summary of the Modernist attitude to history: "Pound believed, and his *Cantos* show, that history was a random succession of periods of enlightenment and darkness. Eliot ridiculed Emerson's hopeful view of history in "Sweeney Erect." Stevens seemed unaware of history. Williams and H. D. had to invent their own eclectic versions of it. Perhaps these are assorted ways of giving up on history. . . ."[26]

So much depends, as Williams might put it, on "giving up on history." Much of Modernism was rooted in this sense of fractured history, fragmentation so pernicious and debilitating that one was thrown back upon the self, itself fractured and vertiginous, and thus upon the ultimate isolation of the individual. In fact, Irving Howe contends in "The Idea of the Modern," that the whole *idea* of the modern revolves around isolation, individuals feeling unmoored and alone, separated not only from each other but also from the structures of government, religion, and philosophy which had given meaning and order to their lives.[27] No wonder that those poets most influential after the Moderns, the New Critics, led what Walter Sutton has called a "conservative counter-revolution" in American poetry.[28] They ignored Eliot's Symbolist-inspired verse and instead focused on his respect for "tradition," his call for an impersonal poetry attained through a systematic "extinction of personality," and his revaluing of the metaphysical tradition in poetry. Why not? Such an aesthetic purchased a return to order, even if it exacted the heavy price of a concerted flight from history. The exodus to pre-Charles I England brought with it an enviably more unified world view, preceding, as it did, the Puritan revolt and its religious and political upheavals, the onslaught of the industrial age, and the horrors of world war. Like the Moderns, the New Critics were nostalgic for an authoritarian and hierarchical rule of order. Much of that nostalgia is present in the Fugitive poets' embracing of the Genteel Tradition and Agrarian ideology, a movement culminating in the manifesto *I'll Take My Stand* (1930), in which twelve Southerners glance back with longing to a preindustrial, moral, and strongly Christian society embodied by the South. One of the New Criticism's most familiar poems, John Crowe Ransom's "Bells for John Whiteside's Daughter," exhibits this nostalgia as well as any poem of the period. Here even the geese the dead girl used to chase about have enough sense to mourn her passing:

> The lazy geese, like a snow cloud
> Dripping their snow on the green grass,
> Tricking and stopping, sleepy and proud,
> Who cried in goose, Alas,
>
> For the tireless heart within the little
> Lady with rod that made them rise
> From their noon apple-dreams, and scuttle,
> Goose-fashion under the skies!

What can be regarded as the most historically engaged poem of the New Critical era, Allen Tate's "Ode to the Confederate Dead," further illustrates the individual's isolation from both the past and an unsatisfying present. Standing at the gate of a Confederate graveyard, the poem's main figure is trapped between the vestige of this heroic past and the befuddling chaos of the moment. Tate contends, in his essay "Narcissus as Narcissus," that the "poem is 'about' solipsism . . . the failure of human personality to function objectively in nature and society."[29] More revealingly, Tate later suggests that the expansive subject of the poem is not exclusively Agrarian or Southern, but instead an evocation of "the cut-offness of the modern 'intellectual man' from the world."[30] If anything, history thus serves to remind us that we're pitifully estranged from our social, political, and aesthetic present.

When the New Critics "fled from Imagism and Chicago," as George Williamson describes it, "into the metaphysical seventeenth century," they escaped chaos and thus reasserted lines of social governance and religious belief seemingly severed by the present culture.[31] Despite the fact Cleanth Brooks insisted that poets needed all the help from historians that they could muster, few poets associated with the New Criticism took his advice. It wasn't until the appearance and tragically short life of Frank Stanford (1948–78) that the Old South had a poet who relentlessly challenged its cultural and social bastions. Further, when Ransom, in *The World's Body*, fervently raised "aesthetic forms that do not serve the principle of utility" above the larger realm of communal life, he was simply codifying poetry's special place outside of, perhaps beyond, temporal matters of history.[32] Poetry was *from* this world but not *of* it, operating, as art must, according to eternal rules. Still, in an attempt to defend poetic mystery against the encroachment of scientific positivism, New Critics concocted an elaborate critical language of "tension," "irony," "paradox"—walling off the poem from the incursions of those who argued either that poetry made no sense or was simply all feeling and no intellect. Even the era's strategies for *reading* poems promoted and exhibited this same insularity. What are the "Intentional Fallacy" and the "Affective Fallacy" if not ways to cut off the poem from history, simultaneously nailing shut portals offered by the writer's biography and the reader's (and the culture's) own contributions as means to enter a poem?

This depersonalization of poetry had predictable but various effects, as later discussions of O'Hara, Lowell, Rich, and Wright will show. In short, most poets of the 1960s freed poetry from the bonds of the rational and chose to immerse themselves in poetry's personal depths. Confessional poetry, and thus private history, became the rage. To some extent it still is: Ask high school students one poet they've read, and, outside of Robert Frost, the most likely response

will come from a list of Confessional poets such as Sylvia Plath or
Anne Sexton. At the same time, however, another movement was
taking hold. Almost any poet worth his/her weight in paperbacks
could dive into the subjective and intuitive mind and surface with a
handful of images, so-called deep images fraught with Jungian associations pulled up from the collective unconscious. Similar to the
Confessional poets, these Deep Image poets rejected outer history in
favor of inner history. Unlike the above, they relied nearly exclusively on the image, or "the clothed percept," as Robert Kelly pronounced it, as a means to communicate their vision.[33] If at one
extreme the New Critics' insistence on rational matters of irony,
tension, and paradox had segregated their poems from history, at the
other, the Deep Imagists' reliance on intuition and subjectivity
limited their commerce with larger matters of communal history.
W. S. Merwin is one exception to this generalization, as the span of
his work from *The Lice* (1967) to *Travels* (1993) shows engagement
with social realities ranging from the plight of rural poor to the cor-
rupt nature of political structures. His recent *Travels* contains a
number of poems directly concerned with historical matters of Co-
lonialism and the ongoing ecological crisis, the latter a major focus
in his personal life as well. Of the remaining Deep Image poets, only
James Wright's poems showing empathy for social outcasts and
workers and those poems indicting the military-industrial complex
demonstrate much awareness of larger social concerns. Paul Breslin
goes as far as to claim that anyone "seeking to refute the assertion
that deep image poetics, by its own implicit logic, excludes representation of social reality could reply, 'What about James Wright?' "[34]

That fact must have settled in Robert Bly's mind, for in his later
poems against the Vietnam War, Bly exhibited a strong social consciousness. However, that was not always the case with Bly. As early
as his well-known 1963 essay, "A Wrong Turning in American
Poetry," Bly was pronouncing that twentieth-century American
poetry had turned away, rather destructively, from the imagination
and intuition to more rational concerns with wit and sophistication.
He distinguished between the move "inward" of Neruda, Lorca, and
Vallejo, for example, and the move "outward" represented, he believed, by the poetry of Ransom and Tate.[35] Curiously, in making
this familiar distinction between poetry issuing from unconscious
impulse and poetry derived from conscious rumination, Bly argued
that one paradoxical effect of the emphasis on conscious modes of
expression is that "there have been almost no poems touching on
political subjects," although such concerns have been present daily.[36]

Politics, Bly reasoned, was a subject too intense and too intimate for poets who (like the New Critics) wish to retain rhetorical detachment from their work—although that fails to explain why most "inward" poets of the deep image also skirted such matters. Nor why, for instance, so many of these poems sound like Bly's "Driving to Town to Mail a Letter":

> It is a cold and snowy night. The main street
>   is deserted.
> The only things moving are swirls of snow.
> As I lift the mailbox door, I feel its cold iron.
> There is privacy I love in the snowy night.
> Driving around, I will waste more time.[37]

No doubt the speaker delightfully undercuts the Puritan ethic by so thoroughly relishing his wasting time, and the poem's thin veneer of calm laid over this almost giddy rebelliousness only accentuates the effect—which surely makes for an interesting poem. Neither aspect, however, has much to do with establishing a working connection with the social world. In fact, the speaker loves most his "privacy," the "deserted" streets, his isolation among the snowy swirls of night. A hermetic impulse governs the poem, despite the speaker's admitted mission of mailing a letter, for even that distant connection seems frail in contrast with his robust aloneness. Though the letter may represent a social connection, it is a private act, carried out in private, and as such promises limited social repercussions. My point here is not to belittle a poem I admire but only to indicate the degree of insularity characteristic of the deep image lyric.

Charles Altieri, in his memorable study of the poetry of the 1970s, *Self and Sensibility in Contemporary American Poetry,* traces the inheritance of this insularity in what he calls the decade's "dominant mode"— the "scenic style."[38] For Altieri, the scenic style portrays a persona constantly transported into visionary states" which eventually "climax in moments of resonant silence."[39] The poem is founded on the believability of the specific scene described and the supposed "naturalness" of the speaker's voice in describing the scene. The implied union of speaker and the poet's "self," Altieri observes, makes for a curious rhetorical manipulation of the reader in which the very fact of rhetoricity is denied. In other words, the poet/speaker seeks to communicate personal experience in a "natural" or "sincere" voice supposedly untainted by rhetorical tricks, evoking "glimpses of a life that makes *isolated* individuality bearable" [my italics].[40] Altieri takes aim on Bly, Wright, William Stafford, Galway Kinnell, Charles

Wright, and others for their attempts to make the individual lyric experience appear representative without engaging more abstract thought or acknowledging rhetoric. What often results is a poetry seduced by the hermetic and thus further removed from the intersection of personal and collective history. Altieri succinctly describes the situation: "The danger in contemporary poetry, and in contemporary culture, is that we see the ironic, depersonalizing forces so clearly that we flee into forms of extreme privacy that we hope are as inviolate as they are inarticulate."[41]

Which brings us more or less to the present state of affairs. By the 1980s, the seductive qualities of "extreme privacy" seemed less alluring than imprisoning. Poets felt cut off from their culture and the public, so much so that it became commonplace for poets to remark wryly that only poets read other poets' books. Poet and critic Dana Gioia, in his provocative essay, "Can Poetry Matter?," aptly summarizes this view: "American poetry now belongs to a subculture. No longer part of the mainstream of artistic and intellectual life, it has become the specialized occupation of a relatively small and isolated group. Little of the frenetic activity it generates ever reaches outside of that closed group. As a class poets are not without cultural status. Like priests in a town of agnostics, they still command a certain residual prestige. But as individual artists they are almost invisible."[42]

Astute as his remarks were, Gioia was somewhat late into the fray, as Joseph Epstein had already pronounced poetry dead in his 1988 *Commentary* article snidely titled, "Who Killed Poetry?"[43] Epstein's essay raised such a fuss it was reprinted in the *Chronicle* of the Associated Writing Programs, the trade paper of the very university creative writing programs that Epstein blamed for the dilution of high poetic art. Epstein's essay engendered, of course, a score of commentaries castigating his conclusion that no more "memorable" poetry was being written and that our poetry thus wallowed in shallow mediocrity. Donald Hall responded brilliantly with his "Death to the Death of Poetry," an essay debunking what Hall calls "every cliché about poetry" that Epstein had assembled in his version of poetry's postmortem.[44] Instead of bemoaning American poetry's death, Hall described its vibrant life: "More than a thousand poetry books appear in this country each year. More people write poetry in this country—publish it, hear it, and presumably read it—than ever before. Let us quickly and loudly admit that no poet sells like Stephen King, that poetry is not as popular as professional wrestling, and that fewer people attend poetry readings in the United States than in Russia. Snore, snore. More people read poetry now in the United States than ever did before."[45] Whatever the reality, several poetic movements rushed in to salvage poetry from its supposed irrelevance. The "New Formalism," advocated by Paul Lake, Timothy Steele, Dana Gioia, and others, proposed determinate meter and rhyme as the means to reinvigorate poetry.[46] Robert McDowell and Mark Jarman's work with their feisty journal, *The Reaper,* led to their polemical and aesthetic championing of narrative poetry, a mode of telling stories in poems that seeks to retake some of the ground lost to fiction in recent years. That movement, not surprisingly, came to be known as the "New Narrative."[47]

Giving these aesthetics their critical due would require more space than is available here. I cite them to underscore the ferment of American poetry at the moment and to emphasize its yet unfolding future. More importantly, however, they illustrate a striking point. These two approaches share one crucial similarity: a curious dependence on technique. Only Jonathan Holden's recent call, in *The Fate of American Poetry,* for a renewed poetry of "moral statement" offers a proposal to revivify the "exhausted lyric tradition" inherited from Modernism in a manner that is not based largely on technique.[48] Technique is our dependable solution to artistic innovation, a recurrent version of Pound's "make it new." As early as 1962, Hall had complained of the "eternal American tic of thinking about art in terms of its techniques."[49] Technique has become an end in itself, merely another measure of surface style owning little of the poet's emotional investment and speaking to readers in only the most superficial terms.

Perhaps L-A-N-G-U-A-G-E poetry, which Bruce Andrews has described as professing "a desire for a social, political dimension in writing—embracing concern for a public, for community goods," offers a viable alternative to the insular poetics of the twentieth century.[50] However, because it is so theoretically charged, emphasizing language and ways of making meaning in often dense and complex forms, L-A-N-G-U-A-G-E poetry hardly promises wide readership. Its difficulty and nonlinearity, while exciting to the specialist, probably appear as elitist as early Modernism to the common reader. Here's Charles Bernstein's "Whose Language":

> Who's on first? The dust descends as the skylight
> caves in. The door closes on a dream of default and
> denunciation (go get those piazzas), hankering after
> frozen (prose) ambiance (ambivalence). Doors to fall
> in, bells to dust, nuances to circumscribe. Only the

real is real: the little girl who cries out "Baby!
Baby!" but forgets to look in the mirror—of a . . .
It doesn't really matter whose, only the appointment
of a skewed and derelict parade. My face turns to
glass, at last.[51]

L-A-N-G-U-A-G-E poets have immersed themselves in the linguistic theory of Saussure and Sapir, the philosophy of Heidegger and
Wittgenstein, and the theory of Foucault, Barthes, and Derrida to
create a poetry driven by the enabling and limiting elements of language itself.[52] Much of this poetry is informed by attention to the
smallest aspects of language, the smallest particles of words themselves, that is, phonemes. By paying such attention to the created
sense of meaning inhering in words, these poets extend the thinking
of Wittgenstein and Saussure regarding the inevitable and arbitrary
distance between the *signifier* used to stand for an idea or thing and
that idea or thing, the *signified*. There's a consequent playfulness
with typology and typos, for example, which lends itself to instruct-
ing readers in the illusion of meaning such language gives. Take, for
instance, "Fractal Diffusion," Christopher Dewdney's poem as "article" that opens with this proposition:

> In this article I am going to reify a progressive
> syllabic/letter transposition in units of ten. Start-
> ing with the letter A and working through the alphabet
> I will replavece eavech letter with ave syllaveble
> normavelly starting with the paverticulaver letter in
> question. The effects will be cumulavetive . . .

and by the time Dewdney has dutifully applied his transpositions
only six letters into the alphabet, ends in chaos and in frustration
(or delight) for the reader:

> Six letttetrs into that avelphavebutett,
> mavenifaretstatvetion petrfaretcotetdio-
> farlowetr ofar farondiouet—ave faraver/
> farettcohetdio cooncolusion.[53]

In another curious fashion, however, with L-A-N-G-U-A-G-E
poetry we find ourselves drawn back to the New Critical era, for in
such poetry, poet and reader alike are cut off from the poem's creation. Both modes operate, to use Gerald Graff's description of the
New Critical poem, under the assumption that "language writes the
poem, not the poet."[54] Though I could scarcely disagree more with
their conclusions, the whole idea of authorship is thus questioned

and reevaluated, in terms likely to show the influence of Marxism and to echo much of Foucault's replacement of the author with an "author-function" derived not from the personal experience and imagination of the individual but from the culture he or she works and lives in.[55] Instead of the poem being the creation of an individual speaker/subject with a particular personality and cache of experiences, such a view holds the speaker him/herself to be the creation of a gathering of historical, social, and cultural discourses. Note the curious swing of the pendulum. If Confessional poetry too thoughtlessly glorified personal experience to the exclusion of the communal, here the communal voice thoroughly subsumes and in effect silences the personal. The individual disappears into the group. In fact, Charles Bernstein suggests, since "there are no thoughts except through language," we are its creation as much as language is our creation to make of, freely, what we will.[56] Thus L-A-N-G-U-A-G-E poets would argue that putting poets and readers back in touch with historical and social contexts is, at root, simply a matter of reawakening both to the language they speak and read, the language through which they come to know the world around them in the most fundamental way.

Some Conclusions and a Beginning

While I am justifiably leary, if not altogether skeptical, of proposing yet another solution to expanding poetry's supposedly dwindling audience, I am anxious to suggest that several recent poets have found varied ways to revitalize American poetry that have less to do with technique than with content—in fact, less to do with content than with reexamining poets' individual aesthetic functions within a communal society. This redefinition amounts to accentuating poets' personal conversation with public culture, a dialogue more complex than that offered by their previous silence on the matter. Robert Pinsky has recently written of the conflicting "responsibilities" of the poet—the need to carry on an art learned, at least partly, from the dead, and the polar need to offer something new to the art, to put forward some original mode to be first accepted then "resisted, violated, and renewed" in the curious, slow motion fury that is aesthetic evolution.[57] Thus Pinsky praises, borrowing Carolyn Forché's term, a "poetry of witness" which may lead engaged poets to write variously of the plight of workers, family oral history, or the Vietnam War. Who's to know? Only the poet, of course, following the need to passionate witness.

Although such a remark may not amuse many of my poet friends who yearn for pure art unsullied by doltish public will, and though admittedly it may not jibe with the mode of some of my own poems, poetry which acknowledges and enacts its role in the sphere of social dialogue promises to enliven both the art and public response to that art. If the era which values interior discourse, hermetic verse, and highly aestheticized subjectivity has largely run its course, let us not grieve. In time, it will return, corrective as always, to extend the dialectical nature of aesthetics that assures a lively and progressive American poetry.

No doubt it's still much too early to speculate about the course of American poetry after the 1990s. Given the pluralistic composition of our society and the increasingly pluralistic nature of our poetry, it's highly unlikely—not to mention wholly unappealing—that a monolithic poetics will emerge to preside over our future. Still, it's tempting to suggest that knowledge of poetry that melds the private and the public ought to complement—if not supplant—knowledge of history as a way to know the course of human deeds and actions. To be sure, I am not suggesting that poetry without an overt historical awareness lacks value. Those personal lyrics testify to the spiritual and emotive blossoming of our lives. What I do believe warrants our attention, and what therefore prompts this book, is the considerable achievement of poets who, in the three decades beginning with the sixties, have struggled to reconnect their poetry to larger historical forces by locating their lives in the intersection of private and public history. These poets have learned to engage the virulent pressures of social fragmentation without turning to bitterness, despair, or self-pity. Just as importantly, they have discovered aesthetic means to address these pressures in their poetry. The kind of poetry that interests me in this study, therefore, is that which acknowledges the inadequacy of "official" or "objective" histories and thus juxtaposes its own in opposition. It is poetry of the present, infused with the passion of the moment, whether it works from recent memory or decades-old chronicle. It is the work of poets whom the past insistently "solicits . . . attracts and torments," poets for whom history, as Croce suggests, has not "lost its quality of being present," its ability to "vibrate in the soul." It is poetry written by those who understand the apparent paradox in Croce's well-known proposition —that " 'every true history is contemporary history' "—to mean that no history can be truly "past" when it animates one's mind and heart, and thus "springs straight from life."[58] It is poetry that embraces the vitality and variety of these worldly acts.

Chapter One

Learning to "Live with What Was Here"

Robert Lowell and Adrienne Rich

The work of Robert Lowell and Adrienne Rich disputes the assumption that "history" always happens to someone else, that what came before matters little to those who inhabit the present, that history's dead are, essentially, dead. Both poets believe it is precisely by engaging the past that the present becomes most passionately alive, intertwining the body of our experience with that of others. True enough, Lowell and Rich draw from this belief dissimilar conclusions regarding the lessons of historical inheritance. On one hand, Lowell represents the final extension of Modernism and the New Criticism, whose aesthetic he eventually abandons but whose elegiac attitude toward history he firmly maintains. For Lowell, knowledge of history's chronicle of despair only accentuates his awareness of the current skein of human mishaps and shortcomings, including his own. As Alan Williamson remarks, Lowell's attitude toward history, much like Freud's, "asks whether the whole project of civilization is worth the cost, being the best of alternatives, or whether, on the contrary, it is—by an internal necessity—suicidal."[1] On the other hand, Rich, younger by twelve years, begins her career in the tow of these same traditions but in time severs lines connecting her to both. Rich discovers in feminism a new optimism in stark contrast to Lowell's pessimism—her belief in the possibility for profound historical change in the roles women assume in our culture. In fact, Rich considers this "act of looking back" at history not as mere episode in "cultural" education but as necessary "act of survival" for women: "We need to know the writing of the past, and know it differently than we have ever known it; not to pass on a tradition, but to break its hold over us."[2]

In these two poets' attitudes toward history, we see figured the salutary close of one guard and the initial surge of another. In sum, Lowell regards history as a burden we humans haul dutifully on our backs, bent double by the weight of history's lessons yet promised scant hope of remedying those failures and thus easing our burden. Rich, to the contrary, insists that knowledge of history grants understanding essential to free oneself from its subtle inscriptions, that in fact such active engagement with history brings enlightened change in the present and future lives of both women and men.

One measure of the literary history shared by Lowell and Rich is indicated by simple chronology. Lowell's third book, *The Mills of the Kavanaughs* appeared in 1951, five years subsequent to his Pulitzer Prize-winning *Lord Weary's Castle* (1946). In 1951, Rich published her first collection, *A Change of World,* in the Yale Younger Poets Series, at a time in which she was still an undergraduate at Radcliffe. Lowell and, to a lesser extent, Rich, must have contributed in sundry ways to Frank O'Hara's conception of mainstream "contemporary poetry" as a "thorn . . . in one's side," something that made doing "everything the opposite" an attractive alternative.[3] Lowell could well have seemed its current "major" poet and Rich (along with Lowell's student Sylvia Plath) its ascendant star. What interests me is the manner in which these poets' subsequent work, altered by their aesthetic engagements with private and public history, helped to make possible a literary environment receptive to O'Hara's publication of *Lunch Poems* in 1964, just thirteen years later.

Lowell began that process through what has by now become a widely studied and much written about literary conversion. Lowell abandoned both the already crumbling New Critical aesthetic and T. S. Eliot's Impersonal Theory with the publication of his *Life Studies* (1959), a collection which won the National Book Award. Lowell's personal poems caused quite a stir for their willingness to hang out for public display the dirty laundry of the Lowell family's past and his own mental turmoil. Critics rushed to coin a term for this poetry, "Confessional," conveying readers' uncomfortable sense of being made priests in the literary confessional, listening intently to the poet's sins and thus offering back a kind of secular absolution.[4] In *Life Studies,* Lowell first evoked the inseparability of public and private history, offering implicit parallels between modern culture's slow motion ruin and that of his family and himself.

Doing so, Lowell seemed to be thumbing his nose at Mr. Eliot, who during his final reading at the Poetry Center in New York had passed on the torch of America's academic poetry directly to Lowell.

Eliot had asked the younger poet, after Lowell's glowing introduction, to remain on stage with him during his reading. "The request, coming from Mr. Eliot," recalls Stanley Kunitz, "had the authority of a dynastic gesture."[5] Lowell's turn toward the personal shouldn't have been so surprising. Despite the attention given Eliot's Impersonal Theory—which had proscribed poets' expressing individual personality in favor of more "universal" statements—"The Waste Land" and "The Love Song of J. Alfred Prufrock" bristle with Eliot's personality in nearly every line. Beneath the persona of Prufrock and the multifarious voices of "The Waste Land," one can detect the trauma Eliot encountered dealing with his unstable first wife, Vivien Haigh-Wood, and his despair of the human condition rooted in the dreariness of London during World War I. He had also disappointed his father by staying in London and not returning to defend his Harvard Ph.D. thesis on the Idealist philosopher F. H. Bradley. Instead, risking his father's anger and potential disinheritance, Eliot had taken on the less notable positions of schoolteacher, reviewer, bank teller, and assistant editor of *The Egoist*. No wonder Eliot in "The Waste Land" might rail against all the "loveless couplings" and feel it necessary to counsel civilization at large to "give," "sympathize," and "control yourself." As his marriage and personal life collapsed to shambles, he saw embodied in Europe's visible destruction a figure of his own personal trials. Even Eliot, years later, secure in a happy second marriage and at the height of a formidable career, came reluctantly to admit the limitations of the Impersonal Theory; he suggested that "The Waste Land" was nothing but "rhythmical grumbling," only a "personal and wholly insignificant grouse against life." Attempting to downplay the cultural significance critics had ascribed to the poem, Eliot curiously achieved just the opposite. His great universal cultural artifact was indeed infused with his individual longing and despondency. In effect, his protests had paradoxically validated the interplay between the personal and the communal.

As early as 1957, on a West coast reading tour, Lowell had noticed that his early poems, when compared to the bardic exhortations of the Beats, appeared to be vestiges of another epoch: ". . . my own poems seemed like prehistoric monsters dragged down into the bog by their ponderous armor."[6] Lowell's choice of the word "prehistoric" to describe the datedness of his early poems carries with it more than the casual allusion to dinosaurs and their eventual extinction. Surely Lowell was referring to the poems' formal metrics and rhyme patterns, their erudition and allusion, and the recurrent religious metaphors. To my mind, however, it was less these techniques than how Lowell used them which enabled him to protect himself from his subjects in a fashion so unlike the Beats. Using these modes of "armor," Lowell was able to view history, and his family's own history, with the detachment and irony one brings to archaeological study. Those poems seemed to issue from an aesthetic itself seduced into believing there was a poetic locale that existed prehistory, or at least a territory of pure art ruled by New Critical principles of tension, paradox, and irony that would balance—perhaps suspend—the pressures of past and present.

This emotional and intellectual teeter-totter drops wildly out of balance with the revelations of *Life Studies*. Both poet and reader are flung to the ground or sent skyward by personal and historical pieces such as "91 Revere Street," Lowell's lengthy prose study of his father and the oddities of his own home life, or by "Waking in the Blue," where Lowell describes a typical day in "the house for the 'mentally ill.'" Elsewhere, in poems such as "Memories of West Street and Lepke," Lowell ventures to make explicit connections between private and public acts. Citing moral grounds, Lowell had chosen conscientious objection and refused induction into the military in World War II (after twice having been refused enlistment). He did so mostly in protest of the Allies' firebombing of Dresden, a private argument he made part of public debate in an open letter to President Roosevelt, as the poem describes:

> These are the tranquillized *Fifties*,
> and I am forty. Ought I to regret my seedtime?
> I was a fire-breathing Catholic C.O.,
> and made my manic statement,
> telling off the state and president, and then
> sat waiting sentence in the bull pen
> beside a Negro boy with curlicues
> of marijuana in his hair.[7]

Looking back on his "seedtime," Lowell reflects from the relative comfort of his present state in the fifties, now "[o]nly teaching on Tuesdays, book-worming / in pajamas fresh out of the washer each morning." He remembers himself being so "out of things" he was unfamiliar with the "Jehovah's Witnesses" and required someone else to point out the gangster Lepke, Murder Incorporated's imprisoned boss, "piling towels on a rack." That the government would imprison Lepke—a man whose profession it was to kill other human beings—along with conscientious objectors who refused to kill, even in wartime, offers the poem's first dose of brutal irony. It's no doubt a biting comment on the skewed values of the government and the military that the murderer Lepke is given special privileges unavailable to the other prisoners: a "portable radio, a dresser, two toy American / flags tied together with a ribbon of Easter palm." Given "toy" symbols of American will and power, Lepke is seemingly rewarded for his willingness to exert power, to murder for his own sordid and unlawful cause that Lowell ironically equates with the larger cause of the American war effort to free the world from such bullying and oppression.

More than anything, the poem is about a disconcerting dissonance between values and actions. The poem goes on to make much of this dissonance, but does so in a way that makes Lowell look surprisingly culpable. Later, Lowell describes Lepke as "[f]labby, bald, lobotomized," a zombie caught between life and death who has come to see the electric chair as an "oasis in his air of lost connections. . . ." What Lowell implies, though does not say directly, is that Lepke appears to be an odd version of himself, for Lowell is painfully aware of his own "lost connections" to that fire-breathing conscientious objector he once was, now resplendent among his own "oasis" of books and the casual grace of one-day-a-week teaching schedules (privileges that parallel those given Lepke). Lowell has become aware of a terrifying dissonance in his own life. Now he's "out of things" in a different way, "tranquillized" by his newfound position and stature and thus estranged from his earlier political engagement. His "memories" of Lepke and West Street jail are just that, memories as removed from his present situation as he is from his former politically engaged role. In remembering his jail time and Lepke, Lowell has censured his present self, pointing toward a willingness to reconnect his former and present selves and perhaps to reconnect himself to the public forum.

In striking ways the "hermit / heiress" of another well-known poem from *Life Studies,* "Skunk Hour," also amounts to a version of Lowell "book-worming" in his fresh "pajamas" and thus retreating from the public world. She too thirsts for "hierarchic privacy" and seems tranquillized "in her dotage":

> Nautilus Island's hermit
> heiress still lives through winter in her Spartan
>   cottage;
> her sheep still graze above the sea.
> Her son's a bishop. Her farmer

is first selectman in our village;
she's in her dotage.

Thirsting for
the hierarchic privacy
of Queen Victoria's century,
she buys up all
the eyesores facing her shore
and lets them fall.

The season's ill—

The old woman represents a troublesome disavowal of the social contract, scorning any meaningful interchange with the community except to make certain her farmer "selectman" partakes in the local government and looks out for her interests. That local homes have fallen to disrepair due to lack of funds or family death means little to her. She merely takes advantage of the situation to ensure and extend her own hermetic lifestyle. In this larger sense the season is truly "ill."

While the heiress turns others' collapse into her good fortune, Lowell views the island's deterioration as possessing implications at once communal and personal. In the homes' decline to shabby "eyesores," Lowell sees an apt symbol for the general decline of American culture. What's more, in the decline of those values and traditions that had once propped up and ordered the old woman's world, Lowell figures his own personal collapse, his disintegration into a state of solipsism. The speaker of "Skunk Hour," like Eliot's Prufrock, direly needs and yet is mortally fearful of interchange with others. That need is embodied in a yearning for love so powerful that it prompts the voyeuristic speaker to cruise a hill where lovers mingle in their steamy "love-cars." What he finds there brings little relief:

A car radio bleats,
"Love, O careless Love. . . ." I hear
my ill-spirit sob in each blood cell,
as if my hand were at its throat. . . .
I myself am hell;

Such separation from others leads to self-absorption, as Lowell's self-pitying remark demonstrates. It leaves the community nearly unpopulated in its disrepair, given over only to "skunks, that search / in the moonlight for a bite to eat." The image echoes Eliot's claim

in "The Waste Land" that modern culture now finds itself in "rats
alley / Where the dead men lost their bones," but, instead of invoking
hopelessness, these skunks offer an instructive example of resource-
fulness in the face of ruin. The mother skunk with her "wedge-head
in a cup / of sour cream" simply "will not scare," and unlike either
Lowell or the heiress, she insistently forages new life out of our culture's debris.

By the time Lowell published *For the Union Dead* in 1964, the
year O'Hara's *Lunch Poems* appeared, his penchant for viewing the
present through eyes trained on the past had become a veritable personal world view. Lowell, surprisingly much like O'Hara, came to
use personal experience to give context to public events. But where
O'Hara celebrates the inimitable pleasure of the moment, even in
the face of Billie Holiday's death or Khrushchev's Cold War ranting,
Lowell dwells on lost pleasure, the moment drained of potency and
value, the redemptive always giving way to the condemnatory. The
beginning of the well-known "For the Union Dead" illustrates this
point:

> The old South Boston Aquarium stands
> in a Sahara of snow now. Its broken windows are boarded.
> The bronze weathervane cod has lost half its scales.
> The airy tanks are dry.
>
> Once my nose crawled like a snail on the glass;
> my hand tingled
> to burst the bubbles
> drifting from the noses of the cowed, compliant fish.[8]

Lowell's ordering of the scenes is instructive. The empty "now"
takes precedence over the formerly brimming "once," so much so
that the aquarium's fall to ruins takes on the character of a personal
affront. The aquarium's decline seems important mainly because it
matters to Lowell, and it matters because Lowell figures his personal
dissolution there.

Against this feeble present Lowell juxtaposes an heroic past, symbolized by Saint-Gaudens' bronze relief of "Colonel Shaw / and his
bell-cheeked Negro infantry," a monument which honors the first
Civil War African-American regiment organized in a free state. Full
of pride and certain of their righteous contribution to the war against
slavery, the unit had marched through Boston en route to battle.
"Two months after," Lowell tells us, "half the regiment was dead."
Despite the ironic deflation of the soldiers' high hopes, the poem

praises the dignity with which these men comported themselves in their struggle for social justice. In particular, that Shaw, a white man, had bravely led his black soldiers into battle must have seemed to Lowell in 1964 a timely and ironic sacrifice. Already the rumblings of America's Civil Rights movement had begun, our country's effort to finish the battle for social equality that had begun a century earlier. In fact, Lowell describes Shaw in terms that accentuate Shaw's usefulness in pointing our country in the proper direction:

> Its Colonel is as lean
> as a compass-needle. . . .
>
> He is out of bounds now. He rejoices in man's lovely,
> peculiar power to choose life and die—
> when he leads his black soldiers to death,
> he cannot bend his back.

It's no secret that Lowell despised militarism, as his poems depicting his family's military heritage and his own conscientious objector status indicate. Still, there's something about the sacrifice of Shaw and his men—their "lovely, peculiar power to choose life and die" —that Lowell honors, their willingness to "give up everything to serve the Republic," as the poem's Latin epigraph extols. Against that kind of selflessness, Lowell notes the lack of monuments for World War II, the "last war," and offers modern culture's crass substitution:

> on Boylston Street, a commercial photograph
> shows Hiroshima boiling
>
> over a Mosler safe, the "Rock of Ages"
> that survived the blast.

In such a world, nuclear holocaust—and all the horror that conflagration implies—is viewed as apt backdrop for commercial advertising. Anything, any horror or joy or sadness or grief—and anything that prompts those human emotions—can be commodified, packaged and sold to the pliant masses. Simply put, even A-bomb carnage can be manipulated to sell a product. This amounts to the packaging of tragedy for profit, what has since become a disquieting tradition of American capitalism. For a recent example, one need only cite the media and commercial flurry surrounding the O. J. Simpson trial to underscore the point.

The image of the Mosler safe conjures up other, equally unsettling associations for Lowell. The idea that in the modern world anyone might secure him/herself away from the world, might be "safe" from the unpredictable workings of the universe, seems dangerous folly to Lowell. Folly because of the necessary bonds of the social contract that link us to our fellows, and dangerous because of the perilous circumstances into which we put ourselves and our society when we attempt to dissolve those bonds. Lowell understands the enticements of such a desire for escape, as his work attests. He also understands the irony of the Mosler company naming its product after the religious hymn "Rock of Ages," which beseeches the Lord for an inviolate place to hide the self from all harm. Lowell knew well enough that none was available nor soon forthcoming.

By the time of the publication of *For the Union Dead,* Lowell had come wholly to doubt the aesthetic efficacy and moral validity of poetry that turned inordinately toward the private to the exclusion of the public, a process which, paradoxically, had begun in the confessional poems of *Life Studies.* He once told interviewer Frederick Seidel, "I don't think a personal history can go on forever, unless you're Walt Whitman and have a way with you. . . . you need something more impersonal."[9] In reviewing *For the Union Dead,* Richard Poirer had called Lowell America's "truest historian," whose imagination could only "be kept sane by reaching some understanding with the past."[10] In the years that followed, Lowell also labored to reach an accommodation with the present, often by inserting himself into public debate with the same vigor and tenacity he brought to his literary work. In the 1960s, for example, Lowell expended some of his own literary capital by protesting the Vietnam War, publicly aligning himself with Dr. Spock and others in the antiwar movement, and marching on the Pentagon. Perhaps his most public gesture was to refuse President Lyndon Johnson's invitation to the White House Festival of the Arts in 1965 to protest the escalation of the Vietnam War. He later campaigned for Eugene McCarthy in the 1968 Democratic primaries and refused to vote for president in that year's election after McCarthy dropped from the race.

Much of Lowell's poetry of the period reflects this involvement in public affairs. His collection, *Notebook 1967-68,* its revision and publication a year later as *Notebook,* and a further revision and enlargement of this volume titled *History* (1973), all show a presiding concern with making sense of the interplay of public and private events, past and present. Lowell makes evident in these books just how thoroughly he inhabits a space intersected by public and private forces and how completely his vision of himself as a human being is figured in their complex interaction.[11] Randall Jarrell had commented early in Lowell's career that Lowell's "completely unscientific but thoroughly historical mind" had in profound ways "condemned" him "both to read history and to repeat it."[12] And to write it, I suggest, especially if one considers the way *History*'s gathering of unrhymed sonnets conflates personal, biblical, and social history, as does the opening poem, titled, appropriately, "History":

> History has to live with what was here,
> clutching and close to fumbling all we had—
> it is so dull and gruesome how we die,
> unlike writing, life never finishes.
> Abel was finished; death is not remote,
> a flash-in-the-pan electrifies the skeptic,
> his cows crowding like skulls against high-voltage wire,
> his baby crying all night like a new machine.
> As in our Bibles, white-faced, predatory,
> the beautiful mist-drunken hunter's moon ascends—
> a child could give it a face: two holes, two holes,
> my eyes, my mouth, between them a skull's no-nose—
> O there's a terrifying innocence in my face
> drenched with the silver salvage of the mornfrost.[13]

The sonnet's cascade of nearly surreal associations falls down the page with the relentless fury of a waterfall, one desolation leading to the next within the surge of emotions surrounding fear of death. Innocents are made skeptics, skeptics suddenly reborn with "terrifying innocence." If history "has to live with what was here," then, the poem implies, so must we. To do so is to live forever aware of time's betrayal in death. Lowell has made cultural and religious history—in this case, Abel's death at his brother's hand—a peculiarly personal affair.

Lowell's reworking of *Notebook* was just as relentless. In compiling *History*, he added eighty poems to the old volume, although he published in the same year two other books, *For Lizzie and Harriet* and *The Dolphin* (which won the Pulitzer Prize). Perhaps not since Whitman had there been a poet so prone to continuous public revision of his work. Lowell's prefatory "Note" to *History* admits that he "plotted" to turn the "jumbled" composition of *Notebook* into something more shapely: "I hope this jumble or jungle is cleared— that I have cut the waste marble from the figure."[14] Lowell's use of a sculptural metaphor hints that he sees the body of his work as just that, a "figure" to be hewn until its true form reveals itself. The simple chronological order of *History* proffers Lowell a means to link past and present in a contiguous and unbroken line. Its sonnets proceed from the ancient past of King David, Solomon, Helen of Troy, and Achilles, through Dante and Anne Boleyn, to Beethoven, Jonathan Edwards, and Abraham Lincoln, and on to Lowell's friends and contemporary figures.[15] Many of these, Lowell says in "Revenant," return to him from the dead with the discomfiting message that "God is not about":

> They come back sometimes, I know they do,
> freed like felons on the first of May. . . .
> I cannot laugh them into laughing back.

Just as often, figures and events of the present day illustrate to Lowell the spiraling descent of modern culture, our godless decline. His poems about the 1968 Democratic and Republican conventions, the withdrawal of McCarthy from the presidential race, and the assassination of Robert Kennedy stand as cases in point. One often feels in reading Lowell's poems the brooding presence of a great ego. No public tragedy is complete without Lowell's evocation of his personal despair, his private shortcomings. In the collapse of public figures Lowell sees his own failures displayed in grand scale, so much so that one wonders whether his empathy for them reflects a corollary need for personal sympathy. Those qualities suffuse "For Eugene McCarthy (July, 1968)," a sonnet reacting to McCarthy's withdrawal from the presidential race in which Lowell had campaigned in his behalf. Notice how Lowell's personal loss stutters through the poem's opening lines, seemingly outweighing the country's loss of a candidate promising beneficial change:

> I love you so. . . . Gone? Who will swear you wouldn't
> have done good to the country, that fulfillment wouldn't
> have done good to you—the father, as Freud says,
> you? We've so little faith that anyone
> ever makes anything better . . . the same and less—
> ambition only makes the ambitious great.
> The state lifts us, we cannot raise the state. . . .

Surely Lowell has himself most in mind when he uses the plural "we" to argue that Americans have "little faith" that any individual can make things "better." He projects his own despair onto the greater populace, half resigned to history's lessons of failure and half defensive of his own.

Among the most memorable of these sonnets on contemporary events is "For Robert Kennedy 1925–68," a poem which directly in-

vokes RFK's historical significance and Lowell's own use of the historian's "bubble":[16]

> Here in my workroom, in its listlessness
> of Vacancy, like the old townhouse one shut for summer,
> airtight and sheeted from the sun and smog,
> far from the hornet yatter of his gang—
> is loneliness, a thin smoke thread of vital
> air. But what will anyone teach you now?
> Doom was woven in your nerves, your shirt,
> woven in the great clan; they too were loyal,
> and you too were loyal to them, to death.
> For them like a prince, you daily left your tower
> to walk through dirt in your best cloth. Untouched,
> alone in my Plutarchan bubble, I miss
> you, you out of Plutarch, made by hand—
> forever approaching our maturity.

It is not accidental that Lowell conjures up Plutarch, who chronicled
the lives of others, for that is very much the role he has taken for
himself in the poems of *History*. And it's not inappropriate for
Lowell to undercut himself and the role he's chosen, shut up in the
"listlessness" of his "airtight" study, giving forth on Robert Kennedy
who left his "tower" to tramp among the "dirt" and rubble of
common people. "Untouched" and safe in his poet's role—and feeling guilty for that—Lowell accords RFK historical status worthy of
inclusion in Plutarch's *Parallel Lives*. As is so often the case in Lowell's work, those he praises and those he condemns actually fore-
ground his own inadequacies. Here, the heroic figure of Robert
Kennedy, the prince who walked in his "best cloth" through the
rabble, serves to highlight Lowell's own flagging loyalty to the
greater cause. Unlike Kennedy who remained "loyal to them," even
as the cause led him "to death," Lowell imagines himself a quitter.
Although Kennedy may seem unreal, almost a godly figure torn
straight "out of Plutarch," he functions as a touchstone for human
frailty, a guiltiness Lowell is more than willing to embody and to
assume. Lowell envisions in Kennedy a suspended figure "forever
approaching" the full measure of his tragically unrealized maturity,
who simultaneously embodies the unachieved maturity forever elud-
ing our culture. Lowell's vision brings no comfort and little resolution, as much as it praises Kennedy, for it represents the flawed and
absolutely unredemptive state of humankind, a perpetual falling
short. This, according to Lowell, is what historical knowledge brings:
knowledge as burden and limit, a casting back of eyes which amounts

to a casting forward. Each Janus-like glance, however, finds always the same disenchanting vision, what Lowell calls, with bitter irony in the poem "End of Year," simply "[o]ne more annus mirabilis."

Adrienne Rich's work looks backward as much as Lowell's, but unlike Lowell, she looks ahead with confidence, imagining for women yet unattained rights of life and expression. Rich has faith in the individual human capacity to change the self and thus alter the culture we breathe like air, the culture that inevitably gives us life. Rich recognizes the way our shared cultural inheritance subtly encodes attitudes toward our own potential, our measure of what it is to be a woman or man living in the late twentieth century and what roles are encompassed by these conceptions. However, as a feminist, Rich focuses on what she sees as the debilitating effects of such historical inscriptions on women. Historical awareness thus becomes a source of political action. Rich refuses the sense of entrapment Lowell garners from historical awareness and insists instead that such awareness offers the means for women to escape the circumscribed roles of mother, help maid, and nurturer to which she believes history has relegated them. Rich encourages women to take a second look at cultural, literary, and social history, advocating a literal "re-vision" that demands "the act of looking back, of seeing with fresh eyes, of entering an old text from a new critical direction. . . . Until we can understand the assumptions in which we are drenched we cannot know ourselves. . . ."[17]

Rich believes the past—which she figures most often as patriarchal culture—has unduly suppressed women. On this score, Rich defines patriarchy at work in the larger culture as any "group or organization in which males hold dominant power and determine what part females shall and shall not play. . . . Such group organization has existed so long that almost all of written history, theology, psychology, and cultural anthropology are founded in its premises and contribute to its survival."[18] As one might suspect, given the wide angle of such a view, Rich defines much of the writing and study of poetry as patriarchal in our society, arguing that men control the means and distribution of power in literary culture. Consequently, in 1970 Rich came to the Women's Liberation Movement, identifying herself, in her own words, as a "radical feminist, and soon after—not as a political act but out of powerful and unmistakable feelings—as a lesbian."[19]

However, early in her career she was the darling of this literary patriarchy. When W. H. Auden chose her first collection, *A Change of World,* for the Yale Series Award, he praised her work in terms that, in retrospect, seem thinly veiled condescension: "The poems in this book are neatly and modestly dressed, speak quietly but do not mumble, respect their elders but are not cowed by them, and do not tell fibs."[20] In literary culture, such patriarchy means simply that a woman—and her poems—must be neat and modest and respect literary tradition, as Auden implies. And she must not tell "fibs"; that is, she must not question the conventional order of things—a curious attitude for Auden to promote, given his own homosexuality.

In application, this notion requires something like "Storm Warnings," a poem from Rich's initial collection. There Rich does in fact tell fibs to keep from speaking outright her own misgivings about women's roles in this order. Rich glazes the poem with a thick icing of symbolism through which she can appear to say one thing and can, perhaps unconsciously, mean another. Here is the poem's opening stanza:

> The glass has been falling all afternoon,
> And knowing better than the instrument
> What winds are walking overhead, what zone
> Of gray unrest is moving across the land,
> I leave the book upon a pillowed chair
> And walk from window to closed window, watching
> Boughs strain against the sky . . .[21]

That sense of "gray unrest," a feeling of impending cataclysm pervades much of Rich's first book, always held in check by the skillful application of protective form. Symbolism, persona, paradox, irony, even determinate rhyme and meter, Rich admits, function like "asbestos gloves" and thus allow her to "handle materials" she otherwise "couldn't pick up barehanded."[22] True enough, the speaker's lighting candles and drawing curtains mirror the actions of someone preparing for an approaching storm. However, given Rich's later realized feminism, those "troubled regions" the speaker inhabits can just as easily refer to any woman's life within what she sees as dominant patriarchy. Likewise, the storm approaching outside can be seen as symbol for the storm raging inside the speaker, who knows she must soon break from her protective shell and enter the conflagration outside the apparent safety of the home in which she nonetheless seems a prisoner. If the reader might otherwise miss this direct comparison between inner and outer weather, Rich states it flat out:

> Weather abroad
> And weather in the heart alike come on
> Regardless of prediction.

At first glance perhaps Rich's reference to the "heart" and not to the head makes the poem read like one bemoaning troubled love rather than sexual or marital politics. The temptation, particularly in 1951, was to see such a piece written by a woman as simply another poem of the broken heart. Still the poem's invocation of "foreseeing and averting change" and elements of "mastery" makes clear that it deals with male-female relationships on a far broader level, and that those women who feel victims of this "mastery" have begun to heed the storm building strength within. The weight of women's prescribed roles wears as heavily on the speaker of "Storm Warnings" as the wedding ring rests "heavily upon" the woman's hand in another familiar poem from *A Change of World,* "Aunt Jennifer's Tigers." There, Aunt Jennifer is defined largely by her relationships with men, her wedding band a stark symbol of how her married life is "ringed with ordeals she was mastered by." Given time and perspective, it's hard to overlook the poignance of Rich's repeating forms of the word "master" in these two early poems. Unlike the "prancing, proud" tigers Aunt Jennifer sews into cloth, the women of these two poems appear all too domesticated, caged within the culture they have accepted without question.

It's little overstatement to say that Rich regards much of culture as a conspiracy meant to condition women to lesser roles in society. Rich describes the nature of her own domestication at the hands of patriarchy by citing the role of learning and approval in a process controlled by men. As Rich sees it, her indoctrination began first with her father, then proceeded to her college teachers and the poets she studied there:

> My own luck was being born white and middle-class into a house full of books, with a father who encouraged me to read and write. So for about twenty years I wrote for a particular man, who criticized and praised me and made me feel I was 'special.' The obverse side of this, of course, was that I tried to please him, or rather not to displease him. . . .

> I know that my style was first formed by male poets: by the men I was reading as an undergraduate—Frost, Dylan Thomas, Donne, Auden, MacNeice, Stevens, Yeats.[23]

What's a wonder is that the "mastery" held so long. Signs of its disintegration are everywhere evident in her early work. Take, for instance, the young woman of "Living in Sin," a poem from Rich's second book, *The Diamond Cutters* (1955). Emotionally shut out by her musician-lover, she turns inefficaciously to typical "women's" chores to control "the minor demons" of a troubled relationship:

> she . . .
> pulled back the sheets and made the bed and found
> a towel to dust the table-top,
> and let the coffee boil over on the stove. . . .
> she woke sometimes to feel the daylight coming
> like a relentless milkman up the stairs.

The woman's reliance on routine, often a useful, mind-numbing tactic, cannot rout the "demons" that haunt her. She awakes in morning not to hope but to the regular (and thus ominous) thudding of the milkman bringing his twice-weekly reminder of her limited sphere, her circumscribed role. Discontent rises like bitter cream to top of those bottles, ready to explode in her face. A terrible readiness permeates these poems, the sense of something about to happen, something on the cusp—a blade ready to free the speaker from routine, but free her to what? This expectancy of great and meaningful events pervades so many of these poems that it's often difficult to gauge whether the much-awaited moments bode evil or good, and for whom. Finally, twelve years after the publication of her first book, the arrival of *Snapshots of a Daughter-in-Law* (1963) effectively delivers an answer. The book is in many ways transitional, mixing poems written in her earlier "asbestos" style with more emotionally and intellectually ragged free verse poems. However, the collection exposes, without protective cover, Rich's complaints about women's limited possibilities. For example, even when the couple of "A Marriage in the Sixties" finally scrapes together enough time to have a conversation, they seem doomed to speak separate languages indecipherable to the other:

> Two strangers, thrust for life upon a rock,
> may have at last the perfect hour of talk
> that language aches for; still
> two minds, two messages.

In "Snapshots of a Daughter-in-Law," the book's title poem, the effect of having "two minds" at odds with one another extends to

individual women themselves. The poem's speaker is torn between
conflicting cultural roles as male vision of a "belle" with "henna-
colored hair" and "peachbud" skin and the woman "crumbling
to pieces under the knife-edge / of mere fact" regarding the limitations of that role. Here that something about to happen has
happened; the blade has fallen and cleaved the speaker in two.
Rich arranges literary and social history to pose her polar "Snapshots of a Daughter-in-Law," and she draws adroitly from sources as
various as Emily Dickinson and Samuel Johnson. The speaker, now
in the so-called prime of life, recognizes how her daughter-in-law
chafes under constraints the speaker has become accustomed to. The
younger woman bangs the "coffee pot into the sink" and

> . . . hears the angels chiding, and looks out
> past the raked gardens to the sloppy sky.
> Only a week since They said *Have no patience.*
>
> The next time it was: *Be insatiable.*
> Then: *Save yourself; others you cannot save.*
> Sometimes she's let the tapstream scald her arm,
> a match burn to her thumbnail,
>
> or held her hand above the kettle's snout
> right in the wooly steam. They are probably angels,
> since nothing hurts her anymore, except
> each morning's grit blowing into her eyes.

The younger woman's self-destructiveness is a function of her entrapment, her self-hatred a measure of the violent wrenching required to contain "two minds" within one person. On one side is
history's vision of women as figures who are forever "*Dulce ridens,
dulce loquens*" ("sweetly laughing, sweetly speaking"), who maintain a pleasing appearance for men by shaving their "legs until they
/ gleam like petrified mammoth-tusk," whose household obliga-
tions revolve around "dusting everything on the whatnot every day
of life." On the other stands Mary Wollstonecraft's desire for women
to have "*in this uncertain world some stay / which cannot be un-
dermined,*" an image of a woman who has spent her life wisely—
not hoarded it, who has not, as Dickinson says, lived her life in the
corner, unused though ready to explode like "a Loaded Gun." The
final point amounts to the sharpest blow, that women come to
realize only in their middle years all that they "might have been."
Elsewhere, Rich summarizes the effects of this kind of historical in-
scription: "Fundamental to women's oppression is the assumption

that we as a group belong to the 'private' sphere of the home, the hearth, the family, the sexual, the emotional, out of which men emerge as adults to act in the 'public' arena of power, the 'real' world . . ."[24] Toward the close of the poem, Rich clarifies the nature of that thing about to happen, the push of expectancy that throttles much of her work and of which I have made much:

> Well,
> she's long about her coming, who must be
> more merciless to herself than history.

That woman, "long about her coming," arrives in Rich's *Diving into the Wreck* (1973), and she goes about the solitary business of reinterpreting history's "myths" from which our culture's definitions of both male and female roles have emerged. Many of those definitions, of course, revolve around and issue from the marriage "pact," and Rich lays much of the blame there. In fact, "From a Survivor," addressed to Rich's husband, a suicide, suggests that the "failures" of the human race are duly bound in marriage:

> The pact that we made was the ordinary pact
> of men & women in those days
>
> I don't know who we thought we were
> that our personalities
> could resist the failures of the race
>
> Lucky or unlucky, we didn't know
> the race had failures of that order
> and that we were going to share them

For Rich, there's nothing "ordinary" about that marriage pact, awash with patriarchal assumptions about the positions men and women take in our culture, nothing about it that ought to go unquestioned or unchallenged. That men and women regard its principles as "ordinary" in fact suggests the rootedness of the problem, the parsing of power, position, and duty that directs our relationships and has done so for generations. Although it is always risky to question the mysterious dynamics of any couple's marriage and/or divorce, note the way Rich uses her late husband as an overarching symbol not only of failed masculine notions of dominance but also of the failed Culture that induced and supported such masculinity. Emotional distance—or perhaps anger—enables her to insert the politics of power even into discussion of his body:

> it is no longer
> the body of a god
> or anything with power over my life

Surely Rich means to regard her husband's body as the seat of his masculinity, and by extension as the source of all male dominance—sexual and political—over women. The poem's title, "From a Survivor," implies that while she survived, he fell victim to the "failures" of the race; that while she was able to extricate herself from culturally imposed roles, he was not.

The most compelling of these poems dealing with cultural issues is undoubtedly the book's title poem, "Diving into the Wreck." There, the female protagonist, having "read the book of myths" and having confronted daily the awful flotsam of our sunken culture, must now dive down to the "wreck" to understand how things got to their present sorry state:

> First having read the book of myths,
> and loaded the camera,
> and checked the edge of the knife-blade,
> I put on
> the body-armor of black rubber
> and the absurd flippers
> the grave and awkward mask.
> I am having to do this
> not like Cousteau with his
> assiduous team
> aboard the sun-flooded schooner
> but here alone.

The gesture is both figurative and real, owing to the kind of active engagement with history that Michel Foucault believes to be the only defense against history's subtle encoding of our lives. For Foucault, the "story" within history is the result of the convergence of great forces in which winner takes all, including the authority to write the history of what happened and what it means for our culture. "The history that bears and determines us," Foucault argues, "has the form of a war rather than that of a language; relations of power, not relations of meaning." History is thus knowable only through the "intelligibility of struggles, of strategies and tactics."[25] What fascinates me about Foucault's theory of history is its central metaphor of war, its dependence on the conception of struggle between competing groups offering competing versions of historical "truth." Foucault's metaphor of history-writing as a form of war proves to be especially appropriate when discussing Rich's poems that reexamine and revise cultural history. The poem's diver, protected by her suit of "armor," seeks nothing less than an understanding of this cultural battle and of how its history has determined the way men and women view their respective societal roles. In such a view, every event (and its history) becomes, as Foucault suggests, "an usurpation of power, the appropriation of a vocabulary turned against those who had once used it."[26] Rich's diver desires to find the words that compose this "vocabulary" of power and thus control its means of distribution:

> I came to explore the wreck.
> The words are purposes.
> The words are maps.
> I came to see the damage done
> and the treasures that prevail. . . .
>
> the thing I came for:
> the wreck and not the story of the wreck
> the thing itself and not the myth . . .

For a while, Rich seems to find the corrective in a kind of androgyny she explicitly grants her diver. As much as anything, it is a measure of reconciliation:

> This is the place.
> And I am here, the mermaid whose dark hair
> streams black, the merman in his armored body
> We circle silently about the wreck
> we dive into the hold.
> I am she: I am he.

That vision of reconciliation between men and women amounts to a re-vision of culture. "This is the place," Rich argues, in which both sexes are able to explore their interests and pursue their individual skills free of prejudice and limiting roles, an optimism that marks the best of Rich's work. If there's one complaint about Rich's poetry, however, it is that Rich fixates on what poet Alicia Ostriker calls an "unrelieved crisis" in the interactions of women and men. Often Rich seems generally to neglect, to the contrary, the considerable merit of "the treasures that prevail" that she points to in "Diving into the Wreck." Ostriker goes on to note the common frame of much of Rich's poetry—"Explicitly or implicitly, since *Snapshots*

Rich's position has depended on the idea of an enemy"—a remark which pointedly echoes Foucault's military metaphor.[27] Occasionally this rhetorical insistence on an "enemy" conceals Rich's poems behind the raised shield and drawn sword of polemics. Even Helen Vendler, generally an admirer of Rich's work, chastises her for the poem "Rape" in *Diving into the Wreck*. In the poem, a woman who has been raped is forced to tell her account of the incident to a male police officer, "a cop who is both prowler and father." That the cop's eyes "grow narrow and glisten," that the "hysteria" of the woman's voice "pleases him," that he is figured as a "warlord" with "one hand" suggestively "touching his gun"—all of this paints the stereotypical portrait of a cop shamefully turned-on by the woman's rape story. By the end of the poem, the woman's description of her assailant has "come to sound like a portrait" of her "confessor," a simplistic conflation of cop and criminal that indicts all police officers and indeed all men in the woman's rape. Vendler's vehement response is to the point: "The poem . . . is . . . untenable propaganda, a grisly indictment, a fictitious and mechanical drama denying the simple fact of possible decency (there are decent cops and decent fathers, and decent brothers too, but they have no place in the consciousness producing this poem."[28]

It's not surprising that Rich's poems have elicited such vitriolic reactions from conservative readers and critics. Her purpose is decidedly to ruffle feathers, to prompt a rethinking of culturally ingrained ideas about women's and men's roles. Adrian Oktenberg argues, in fact, that Rich's goal is actually double: to effect "disloyalty" to the dominant patriarchal civilization among both women and men, and to "grasp and place beside it, as opposition and reproach, another conception of civilization—one that is woman-centered, woman-identified, woman created."[29]

If the central metaphor of battle still holds, then Rich is likely to take as many shots as she gives. Her more recent poetry shows continued interest in dialogue with history and culture, evidence that she has not made an easy accommodation with either. Many poems from *The Dream of a Common Language* (1978), *A Wild Patience Has Taken Me This Far* (1981), *Your Native Land, Your Life* (1986), and *An Atlas of the Difficult World* (1991) mirror the experiments with dialogic form undertaken by other poets in this study, particularly Philip Levine and Carolyn Forché.

One striking example is Rich's series of "Twenty-One Love Poems," included in *The Dream of a Common Language*, which demonstrate that she has as acute a sense of literary history as O'Hara or James Wright. Rich's poems deliberately play off associations with the patriarchal tradition of the Elizabethan love sonnet. In Rich's series, however, the speaker directly addresses a lesbian lover, charting the heady rise of the relationship and its painful decline as poignantly as any male poet's recounting of his love affair with a lovely maiden. Rich's dialogue is thus doubled—enabling her to speak both to the lover and to the patriarchal literary history she inherits. In doing so, Rich provides a tart reply to Auden's characterization of her early work as "neatly and modestly dressed," and she proves, in effect, that she has learned well what it means for poems to "not tell fibs." She also undertakes to regain the "power" and "vocabulary" Foucault believes usurped by writing of conventional cultural history, appropriating the language of traditional male-female love poems to serve her own purposes, as she does in the lush and sensual language of number XI of the series:

> Every peak is a crater. This is the law of volcanoes,
> making them eternally and visibly female.
> No height without depth, without a burning core,
> though our straw soles shred on the hardened lava.
> I want to travel with you to every sacred mountain
> smoking within like the sibyl stooped over her tripod,
> I want to reach for your hand as we scale the path,
> to feel your arteries glowing in my clasp,
> never failing to note the small, jewel-like flower
> unfamiliar to us, nameless till we rename her,
> that clings to the slowly altering rock—
> that detail outside ourselves that brings us to ourselves,
> was here before us, knew we could come, and sees beyond us.[30]

If anything, the poem's language and images are more overtly sentimental than that of most heterosexual love poems written by contemporary male poets, for whom the genre has become increasingly suspect if not altogether bankrupt. In essence, Rich gets away with what those poets no longer can. By the sheer excessiveness of "burning" cores, "glowing" arteries, and "sacred" mountains, Rich strives to appropriate, as Foucault would have it, both the authority of Elizabethan love poems and the validity of their social contract.

In the apparent paradox of renaming what had before been "nameless," Rich also provides a fitting metaphor for the kind of historical "re-vision" she has worked toward since 1963. What Rich contends has been overlooked, neglected, and dismissed into namelessness by patriarchal culture is given, by women, a new name, "jewel-like" and welcome. The flower is both vision and re-vision of what roles women might very well attain in the "slowly altering" future that lies "beyond." More importantly, the flower symbolizes the optimism Rich derives from history, an optimism in vivid contrast to Lowell's despair of things ever changing for the "better."[31] Rich's optimism regarding women's ability to break from an oppressive tradition has only strengthened in her recent work. Marianne Whelchel argues that, by using women's history in her poetry, Rich "participates in the movement among feminists—historians, sociologists, anthropologists—to reclaim, preserve, and evaluate women's lives."[32] Increasingly, though, Rich has turned to prose as another means to achieve this goal, often linking private and public events in the process. In fact, Rich describes her prose work, *Of Woman Born: Motherhood as Experience and Institution* (1976, reissued 1986), as merging these very modes, a gathering of "personal testimony mingled with research."[33]

Through the work of Lowell and Rich, readers of American poetry gain a singular notion of the way poets may effectively hold dialogue with culture and history. Their poetry stands as antidote to the enticing insularity of the "hermetic" mode by which poets hope to abandon their communal function in favor of the pristine woodlands of "pure" art. As such, their examples prove instructive if only for their variety. When Lowell, speaking as inheritor of the Eliotic tradition, suggests that all of us must learn "to live with what was here," he has in mind a coming to terms with history that implicitly questions the possibility of remedying civilization's failures. For Rich, however, living "with what was here" means precisely to change the present, to alter and remake its conventions for our future's sake— essentially, choosing *not* to live passively with history's inheritance. Succeeding chapters examine how three poets born to Rich's generation—Frank O'Hara, James Wright and Philip Levine—also began to negotiate, at roughly the same time, the intersection of private and public history in their lives and art. That O'Hara, Rich, Wright, and Levine were able to do so, in manifestly similar and yet undeniably unique ways, nevertheless has much to do with the aesthetic courage and inventiveness of Lowell.

Chapter Two

"Everything the Opposite" of History

A Literary Basis for the Anti-Literary
in Frank O'Hara's *Lunch Poems*

It may seem surprising to include within a study of "history" in contemporary poetry a poet who would seem deliberately and assiduously to refuse the public in favor of the private. True enough, O'Hara, more than most American poets, shows a fondness for spritzing his poems with references to friends and events in his life, implicitly valuing the personal over the communal experience. It is precisely this choice of the personal that interests me, not only for its aesthetic but also its historical implications. O'Hara's privileging of private over "objective" history stems from his vital opposition to another kind of history: literary history. By 1964, when Frank O'Hara's *Lunch Poems* appeared, American poetry was already embroiled in a wrenching poetic revolution. The rebellion had been initiated variously in the fifties by the Beats, by Charles Olson's theory and practice of projective verse, by the Black Mountain poets of the Objectivist tradition issuing from William Carlos Williams, and by Robert Bly and James Wright, who late in the decade abandoned the "square poem" for an imagistic, intuitive mode modeled after foreign influences such as Georg Trakl, Pablo Neruda, and Cesar Vallejo.[1]

Still, O'Hara's meticulous dating of each piece in *Lunch Poems* made abundantly obvious that he was one of the first poets to abjure the New Critical manners that had dominated American poetry since the thirties and that, in the mid- to late fifties, no one else was doing anything quite like him. John Ashbery, in fact, contends that O'Hara's poetry is "anything but literary," that it owes its peculiar character to a "modern tradition which is anti-literary and anti-artistic."[2]

One sensible way to define the "anti-literary" quality of O'Hara's work is to delineate what then-prevalent literary manners it rejects.

Certainly, the majority of pieces in *Lunch Poems* refuse both regular metric and rhyme patterns; they make use of varied language, welcoming both hieratic and demotic phrasings; and they abandon the then-popular mythic reference in favor of more personal allusion, often to close friends and familiar New York locations.

Citing these points of departure from the dominant literary mode of the fifties begins to establish the rebelliousness of O'Hara's work by highlighting what the Russian critic Jurij Lotman calls "minus-devices," an artist's "consistent conscious rejection" of accepted literary values.[3] However, such matters concern mostly form and structure, and though helpful in appreciating the uniqueness of O'Hara's work, they fall short of identifying what gives his work its pervasive insouciance and occasional joy, its air of passionate giddiness so unlike the dour metaphysical ruminations of many poets of the fifties.

A more promising approach lies in applying Lotman's theory of aesthetic evolution, especially his conception of the "minus-device," not to form but to the epistemological and ontological concerns that underlie O'Hara's rebellion against the dominant mode. Such a study reveals a compelling basis for O'Hara's uniqueness: his deeply held conviction that the individual self matters, and that experience, though not necessarily a source of instruction for the individual, nevertheless weaves the very fabric of selfhood. When O'Hara does refer to elements of larger, public history swirling about him, he does so either to accentuate the significance of individual experience or to set himself in opposition to the era's values. These convictions, though wholly personal in origin, contribute to the anti-literary stance of O'Hara's poetry—and conversely—enhance its literary appeal.

It has become an academic truism, no less true for its wide acceptance, that the experiments of modernism had run aground by the forties and fifties, abandoned by captain and crew, left foundering by the major figure of the day, T. S. Eliot. In general, many writers had embraced a far-reaching retrenchment to formalism, a move applauded by the great majority of critics. Many of those critics were also poets, and vice versa, a situation which created a bizarre kind of inbreeding among American writers. A new (and formidable) generation of poet/critics appeared. Their aesthetics were based largely on the New Critical principles of irony, paradox, and tension; an appreciation for the seventeenth-century metaphysical poets; and a firm belief that poets were far better off thinking than emoting in a poem (so much so that feeling became equated with unsophistication, innocence, and contemptible weakness).

John Crowe Ransom, Allen Tate, Yvor Winters, and the others may themselves have been on solid ground reacting against the excesses of nineteenth-century Romanticism, poetry where emotion often came easily and thoughtlessly, but they so narrowed the channel with their poetic prescriptions that only poems of a certain size and draft could pass through into journal publication and readers' hands. It was against such constraints that Frank O'Hara reacted, following the pattern that Jurij Lotman identifies in succinct terms: "All rebellions in art against the original type have rallied around the banner of 'naturalness' and 'simplicity,' against the oppressive and 'artificial' limits of the preceding period."[4] Perhaps more importantly for our conception of how aesthetic matters evolve, Lotman emphatically argues that such rebellions can never begin or long exist in isolation. Each rebellion is inextricably tied to the earlier mode it reacts against as a positive charge is tied to a negative, therefore making impossible the definition of one mode without invoking the other.

One might argue, then, that O'Hara's decision to avoid rhyme in his poems is directly bound to the choice of the earlier generation to make this formal concern a hallmark of its poetics. When put into practice in his work, O'Hara's aesthetic decision becomes what Lotman calls a "minus-device," what can be viewed as the absence of rhyme or the presence of "non-rhyme."[5] The artistic effect of any device or minus-device, Lotman tells us, is "always a relation" both bearing and borne upon by forces such as the aesthetic norms of an era and readers' expectations.[6] These "extra-textual" matters tie the particular poetic elements (or artistic choices) of a poem to the larger set of poetic elements the poet has to choose from. Simply put, O'Hara's choosing to model his early work after Rimbaud and Mallarmé may negate but does not sever his ties to the more conservative aesthetics of the era.

This may be a highfalutin way of saying that, even when O'Hara began writing a poetry that broke the currently accepted rules, the literary and artistic value of his work was still largely dependent on those rules to give it definition, or rather, that his breaking of the rules gave his work its necessary literary quality. It may be somewhat misleading to think of O'Hara as "anti-literary and anti-poetic," as Ashbery describes him; he rebels less against "literature" and "poetry" than against the definition (and limits) given those terms by the dominant literary establishment.

O'Hara himself seemed to realize this, for he admitted that he owned a "dislike" for "a great deal of contemporary poetry . . . but it is a useful thorn to have in one's side."[7] That "useful thorn" gave him something to respond to, something to help clarify his own artistic principles, as it were, by negation. O'Hara says as much in his unpublished statement for the Paterson Society in responding to a question about his "convictions concerning form, measure, sound": "well, if I went into that thoroughly enough nobody would ever want to read the poems I've already written, they would have been so thoroughly described, and I would have to do everything the opposite in the future to avoid my own boredom, and where would I be? That's where I am anyway, I suppose, but at least this way it's not self-induced."[8] Doing "everything the opposite" of the dominant mode amounted to an aesthetics of choice for O'Hara. But because so much of what O'Hara chose to omit from his work and so much of what he chose to replace it with violated conventional critics' expectations of poetry, his work was met, at least initially, by what Ashbery describes as the "friendly silence reserved for the thoroughly unacceptable guest."[9] However, O'Hara understood more clearly than those critics that his work was artistic because it did not pretend to be artful, that it was most poetic in its negative relation to then-fashionable poetics.

This negative relation to the aesthetics of the dominant mode, as I've asserted, involves more than simple matters of form. It seems to me to involve the relation of the poetic self to the experiential world, and to demand that the poem actually be an experience in itself, rather than merely explain (or contain) experience. In an era in which poets were both fearful of experience and fond of ruminating upon it at a safe intellectual distance, O'Hara's aesthetic offered life as the subject, experience unmediated by reason and rational discourse. If rhetoric was to be found in O'Hara's poems, it was, to borrow Lotman's terminology, a form of "non-rhetoric" that refused to separate the act of writing from the act of living. O'Hara rejected the kind of aesthetic "decadence" that Robert Hass has described as a "cultural disease" which "flourishes when the life of the spirit . . . retreats or is driven from public life, where it ought, naturally, to manifest itself."[10] O'Hara's poetry most differs from the dominant mode precisely in this attitude toward the "Jumble Shop" of experience, and this attitude contributes to the intimacy between writer and reader in his poems, as well as to his tenuously maintained joy in an age shamefully prone to anxiety attacks.

In a perhaps unexpected way, O'Hara is a poet of the Emersonian tradition, for he takes Emerson's insistence on the primacy of experience and uses it as a cornerstone of his aesthetics. As with Emer-

son, what one sees and what one does matter to O'Hara. But while
Emerson believed that some version of personal truth would issue
from such attention, O'Hara is less sure of the results and more concerned with the action as a reward in itself. When O'Hara says, "I
am mainly preoccupied with the world as I experience it," he is af-
firming his belief in the primacy of the experiential world and his
subjective apprehension of it.[11] And unlike the New Critical poem's
willful suspension of dichotomous forces, things actually happen in
an O'Hara poem. While John Crowe Ransom's poem "Spectral
Lovers," for example, leaves the lovers eternally separated by a terrifying dialectic between passion and morality, the lovers of O'Hara's
"St. Paul and All That" do meet, do have a relationship, and one of
them does feel the pangs of separation—but only *after* the consum-
mation of their love.

Many of the pieces in *Lunch Poems* contain a seemingly discon-
nected array of experiences bounded by time—often, appropriately,
the length of O'Hara's lunch hour—experiences "all jumbled / together like life is a Jumble Shop."[12] Here, the public realm seems
forever subject to the whims of the poet's attention, or inattention.
One of these is "A Step Away from Them," which begins by setting
both time and scene in elaborate detail:

> It's my lunch hour, so I go
> for a walk among the hum-colored
> cabs. First, down the sidewalk
> where laborers feed their dirty
> glistening torsos sandwiches
> and Coca-Cola, with yellow helmets
> on. They protect them from falling
> bricks, I guess. Then onto the
> avenue where skirts are flipping
> above heels and blow up over
> grates. The sun is hot, but the
> cabs stir up the air. I look
> at bargains in wristwatches. There
> are cats playing in sawdust.

Borrowing a line from the poem itself, one could easily call this
an example of O'Hara's "I look" poems. His ostensible intention
for the poem and its impetus, at least initially, are identical, and
both seem purely visual. Still, amidst the glow of "neon in day-
light" and the smoke of a sign, the "blonde chorus girl" and the
"lady in foxes," time suddenly and sullenly rears its ugly head:

O'Hara, dead center in "Times Square," becomes aware it is "12:40 of / a Thursday" (and he dates the poem 1956). Public reality, figured by Times Square, Coca-Cola, and sweating workers building the palaces of capitalism, simply evaporates in the sudden heat of this very personal perception of time. He is made fitfully aware that time imposes limits. On the most mundane level, it brackets the exhilarating hour of his lunch, and in a larger way, brackets his own lifetime as it already has those of his deceased friends Bunny Lang and Jackson Pollock, of whom he thinks while walking on the "beautiful and warm" avenue before heading "back to work." Quickly, though his "heart" is in his "pocket," O'Hara moves from the death of his friends to safer, more objective matters such as "BULLFIGHT" posters and "papaya juice."

Of O'Hara's poetry, Helen Vendler has remarked, "the wish *not* to impute significance has rarely been stronger in lyric poetry. It happened, it went like this, it's over."[13] However, as "A Step Away from Them" demonstrates, even O'Hara's insistence on aesthetic immediacy and spontaneity can lend itself to epiphany, though he may consciously shy from it in his poems and deny it in his prose. O'Hara, in fact, argues against reading metaphysical moments into his poems: "What is happening to me, allowing for lies and exaggerations which I try to avoid, goes into my poems. I don't think my experiences are clarified or made beautiful for myself or anyone else."[14]

One cannot dispute that O'Hara, much as he described his painter friend Larry Rivers, would rather "see something" than abstractly conceptualize when he creates art.[15] He is intent upon paying attention to himself and to the world with which he interacts. And if any truth is to be perceived from that act of seeing, it resides mainly if not solely in the moment itself; the poet, or any person for that matter, cannot extract truth from a single instant of time and apply it formulaically to other occasions. Life does not lend itself to rule making. Though O'Hara himself might have objected to the use of a philosophical term to describe such an attitude, it amounts to an epistemological decision about how one knows the world and the self. He seems to imply that only in attention to the moment can one know life, and that to know life one must live it passionately and attentively in the face of death. "The Day Lady Died," another poem of the "Jumble Shop" which displays O'Hara's obsession with time and his characteristic frenetic pacing, clarifies this point. Again note the collapsing of private and public history:

It is 12:20 in New York a Friday
three days after Bastille Day, yes
it is 1959 and I go get a shoeshine
because I will get off the 4:19 in Easthampton
at 7:15 and then go straight to dinner
and I don't know the people who will feed me

I walk up the muggy street beginning to sun
and have a hamburger and a malted and buy
an ugly NEW WORLD WRITING to see what the poets
in Ghana are doing these days
                        I go on to the bank
and Miss Stillwagon (first name Linda I once heard)
doesn't even look up my balance for once in her life
and in the GOLDEN GRIFFIN I get a little Verlaine
for Patsy with drawings by Bonnard although I do
think of Hesiod, trans. Richard Lattimore or
Brendan Behan's new play or *Le Balcon or Les Nègres*
of Genet, but I don't, I stick with Verlaine
after practically going to sleep with quandariness

and for Mike I just stroll into the PARK LANE
Liquor Store and ask for a bottle of Strega and
then I go back where I came from to 6th Avenue
and the tobacconist in the Ziegfeld Theatre and
casually ask for a carton of Gauloises and a carton
of Picayunes, and a NEW YORK POST with her face on it

and I am sweating a lot by now and thinking of
leaning on the john door in the 5 SPOT
while she whispered a song along the keyboard
to Mal Waldron and everyone and I stopped breathing

Amidst the swirl of dates and times, O'Hara purposefully mixes an event of great historical consequence—Bastille Day—with the pleasurable but quotidian concerns of his day, thereby implicitly equating the two. Even more suggestive is O'Hara's setting these events three days "after" the anniversary of Bastille Day, after the historical rebellion remembered as much for its excessiveness as for its salutary results. O'Hara may well be seeking personal freedom from an oppressive hierarchy whose mode is not monarchial but rather temporal. To inhabit the moment so vibrantly, unburdened of bank balance worries and concerned only with the amenities of one's own social calendar, is for O'Hara expressive of ultimate personal agency. O'Hara's repeated references to time and to train schedules, however, subtly intimate that this freedom is itself constrained by larger and more unsettling forces.

Still, the tone at the opening of the poem is giddy and excited. After all, this is a somewhat glib speaker who is readying himself for dinner at the home of someone he doesn't know, who can smart-aleckly refer to the "poets / of Ghana," who is prone to "stroll" and "casually ask" for cigarettes, and who can "practically" go "to sleep with quandariness" over the simple decision of what book to buy a friend. This is not a speaker burdened with metaphysical deliberations about the meaning of life.

Even when he sees the "NEW YORK POST with her face on it," he refuses to break into discourse on the brevity of human life, "thinking," instead, in visual and sensory images. Nothing of the larger historical context of Holiday's life enters the poet's mind. Not a word of her rape at ten years of age and her turn to prostitution to survive. Nothing of her terrible addictions and the hounding they brought from the FBI, the mismanagement of her career and finances by her handlers. Nothing of her cultural status as an African-American artist whose music crossed the color line to attract white audiences. None of these subjects seems the proper province for a poetics in which personal experience gives context to public events. O'Hara's aesthetics thus propose an oppositional form of history based mainly, as he admits, on "the world as I experience it." Clearly he is moved by Holiday's death, though he is less inclined to focus on that event than on how he learned of it. Those circumstances, however, quickly bring to mind a personal celebration of her art and life, a memory replete with erotic overtones. He recalls an instance when he heard Billie Holiday sing so sweetly that life itself seemed to halt in deathly pause while "everyone and I stopped breathing." Surprisingly, the pronoun "everyone" subtly conjoins his very private epiphany with a shared, communal experience.[16]

Up to the final line, O'Hara had offered the reader an ontological account of selfhood based largely on a narrative retelling of the way the individual fragments of his day melded into a mysteriously unified whole. But at this juncture, where anticipation and profound loss meet head on, the collision results in image, scene, a moment of experience which itself is of ultimate value. The present moment and the remembered one do not require metaphysical rumination in order to clarify them. That kind of deliberation has preceded the poem onto the page: the understanding that life is unpredictable and crass, capable of imparting immense pleasure and equally formidable pain. Although O'Hara may very well have agreed with the Heraclitean conception of a universe forever in the process of change, he would never use Heraclitus's fragments as poetic epigraphs (as Eliot did) or allow such thinking to impose an overtly philosophical structure on his work. O'Hara has already decided on these epistemological and ontological issues before the poem began. And more importantly, they were first of all personal values, which naturally (but secondarily) gave form to artistic values.

O'Hara lives in a world of flux and his poems do too. O'Hara means for the aesthetics of composition I've called the "Jumble Shop" to enable his poetry to express life in all its beauty and terror, but unlike a great majority of the poets of the period, he never means for his poems to replace experience. He confides that "it's a pretty depressing day, you must admit, when you feel you relate more to poetry than to life."[17] For O'Hara the experience always means more than the poem which embodies it, an attitude which accounts for the spontaneous way he wrote many of his poems in crowded rooms or noisy bars, and which may also account for his haphazard manner of saving (and often misplacing) them, as if the experiences that go into a poem always surmount the poem in importance.

Most American poets in the fifties concerned themselves with retaining a distance from their readers. Whether by using rhetorical means, a detached, observant tone, or even the very formal structure of the poem, many poets sought to distance themselves not only from the experiences they spoke of but also from the reader they spoke to. This kind of "strategy," as Adrienne Rich refers to it, functioned like "asbestos gloves" allowing the poet to deal with issues she/he couldn't deal with "barehanded."[18] It was a defensive tactic meant to insulate the writer from both world and audience—a method derived, no doubt, from Eliot's insistence that the act of poetry required an "extinction" rather than an "expression" of personality.

Frank O'Hara had little patience with such isolationist strategies resulting from the intellectual excesses of an overly aestheticized art. O'Hara (more than slightly tongue-in-cheek) founded his own poetic movement, which he called "Personism," based on the belief that a poem belonged "between two persons not two pages."[19] Even though O'Hara protested that "Personism" had nothing to do with "intimacy," one of its basic tenets is that a poem should "address itself to one person (other than the poet himself), thus evoking overtones of love without destroying love's life-giving vulgarity."[20] The dialogic effect, not surprisingly, is to increase the intimacy of the utterance and to accentuate the vulnerability of the speaker. One curious corollary effect is that in addressing his remarks to someone else, O'Hara can often more clearly define his own personality, almost as if he were conversing with himself.

O'Hara claimed a great admiration for Pasternak's poems and an equal appreciation for Pasternak's attitudes regarding the role of the poet. In his essay "About Zhivago and His Poems," O'Hara praises Pasternak for his "belief that a poet must first be a person, that his writings make him a poet, not his acting the role."[21] From Pasternak, O'Hara learns a crucial lesson that sets him apart from the rhetorically detached poets of the fifties whom James Wright once ruefully labelled the "safe boys":[22] "Life is not a landscape before which the poet postures, but the very condition of his inspiration in a deeply personal way."[23] The opening lines of O'Hara's "St. Paul and All That," addressed in epistolary form to an absent lover, reveal O'Hara's deeply personal and intimate mode of expression:

Totally abashed and smiling

                                        I walk in
                                        sit down and
                                        face the frigidaire

            it's April
            no May
            it's May
such little things have to be established in morning
after the big things of night
                                do you want me to come? when
I think of all the things I've been thinking of I feel insane

Despite the invocation of St. Paul in the poem's title, the great weight of Paul's religious and intellectual discourse is absent or at best implicit in the body of the poem, for truly the human body and its impulses dominate the speaker's attention. Again "history" serves as a useful backdrop for the speaker's experience, foregrounding all the more his opposition to Paul's pronouncements on the ascetic life. The poem's language and its form are passionate and open, exemplary of the kind of pleasurable displacement that love can bring. As the poem closes, the address becomes even more painfully vulnerable and overtly sexual when the speaker recalls how a friend came to the apartment during his lover's absence and said, "hey, / there's no dancer in that bed":

you never come when you say you'll come but on the other hand
                                                    you do come

Poems invoking such intimate forms of address between two lovers, replete with the sexual innuendo of the repeated "come" and
the open sentiment, might have seemed brash and indecent to many
readers weaned on the more decorous and conservative work of the
era. O'Hara seems clearly to understand how his poetry stood in opposition as well to the largely conservative social and political climate of the late fifties. Certainly his awareness of himself as a gay
man in the buttoned-down fifties must have increased his sense of
being marginalized from the dominant culture. O'Hara genuinely
relishes the shock value of his work, often showing a playful attitude toward his readers' expectations of good art and moral propri-
ety. His "Ave Maria" is a splendid example of such a poem, for
O'Hara addresses the mothers of America and somewhat facetiously
urges them to allow their children to go to the movies, and implicitly, to let them experience the "darker joys" of life. "Ave Maria"
begins innocently enough:

Mothers of America
                let your kids go to the movies!
get them out of the house so they won't know what you're up to
it's true that fresh air is good for the body
                                        but what about the soul
that grows in darkness, embossed by silvery images
and when you grow old as grow old you must
                                        they won't hate you
they won't criticize you they won't know
                        they'll be in some glamorous country
they first saw on Saturday afternoon or playing hookey

But when the "darkness" of the movie house metaphorically expands to include the possibility of "the little tykes" being picked up
and having "their first sexual experience" with a "pleasant stranger
whose apartment is in the / Heaven on Earth Bldg," O'Hara knows
that few mothers would agree that the experience would be "sheer
gravy" and "truly" entertaining for their children. And although he
ends the poem humorously by playfully threatening the possibility of
family breakup "if you don't take this advice," O'Hara makes a serious point about the necessity and beauty of human sexuality, arguing that "keeping them from the darker joys" is itself a truly
"unforgivable" sin.

As with many of O'Hara's poems that operate as supposed dialogues with persons who are absent or cannot readily reply, "Ave Maria" reveals more about O'Hara and his attitudes than a simple monologue ever could. The form of the poem enables him to address himself as well as his audience, to examine his own ideas regarding the value of fantasy and the beauty of sexuality, and thereby define the essence of his self. An unexpected benefit of "Personism," it would seem, is the manner in which the act of addressing another human being aids and induces a definition of one's own person.

One final and perhaps largely intangible quality separates O'Hara's poetry from the majority of the work being written in the fifties: his acceptance of human loneliness and suffering and his insistence on celebrating life anyway. One must remember that, in the era of the Cold War, hope and possibility were in scant supply, and poets spouting these attitudes were regarded as unsophisticated and jejune. R. W. B. Lewis aptly summarizes the era's pervasive despondency in his book *The American Adam,* inveighing against the "mordant" and "chilling skepticism of the mid-twentieth century" as one of "the modes of death."[24] O'Hara himself was not immune to the impulses of the day, for as Richard Howard reminds us, O'Hara admitted in his poem "Rhapsody" to being drawn toward "the enormous bliss of American death."[25] Some poems in *Lunch* show a depth of despair that approaches utter desperation, as does "Poem en Forme de Saw," where O'Hara imagines himself as "alone as a tree bumping another tree in a storm" and confesses "I'm so damned empty."

More often, O'Hara confronts life's equal capacity for beauty and terror with a kind of joyous good will. Structurally, he links these disparate feelings by use of oxymoron, discovering that in the throes of loneliness for his lover he can still awaken "totally abashed and smiling," and can learn to appreciate the "pleasurable anxiety" of being caught in the middle of an uncertain love affair ("St. Paul and All That"). While many poets were circling their wagons in the era Auden labelled the "Age of Anxiety," O'Hara takes on the Cold War with ebullient good will. Far from despondent at the thought of thousands of nuclear warheads aimed at the United States, many, of course, pointed directly at his beloved New York, O'Hara espouses joy in the moment that to some must have seemed hopelessly naive, as is evident in "Poem (Khrushchev is coming on the right day!)":

Khrushchev is coming on the right day!
                                        the cool graced light

is pushed off the enormous glass piers by hard wind
and everything is tossing, hurrying on up
                                        this country
has everything but *politesse,* a Puerto Rican cab driver says
and five different girls I see
                        look like Piedie Gimbel
with her blonde hair tossing too,
                                as she looked when I pushed
her little daughter on the swing on the lawn it was also windy

In the face of such "graced light" and blustery wind, Khrushchev
has no choice but to seek peace and cooperation, O'Hara implies,
for their magic is as irresistible as Piedie Gimbel's "little daughter"
in flight on her swing. No mention of Khrushchev's pounding his
shoe on the podium at the United Nations, not a word of his threat
that the Soviet Union will "bury" our country. By the poem's close,
however, "as the train bears Khrushchev on to Pennsylvania Sta-
tion," the poet shows himself to be aware of his own lyric impulses.
He laces the final lines with the conditional "seems" and fesses up
to his own tendency to be "foolish":

> and the light seems to be eternal
> and joy seems to be inexorable
> I am foolish enough to always find it in wind

Still, O'Hara could affirm life in a more stoic fashion, as in
"Song," where he brushes aside the dirtiness of New York City by
comparing it to an "attractive" person with bad character. Given
the choice of suffocating oneself or breathing New York's dirty air,
O'Hara asks his readers, "you don't refuse to breathe do you." If, as
he contends in "Adieu to Norman, Bon Jour to Joan and Jean-
Paul," "the only thing to do is simply to continue," O'Hara bases
that attitude partly on stoicism and partly on hopefulness. His hap-
piness is tenuous at best, dependent on the possibility of possibility:
"surely we shall not continue to be unhappy / we shall be happy."
And even though he can't convince himself that "everything / continues to be possible" (he says, "I don't believe it"), he does believe
some things are possible.

O'Hara's joy is sophisticated and qualified, rooted in the dirt and
noise and excitement of New York life. Many poets of the fifties
sought to make their well-wrought poems timeless artifacts almost
too pure for the world as it is. Many more cherished the thought
that art might help them rise above the fallen earth to an ideal state
of grace. The idea of ascendence intrigued O'Hara also, to be "a

part of the treetops and the blueness, invisible." But unlike most of
them, O'Hara's angel always returned to the earth where he belonged, as he reveals in "Three Airs":

Oh to be an angel (if there were any!), and go
straight up into the sky and look around and then come down . . .
                            silent, listening to
              the air becoming no air becoming air again

Basing an aesthetics on the poetics of experience in an age fearful
of experience was risky business indeed, and Frank O'Hara understood that. He once felt compelled to explain the "very jumbled"
nature of his long poem "Second Avenue"[26] by saying that "actually
everything in it happened to me or I felt happening (saw, imagined)
on Second Avenue." In other words, he aspired for "the poem to be
the subject, not just about it."[27]

If O'Hara's poetry is at all "anti-literary," the source of its rebellion lies in his conscious refusal of the conservative and often des-
pairing poetic mode of the day. And if Lotman's theory of the
"minus-device" can help us understand the nature of O'Hara's personal artistic battles, that theory works best and enlightens most
when applied less to matters of form than to more epistemological
matters concerning how the self interacts with and is shaped by experience. What remains significant, finally, is the essential literary
quality of O'Hara's anti-literary contribution to American poetry.
Against what current critics might call the ruling hegemony of the
day, O'Hara created poetry bound to the "Jumble Shop" of experience, demonstrated how a poem could be an intimate intercourse
between two persons, and asserted that joy, as foolish as it may
sound to say so, is as necessary and vital to life as lunch.

O'Hara was fully aware of how his belief in the primacy of personal experience opposed the then-dominant aesthetics of "universal" or "impersonal" poetry. In other words, he understood literary
history. That very understanding in turn dictated how he freely used
private and largely ignored public history in his poems. For O'Hara,
personal experience always and necessarily gave context to public
events. To engage Frank O'Hara and his *Lunch Poems* is to encounter a poet exemplary of the ascendency in the sixties and seventies of
a poetry founded in personal, subjective, and intuitive impulses.
Other poets found different means and motivation for working in
the charged field where literary, private, and public history intersect.
In the chapters that follow, we'll see this dialogue carried out in
equally intimate and increasingly public terms.

Chapter Three

"A Dark River of Labor"

Work and Workers in
James Wright's Poetry

Many of James Wright's early poems introduced uncommonly common subjects, populated as they were by a murderer, a prostitute, a lesbian, an escaped convict, and an occasional drunk. Even W. H. Auden, who chose Wright's *The Green Wall* as the Yale Series winner, couldn't help but notice Wright's affinity for chronicling the lives of "social outsiders," those who "play no part in ruling the City" and no part in making its "history."[1] As Wright matured, beginning with the unpublished collection *Amenities of Stone* (1961–62) and its successor *The Branch Will Not Break* (1963), this attention took keener focus, often directing his eye to the "lives / Of the unnamed poor."[2]

These coal miners, small farmers, housewives, and factory hands were "outsiders" largely because they lacked access to society's "ruling" circle of power and to the pen that wrote its "history." Growing up in the mill and factory town of Martins Ferry, Ohio, Wright, of course, experienced firsthand the hard life of America's working poor. He saw the physical, emotional, and spiritual toll exacted on his father by years of labor at Hazel-Atlas Glass, where he once briefly worked himself. Only through the grace of the G.I. Bill was Wright able to attend Kenyon College and, in effect, trade his father's factory for a factory of another sort, one where words were both tool and end product.

Wright's escape from the Ohio River Valley, and from the industrial greed that polluted it, was never complete, nor did he want it to be. His poems insistently return to the work and workers he knew in Ohio, indicting in the process a capitalistic system that devalues both. What's most striking about these poems, however, is the manner in which Wright inextricably binds his empathy for those chained to the machinery of capitalism to his own pressing guilt for having escaped that fate. Recognizing that his personal guilt has its source in larger social realities, Wright refuses to separate the private from the public self.

One goal of poetry such as Wright's is to subvert the silencing of "outsiders" that Auden, perhaps unwittingly, alludes to in his introduction to *The Green Wall*. Giving voice to the voiceless fulfills James Scully's call for a "dissident poetry" that "breaks silences: speaking for, or at best with, the silenced."[3] The act of writing "history" thus takes broad sweep in Wright's poems, including not only the communal but also the personal. History becomes inclusive and embracing, drenched with the peculiar spirit of a time, its sources and its future. Wright would take quite seriously C. K. Williams' injunction that history is the proper arena for "our most profound ideas and ideals," for it grants fundamental grounding, the means of connection to what Williams calls "concrete historical reality with its necessities and its responsibilities and demands."[4] For Wright, that meant acknowledging, as he did in an interview with Dave Smith, the unsettling truth about his home, a town where "people were quite shockingly separated from each other along class lines."[5] His uneasy sense of himself as risen from an underclass indisputably affected his aesthetics and, just as importantly, his attitude toward a poet's responsibility to a place and its people.

Perhaps the poem that epitomizes this merging of communal and personal, of the spirit of place and the citizens who live there is Wright's widely recognized "Autumn Begins in Martins Ferry, Ohio." The poem is brief enough to quote in its entirety:

> In the Shreve High football stadium,
> I think of Polacks nursing long beers in Tiltonsville,
> And gray faces of Negroes in the blast furnace at Benwood,
> And the ruptured night watchman at Wheeling Steel,
> Dreaming of heroes.
>
> All the proud fathers are ashamed to go home.
> Their women cluck like starved pullets
> Dying for love.
>
> Therefore,
> Their sons grow suicidally beautiful
> At the beginning of October,
> And gallop terribly against each other's bodies.

Characteristic of many poems in *The Branch Will Not Break*, "Autumn Begins" moves elliptically, almost reticently, as if the white spaces of silence paradoxically enlarge and embolden what is spoken in the poem. Returned to the scene of his youth, Wright finds himself afforded a perspective not available to the locals. Now curiously outside of the outsiders, he calls the ballplayers "their sons," not claiming them personally as "mine" or collectively as "ours." He comes to recognize the ritualized violence of football as an emblem of the larger competitiveness of capitalism, a system that, particularly in the mill and factory town of Martins Ferry, necessarily produces more losers than winners. Workers, driven to the refuge of "long beers" or made pallid by the "blast furnace" of their workplace, have come to realize that for them the American dream has been irreparably "ruptured." The residue of their grinding, physically debilitating work carries over to the home front, ineffectuating even the men's relations with their wives. The wives suffer, too, both in need of their husbands' love and in empathetic love for them.[6]

Of course, all this has not been lost on the sons, who know as well as anyone that to dream of "heroes" in our society, whether in athletics or in business, is to dream of the wealthy. Soon to be defeated by the economics of hard labor, they partake of their own "suicidally beautiful" ritual, hoping that they, unlike their fathers, will break the cycle of repression. The boys seize football as the last chance to elude their fate—whether by earning the adulation that accompanies football heroes through adulthood, or by literally escaping the region through a college football scholarship. Wright, who watched future Cleveland Browns placekicker Lou Groza star on his own high school team, appreciated the allure of the latter and readily admitted it: "I realize that . . . our problem when we were boys in Martins Ferry, Ohio, in that industrial area enclosed by the foothills of the Appalachians on both sides, near that big river, was to get out. It has become plain to me that football helped many people to get out. And many of these people came from desperately poor families."[7]

Any cautious critic would do well to question whether Wright, a former semi-pro player in the Ohio River Valley, might have exaggerated the contribution of football in particular, and sports in general, to the upward mobility of the region's youth. That critic need only turn to higher authority, none other than *Sports Illustrated,* to adduce the following facts from Ron Fimrite's "The Valley Boys," which chronicles the early lives and later successes of

some of the area's most renowned professional athletes.[8] Martins
Ferry, and its neighboring towns along the Upper Ohio River Valley,
have produced an astounding number of accomplished athletes, six
chief among them: Phil and Joe Niekro, the winningest pitching
brothers in the history of major league baseball; John Havlicek, college, Olympic, and Boston Celtics star, and member of the Basketball Hall of Fame; Bill Mazeroski, eight-time Gold Glove-winning
second baseman for the Pittsburgh Pirates and the hero of the 1960
World Series; Alex Groza, a talented basketball player whose career
was ruined by his involvement with fixing games while in college;
and of course, Lou Groza, third-ranking scorer in professional football history and member of the Pro Football Hall of Fame. It's clear
that while "Autumn Begins in Martins Ferry, Ohio" may indeed
chastise the prevailing economics of repression, it also subtly celebrates the communal spirit and individual will of the region's inhabitants. In Fimrite's opening description of Martins Ferry, one can detect a similar acknowledgment of communal and individual will.
The physical lay of the town so plainly embodies the intangible
mood of its inhabitants that even a sportswriter, there ostensibly to
reminisce about the youthful glories of aging athletes, becomes intoxicated with its potent brew of melancholy and pride:

> The beauty of the place is that time has passed it by. Martins
> Ferry, Ohio, and its sister villages on the broad banks of the
> murky Ohio River have the look and feel of 19th-century mill
> towns, which is exactly what they were. The houses are built of
> wood, with peaked roofs and grand porches, and the best ones
> look as if they will stand forever. The others are tumbledown
> and grimy and so fragile in their decay that it seems a brisk
> wind might turn them to rubble. But they, too, have somehow
> withstood the ravages of the decades.[9]

Fimrite clearly imagines that the townfolks, like the houses they live
in, have "withstood" much over time. The town, layered on steep
hills, climbs from board-flat land closest to the river and angles uphill. Climbing the social ladder possesses a literal meaning in Martins Ferry: Those with means and money—mostly the mill owners
and bosses—built their houses uphill above the smoke and grime
emanating from the mills splayed along the lowlands near the Ohio.
The richer one was, the higher one rose above the soot and dirt. In-
versely, the poorer one was, the closer one lived to the mills and factories belching purple-gray clouds into stagnant air.[10] The Groza
family numbered among the latter, as Lou describes:

We grew up across the street from the steel mill in Martins Ferry. We lived above my dad's tavern. . . . We played tackle [football], without pads, on a place along the River called Mill Field. They dumped ash from the blast furnaces right next to it, at the cinder dump, so it was always dusty there. There was no grass, and when the river would rise, the field would first get muddy, then dry and cracked. We'd be filthy after a game, then we'd dive into the river to wash, and go home.[11]

Even though the Martins Ferry lowlands were coated with foul dust, or perhaps partly because of that, area youths developed a scorn for things soft, things beautiful and useless—a fact which makes Wright's becoming a poet all the more remarkable and his peculiar obsession with beauty commingled with ugliness all the more understandable. Lou Groza's subtle mention of the fact the boys played tackle football "without pads" points to this toughness, an attitude demanding that the boys (and their fathers) take life's worst shots and merely bite their lips in response. No tears, certainly none in public.

This necessary strength and forbearance permeates the psyche of the place and its people. Fathers teach their sons that there is no easy way out, literally or figuratively. Everything has to be worked for, labored for at great cost to body and soul. Those "proud fathers," although they may indeed be "ashamed to go home," as Wright's poem suggests, do drag themselves back there, wearied by the day's labor, only to find other responsibilities awaiting them. Not washing dishes or mowing the few spindles of grass able to sprout through layers of steel dust, but ball-playing instead. Phil Niekros' recollection of his father's nightly return recounts a scene probably common to the area: "Our dad would come home at 5:00 or 5:30 from the mines, and he'd be black with coal dust. He'd go upstairs and wash and then rest for a while—sometimes he'd just fall asleep on the floor. But he'd always come down and play catch with us in the backyard."[12] Precisely because athletics "was a way out of the ghetto, much as it is now for blacks," as Alex Groza remarks, that game of catch took on economic and social undertones deeper than those of simple fatherly devotion.[13] One can decipher these patterns repeating themselves, with a keenness all the more distressing because it's cyclic, in the comments of high school baseball player Jason Ellis: "All of us have goals to make it to some big school somewhere else. For me it will be the Air Force Academy or Notre Dame. . . . Oh, I know there's a lot of tradition here. I think everybody in the whole town has an autograph from the Niekros. But what I'm going to try to do is try to make it out of the Valley just like they did. . . . I don't look down on it though. It's where I'm from.''[14] It is striking to note how closely Ellis' remarks echo both the theme of Wright's poem and his statement to Dave Smith that sports success was a vehicle for local kids to "get out" of the Valley. Similarly, the understated pride of "Autumn Begins" is evident in Ellis' final comment, for the poem, both celebratory and plangent, is Wright's clearest evocation of "where I'm from."

"Autumn Begins" was meant to be included in Wright's unpublished collection, *Amenities of Stone* (1961–62), the precursor to *Branch* which he withdrew from publication at Wesleyan University Press, and its theme is representative of the manuscript. I have lavished so much attention on this relatively brief poem not only because it succinctly encapsulates social conditions in Wright's Ohio River Valley but also because it signals a striking shift in his personal attitude toward the region's public history he shares. In fact, of the sixty-seven poems in the 5 March 1961 version of the *Amenities* manuscript, at least twelve can be said to address the fate and circumstances of the working class. The titles of just a few poems make this evident: "On the Foreclosure of a Mortgage in the Suburbs," "The American Dream," "The Mill Field at Aetnaville, Ohio: 1960," "Miners," and "People Are Sick of Pretending That They Love the Boss."[15] The titles alone demonstrate that the redefinition of poetic self Wright had undertaken in *Amenities* necessarily involved a concomitant reexamination of his relationship to a place and its people.

What occasioned this transformation, though the source of much critical discussion, remains largely speculation. Certainly Wright had lost faith in the odd sort of ventriloquist act he had performed, to general acclaim, in *The Green Wall* (1957) and *Saint Judas* (1959). There he spoke his poems in the voices of Frost and Robinson, but also Herrick, Donne, and his former teachers Theodore Roethke and John Crowe Ransom—none of whom, to be honest, spoke much like the folks back home. Like most young poets, Wright tried on the familiar voices of other poets as a way of finding his own. Surely his work translating Trakl, Lorca, Neruda, Vallejo, and others exposed him to ways of writing and thinking about poems that both startled him and vivified his own conception of what a poem might do and say, as well as what it need not do and say. Wright clearly was looking around for models, as his remarkable association with Robert Bly indicates, though he was looking less for a guru than for someone whose ideas resembled his own emerging sense of the responsibilities and possibilities of poetry.

Wright may have found someone like that in John Knoepfle, a quiet and somewhat shy poet who had collaborated with Wright and Bly in translating Vallejo, and who would later become an occasional visitor, along with Wright and John Logan, to Bly's farm. Not only was Knoepfle interested in translation, but he also had embarked on an ambitious project to record the oral histories of men who had worked as captains, mates, rousters, etc., on side and sternwheel boats on the Ohio River. From that experience, Knoepfle had begun to write what he called "river poems," often using the men's work stories as their basis. Wright himself had seen these poems, and, in a letter of April 1961, during the period of his own struggle with *Amenities,* Wright wrote Knoepfle, "I want to say that I have admired your translations very much, and your poetry also, particularly the group of river poems. . . ."[16] Wright may have been referring specifically to a group of Knoepfle's river poems published the previous month in *Audit.* That group included the poem "Sons of Kanawha," whose subject is the Kanawha Valley men who worked pumps at a dam site above Cincinnati during World War I, when getting coal supplies downstream from Pittsburgh to New Orleans proved crucial to the war effort. Many of the men died of flu contracted from laboring at the pumps, indirect victims of the war, as the poem's second and third stanzas explain:

> They volunteered on pumps
> to dry the coffers when
> Ohio's dams went up with
> Wilson's war and coal
> from Pittsburgh needed
> good water all the way
> to Cairo. No one asked
> the price they paid.
>
> There were rooms where
> no doctors came when flu
> soiled their sleep and
> gas lamps sputtered with
> lost light for their eyes,
> coins for the dead. . . .

What's most notable about the poem is the manner in which Knoepfle weaves together the sacred trinity of Wright's own Ohio River Valley poems: work(ers), the Ohio River, and death. My point is not at all that Wright got his ideas from Knoepfle (he didn't), but that Wright surely noticed Knoepfle had studied the Valley and its workers and come to similar conclusions about the state of things in his home country. In effect, Knoepfle's poems confirmed Wright's own beliefs about the dire conditions for workers in the Ohio River Valley. Having that confirmation must have strengthened Wright's resolve to speak of this place and for these people, which, after all, were his place and his people.

Wright's own poems about work and workers, as they appear in *Amenities*, are bleak and imagistic, and often quite idiosyncratic in their choice of images. Most of them show an unguarded, almost shocking will to speak the truth about the life of the working class. The unpublished "People Are Sick of Pretending That They Love the Boss," for example, closes with this stomach-churning scene:

> A merchant seaman
> Leans on a fire hydrant
> And throws up,
> Alone,
> Murmuring
> The names of items on his mother's shopping list,
> Over and over.

And here is the dreary, though understated, opening of "On the Foreclosure of a Mortgage in the Suburbs": "The friends of my childhood / One after another have fallen behind / Payments / And stones." Again Wright mingles death and need of money, and he does so with characteristic, albeit bitter, wit.

One other unpublished poem from *Amenities*, "The Continental Can Company at Six O'Clock," describes—in violent and incendiary images—the dehumanizing process that eventually overwhelmed those friends who didn't get out. Handwritten, passionately scribbled on the bottom of a draft of another poem titled "Rain" (a version of which eventually appeared in *Branch*), the poem boldly conflates the polluted Ohio River and the area's exploited workers, implying their mutual victimization at the hands of the wealthy and powerful. When the speaker observes workers driving away from a day's labor, he witnesses a pernicious transformation:

> The faces fall down the ramp into the yard
> Beside the river.
> Headlights roil over the water,
> And the faces divide into drops of blood,
> That fall over the high voltage wires of the fence
> Into the river.
> The water darkens to red fire.

And the blast furnaces of Benwood are lunging at the sky,
Animals blinded with anger.
Suddenly the faces flood into one dark red face.
The hood of each car is a dark sloop bearing a coffin
Toward the river.
This is October, the restless flames of dead blow torches
have scarred the wind.
Men are dying without ever knowing it.
America, America,
It is raining
In the river.[17]

The workplace itself has become bestial, a violent animal that swallows workers in the morning and spits them up, bloodied by the experience, at shift's end. Even then the workers are not free. Wright negates the stereotypic association of the work day's end with freedom and rebirth, effectively eliminating the only escape available to these workers. In fact, numbed by a day's grueling labor, they drive off, at the wheel of their car become boat become coffin, to a kind of death-in-life, unaware of their fate.

Wright feared this fate for himself and mourned it for others. Donald Hall, in his introduction to Wright's *Above the River: The Complete Poems,* quotes from a Wright letter which elaborates the dailiness of the process and its cruel results: "I knew musicians and possible poets and even ordinary lovable human beings, and saw them with brutal regularity going into Wheeling Steel, and turning into stupid and resigned slobs with beer bellies and glassy eyes." Elsewhere in the same letter, Wright reveals how darkly he viewed the situation back home: ". . . nothing but the Ohio Valley (i.e., death, real death to the soul) on one side and life (escape to my own life . . .) on the other."[18]

By embellishing its flow with a bleak rain of coffins, Wright equates the Ohio River with the mythic Styx. Thus joined, the Ohio and the Styx become what Wright, in "Prayer to the Good Poet," later calls a "dark river of labor," ferrying away the broken and defeated. This image, pervasive throughout his work, serves as the focal point of the haunting collection *Shall We Gather at the River* (1968), a book decrying the fate of "legless beggars" and "Poor Washed Up by Chicago Winter." To Wright, release from such a place into the heavenly "other world" must have seemed an enticing alternative to enduring this world's sufferings, which surely accounts for Wright's inability to grieve the death of Willy Lyons, his "uncle, a craftsman of hammers and wood."

In the poem that bears his name, Willy has died with little to show for his years as a low-paid carpenter; "nothing," Wright says, with bilious irony, "but one cracked ball-peen hammer" and a suit his son "inherited, / For a small fee, from Hesslop's Funeral Home." At Willy's passing, Wright's mother weeps "with anger," fitfully mourning his death less than the hardscrabble life of poverty he had been forced to live in the Ohio River Valley.

Unlike his mother, Wright appreciates that by dying Willy has, in effect, freed himself from an unforgiving life controlled by economic forces. In the poem, Wright imagines "roan horses," often a figure of redemption in his poetry, "plod[ding] slowly" to the Styx to greet Willy's coffin. Instead of carrying Willy into the promised land, the horses mistake the coffin for a "horse trough drifted to shore" and find it empty, a detail which nicely salvages the poem from the possibility of sentimental excess. More importantly, though, Wright grants Willy in death a degree of personal agency simply not available to him in life. To gain redemption, Willy requires neither the mystic blessing of the "roan horses," nor the clink of coins needed to pay Charon, ferryman of the dead. He works patiently and with care, planing trees by the water's edge, "fitting his boat together" for the crossing to heavenly reward.

In crafting his own death ship, Willy escapes from what any good Marxist would surely label the commodification of labor, that process of reification whereby unique human activities forfeit their various qualitative differences in favor of a single quantitative measure of value—that is, how much one is paid for doing them. Pointedly, Wright, either by aesthetic choice or political inclination, avoids that sort of rhetoric. Though clearly aware of class distinctions and the role work has in them, Wright abjures political theory in favor of a deeply human, though spiritual, faith. He enables Willy to discover in death, in the release from earthly strictures, that craftsmanship itself possesses an immanent and redemptive value not bound to wage. If the poem is a version of American tragedy, it's also strangely, and ironically, beautiful.

In the books up to and including *Shall We Gather at the River,* Wright's attraction to forms of escape influences much of his poetry concerning work and workers. It also begins to distinguish his poetry of the working class from that of others writing on the same subject, in particular Philip Levine. If, at this stage of his career, Wright frequently yearns for escape, Levine prefers to stay put, sanctioning a kind of fight against authority and privilege that eludes Wright. One need only examine the function of animals in both poets' early work to see this distinction. Levine's lion in "They Feed They Lion" returns full of racial and class anger to riot Detroit like a contemporary version of Yeats's great beast. In "The Fox," the besieged animal turns to face his pursuers, "shouting and refusing / to budge, feeling the dignity / of the small creature menaced / by the many and larger."[19] Wright's animals, on the other hand, often serve as mythologized and beatific sources of transcendence, like the "Indian ponies" of his well-known "A Blessing," or the "great white bird" that he asks in "The Minneapolis Poem" to lift him away from the "police" to safety among the "secrets of the wheat and . . . the unnamed poor." In nearly every instance, these animals offer means for Wright to break free of the discomfiting reality of this world, a way to distance himself from gloomy Ohio. Unlike Levine, who still loosely considers himself a member of the working class and therefore speaks *with* them, Wright seems to regard himself as painfully outside of the outsiders and, as such, speaks *for* them.

While the quest for release compels much of Wright's poetry, so does the guilt associated with successfully achieving it. In fact, the tension that animates Wright's relationship with the Ohio River Valley can be attributed to his own physical if not spiritual escape from it. Wright, unlike many of his boyhood friends, did "get out." The mere grace, perhaps the luck, of that release infuses "The Flying Eagles of Troop 62" with a ranging, self-reflective intelligence. Appearing in *To a Blossoming Pear Tree* (1977), the prose poem is devoted to Wright's Scoutmaster, Ralph Neal, who "knew he would never himself get out of that slime hole of a river valley," or who "maybe . . . didn't want to." Ralph Neal stayed because of his Scout troop—boys he loved, Wright explains, mostly for the awful "knowledge of what would become of" them. And Ralph Neal was right, on both counts.

After Wright admits, almost ashamedly, that his "portrait hangs" in the Martins Ferry Public Library,[20] he then offers a broken litany of what happened to those who stayed there: "Dickey Beck, a three-time loser at housebreaking, was doing life at the State Pen"; "Dale Headley was driving one of those milk trucks where the driver has to stand up all day and rattle his spine"; "Hub Snodgrass was still dragging himself home to . . . spend a good hour still trying to scrape the Laughlin steel dust out of his pale skin"; and "Mike Kottelos was making book."

Making "book" in a different fashion, Wright records his friends' heroically unheroic history. Woven within it are the implicit failures of education, of religion, of capitalism, even of the Boy Scout system and—by extension—the generalized failure of America, "the very name of" which, Wright tells us, "often makes me sick." The poem might end here, easily dismissed, its tenor that of a familiar and myopic protest poem. But there's the matter of Ralph Neal, whom Wright conspicuously calls "an American." Dedicating himself to the boys, Neal illustrates "the most sublime of ethical ideals" by refusing to abandon them, behaving much like the poem's saint who refuses "Nirvana" when he realizes his rabid, "scruffy" dog can't "accompany him into perfect peace." Surely such loyalty became most honorable and most compelling to Wright in light of his own escape.

It's worth noting that Ralph Neal's actions earned no monetary reward. His was volunteer work, offering just the kind of intrinsic satisfaction that capitalism most often imperils. It's this humanity Wright admires in Ralph Neal, his ability to elude economic and spiritual bankruptcy without departing the earth altogether. In his late work, in fact, Wright comes to admire this determination to stay put, to endure the travails life foists upon us; gradually but certainly, this attitude counterbalances his yearning for escape.

The turnabout must have taken Wright by surprise, for in "The Old WPA Swimming Pool in Martins Ferry, Ohio," a poem appearing in *Two Citizens* (1973), Wright is "almost afraid to write down" what amounts to an epiphanic moment of spiritual rebirth. In the midst of the Great Depression, Wright's father and uncles had found work with the WPA digging a swimming pool next to the hopelessly polluted Ohio River, which, Wright tells us, was already "dying." For once, "that hole in the ground" isn't a grave. Instead, filled with water, it becomes a sort of New Deal baptismal font—providing salaries to sustain the out-of-work men and their families, and offering them the literal and figurative opportunity to rinse themselves in its redemptive waters. Diving deep, Wright himself "rose" to epiphany, delivered by a little girl's solemn—and practical—advice: "Take care now, / Be patient, and live."

Wright's father, who, he tells us in "Two Postures Beside a Fire," "broke stones, / Wrestled and mastered great machines," is the model for this way of life, a worker perhaps weary but decidedly not broken. Wright came to admire the way his father dealt with thwarted dreams and still refused to give in. In the prose poem "Honey," included in the posthumous *This Journey* (1982), Wright recounts one story exemplifying his father's response to the frustration of being without work:

I heard my father offer to murder his future son-in-law. . . . They were fighting with each other because one strong man, a factory worker, was laid off from his work, and the other strong man, the driver of a coal truck, was laid off from his work. They were both determined to live their lives, and so they glared at each other and said they were going to live, come hell or high water. High water is not trite in southern Ohio. Nothing is trite along a river.

Prompted by the loss of work during the Great Depression, the incident starkly demonstrates the two men's will to make a living, no matter what the physical and emotional costs. Still, the most curious aspect of the poem is not Wright's memory of the event itself, but his recollection of another incident, occurring near his father's death, in which his father subtly resolves the earlier dispute: "My father died at the age of eighty. One of the last things he did in his life was to call his fifty-eight-year-old son-in-law 'honey.'" The father's gesture of reconciliation is informed as much by stubbornness as by tenderness, for as Wright says at the poem's close, the real lesson here is this: "My father died a good death. To die a good death means to live one's life. I don't say a good life. // I say a life."

Wright's *This Journey* is replete with poems revealing his admiration for others who stay put, resolutely determined to resist any trial they encounter, those who show a muted, perhaps understated, courage in the face of adversity. If Wright never fully refuses the enticements of transcendence, he has, by this time, begun to amass a solemn list of those creatures and things that keep themselves firmly rooted to a place, even an irreparably ugly place. Things that have "withstood," as Fimrite suggests, all that life has thrown at them. In the poem "The Sumac in Ohio," for example, Wright discovers a grove of sumac opening their buds along the inhospitable slopes of a gulley in Ohio, impervious to the effects of "sap and coal smoke and soot from Wheeling Steel," their skin so tough it "will turn aside hatchets and knife blades." And in "A Finch Sitting Out a Windstorm," he celebrates as well the "damned fool" finch who dares to "return / The glare" of a windstorm, clamps his claws "so stubbornly" around a branch, and "refuses to move"—all the while rejecting Wright's halfhearted advice to "Give up, drift, / Get out."

Throughout his career, James Wright was compelled to write poems about the work and workers of Martins Ferry, the presiding spirit of a place he both dearly loved and hated. He loved the place for the resoluteness of the people who worked there and the stubborn beauty of the landscape. He hated it for the terrible ravages inflicted by grinding factory labor upon those people and the environment. His escape from that work and that place was itself the source of his most wrenching personal debate, the wellspring of both pride and shame, relief and a pertinacious guilt that reveals itself in his poems—perhaps nowhere more tellingly than in "Prayer to the Good Poet." Addressed to Horace, the poem asks the ancient poet to welcome Wright's seriously ill father into heaven, imploring him "to gather my father to your bosom." His father had reached the end of his own "dark river of labor" beside the Ohio where he once gathered his sons to swim, and now must cross the Styx into the afterlife. It's no accident Wright wishes to introduce his father to Horace: in doing so, he links his paternal and literary fathers. More importantly, in bringing the two together, he reconciles the work and place he escaped from and those he escaped to, and is able to confess, revealingly, to Horace:

> I once worked in the factory that he worked in.
> Now I work in the factory that you live in.
> Some people think poetry is easy,
> But you two didn't.

Absolved by his two fathers of having chosen the "easy" life over an honest day's work, Wright frees himself to speak for the "silenced" he left behind. In writing a personal and communal history of the working class in the Ohio River Valley, Wright spurns a glib, stereotypical presentation of oppressor and oppressed, and likewise rejects the easy solace of Marxist rhetoric. If the broken lives of the exploited must be recorded, so also must the lives of those who, by strength of will and moral conviction, refuse to succumb to exploitation.

Chapter Four

Why "Nothing is Past"

Philip Levine's Conversation with History

Three-quarters of the way through Philip Levine's "The Present," a poem recounting the bloody memory of what happened when "Froggy Frenchman" fell from a high pallet at work, Levine shares a secret with his readers, "I began this poem in the present / because nothing is past."[1] On a rhetorical level, Levine addresses his readers merely to let them know why, given the possibilities available to him, he chose present tense for a poem devoted to events long past. It's a way of saying, "Here's how this poem works," and though the remark surprises, it hardly smacks of the memorable. However, on an aesthetic plane, these lines reveal Levine's fundamental attitude towards the way the past impinges upon the present, enlivening, deepening, and sometimes haunting our lives. The past has never truly left us, Levine implies, and we can never flee from it.

In this larger sense, then, Levine has staked out a position on the interplay of history and the poet's own historical consciousness, insisting on a kind of dialogue with the people and events that compose the past and continue to shape the present. No solipsist, Levine is looking for an understanding of self that transcends the self, one that takes into account both the individual's place in history and history's place within the individual. In this way, Levine's thinking resembles Hans-Georg Gadamer's conception of the individual's relationship to history and its texts. Like Levine, Gadamer regards this process as a dialogue between the past and the present. In his *Truth and Method,* Gadamer makes this encounter an even more intimate affair, describing it as a "conversation," ideally one in which a person comes "to experience the 'Thou' truly as 'Thou,' i.e. not to overlook his claim and listen to what he has to say to us."[2] It was Gadamer, after all, who once called history itself "the conversation that we are." Still, while Gadamer concerns himself mostly with how one reads and interprets a text, Levine demonstrates how this process applies as well to the creation of an artistic text, to the making of a poem.

Moreover, Levine apprehends one aspect of this conversation that Gadamer complacently overlooks: that often the dialogue excludes the disempowered, the poor and the marginalized, those who have by some intentional or unintentional means been silenced by the exercise of power. Recorded history is rarely written by or about those individuals disenfranchised from the realms of political or economic power. Levine's poetry, compelled by moral and aesthetic urgency, therefore directly engages those individuals in poetic conversation. Whereas James Wright often spoke *for* the silenced, Levine instead speaks directly *to* and *with* them. What most interest me are those poems in which the speaker addresses an historical "you" in a kind of dialogic act. Sometimes that "you" says nothing in the conversation, other times a dialogue ensues, and occasionally the reader is the "you" the poem addresses. These poems provide a forum for Levine both to intermingle the private and the cultural and to interact with history—offering, in the process, an aesthetic means for him to personalize the historical and historicize the personal.

Gadamer regards this process as a "fusion" of historical "horizons": that which the individual brings to the subject and that of the subject which speaks to him.[3] In fact, Gadamer believes only a fool would consider these horizons as separate. Our individual horizon, what he calls "everything that can be seen from a particular vantage point," always exists within "one great horizon that moves from within," always remains part and parcel of "a single horizon that embraces everything contained in historical consciousness."[4] Understanding takes place when our own personal horizon of historical meanings and assumptions comes to be seen as "only something laid over a continuing tradition" and when our horizon fuses with that of the historical subject we are examining, whether it is a text, an event, or a person.[5] Gadamer refers to this simultaneous projection and removal of horizons as "effective-history."[6]

This may be a somewhat fancified way of saying that we come to see history as part of us and ourselves as part of history. Once we realize that "the present is being continually formed" by our "encounter with the past," as Gadamer asserts, we come to see how these horizons which we thought to be discrete actually define, inform, and shape each other.[7] Because the present requires the past to give it depth and perspective, and vice versa, understanding always issues from a "fusion" of these horizons which we imagine to exist by themselves. Levine's version of this is simply: "nothing is past."

Frequently these poems that converse with history examine the process by which human beings, burdened by oppressive economic and political forces and often nearly broken by them, still retain their essential human dignity. This idea surges like an undercurrent beneath much of Levine's poetry. Because it is a belief continually submitted to questioning, prodding, and belligerent testing, it charges his poems with poles of joy and anger, faith and despair, affirmation and resignation. For many poets such a compulsion might remain unfocused, a theme that inadvertently crosses wires and brings forth occasional sparks. Levine, however, claims both a personal source and an historical focus for his attentions: the Spanish Civil War. In his youth, Levine found in the Spanish anarchist's politics a system that promised to avoid the abuses of capitalism, fascism, and communism, a way of life he describes to an interviewer as having "to do with the end of ownership, the end of competitiveness, the end of a great deal of things that are ugly."[8] Levine goes on to say that his "obsession" with the war gained poignancy while he was growing up Jewish in the "extraordinarily anti-Semitic city" of Detroit, largely because the Spanish anarchists seemed to be the only ones willing to fight the fascism already spreading like plague through Europe and potentially, he feared, "reaching right into my house and snuffing me out."[9]

If, as in the poem "To P.L., 1916–1937," originally published in *They Feed They Lion* (1972), the historical figure remains silent, a conversation takes place just as surely as though the two were sitting face to face, over a cup of coffee, in a kitchen dark but for the light above the sink. And perhaps Levine did converse with P.L. before the man's death, for Levine reveals to Studs Terkel that P.L. was the "older brother of my closest friend," one of those men from Levine's Detroit neighborhood who "went off to fight for a free Spain and didn't come home."[10] Vividly imagining the soldier's death, the speaker fashions a kind of dialogue with the dead man in which one of the parties (necessarily) remains silent in much the same way as the Russian theorist M. M. Bakhtin describes below: "Imagine a dialogue of two persons in which the statements of the second person are omitted. . . . The second speaker is present invisibly. . . . We sense that there is a conversation, although only one person is speaking, and it is a conversation of the most intense kind, for each present, uttered word responds and reacts with its every fiber to the invisible speaker. . . ."[11]

The poem opens by graphically recounting P.L.'s lonely death in the snow, with "one side of your face / frozen to the ground," and then describes the casual way "they . . . bundled you / in canvas,

and threw you away."[12] It's interesting to note that the poem begins
with P.L. already dead, his sacrifice on the altar of democracy as
complete as it was apparently futile. What the speaker focuses on in
this conversation, and what he in effect thinks P.L. ought to know,
is what happened *after* his sacrificial death for the republic.

Here the speaker envisions, in the person of an "old country
woman / of the Aragon," an utterly pragmatic way in which good
comes out of such abject defeat. The woman relieves the dead man
of his Wellington boots, his hunting socks, and a knife he had worn
on his right hip, laughing ambivalently at the thought of the knife
even "though she had no meat to cut." In her poverty, caught in the
middle of a violent and pitiful battle for freedom, the woman comes
to see the dead man as an angel who has, through his passing, delivered unto her a tangible means of sustenance more valuable than
mere rhetoric. Believing she "understood" the true nature of P.L.'s
sacrifice, the old woman wears the boots and socks, and then passes
them down to her nephew in a trail of inheritance which extends the
traditional notion of family.

It's worth mentioning that Levine and P.L. share initials, for their
identities tend to mingle by the poem's end. Like P.L., described
here as "a soldier of the republic," Levine sees himself as a kind of
soldier in the cause of social equality, as his many poems of the
working class demonstrate. Moreover, the Spanish Civil War, which
Levine calls "the most meaningful war I can remember," embodies
all of the qualities most evocative in his world view: the pugnacity
of the little guy against overwhelming odds, the obstinate human
will for social democracy, and the unrelenting force used to squash
such citizen rebellions.[13] Levine wants P.L. to know simply that,
despite his death and the anarchists' defeat, the human spirit remains fiercely unbroken. What's more, the dead man's inheritance
proffers to this day a tangible as well as spiritual utility:

> The knife is still used, the black handle
> almost white, the blade
> worn thin because there is meat to cut.

Here the battle knife becomes the table knife—enacting a transformation as regenerative as the more familiar conversion of swords
into ploughshares. In a larger sense, the poem achieves Gadamer's
"fusion" of historical horizons; simply put, the poem's conversation
with history asserts that the past is not past. Certainly not for the
old woman, who years later sees in her mind's eye the dead man's
"tight fists / that had fallen side by side" and must turn in grief

from her bread and soup. Surely not for Levine, who, even after the woman's death, memorializes the spot where the man lay dead:

> Without laughter she is gone
> ten years now,
> and on the road to Huesca in spring
> there is no one to look for you
> among the wild jonquils, the curling
> grasses at the road side,
> and the blood red poppies, no one
> to look on the farthest tip
> of wind breathing down from the mountains
> and shaking the stunted pines you hid among.

To say the poem is political is no revelation, though the terms of its rebellion have less to do with overthrowing governments than with freeing the human heart. Its politics are implicit, inherent to Levine's conception of writing, for "just the writing of a poem is a political act. . . . if a man or a woman insists on depicting the truth, that in itself is a kind of political act."[14] In "Gift for a Believer," a poem addressed to the anarchist artist Flavio Costantini, Levine labors to depict such "truth," linking the fates of Jews under Nazism and all those who suffered under Spanish fascism.

The poem surveys the pitiable results of the Spanish anarchists'— and his own—dream for a "new world."[15] It offers a cracked litany of those who were in one way or another defeated by the fascist system, including "Santo Caserio / who lost his head for knifing / the President of France, the ambassador / to hell," Ferrer Guardia, the leader of a Spanish free school that taught the "children to question" fascism, and Francisco Ascaso, killed during the "storming" of a fascist barracks. Troubled by the broken promise of these lives, the speaker dwells on a dream of Costantini's in which the anarchist Durruti voices his most solemn pledge:

> In your vision Durruti whispered
> to an old woman that he would
> never forget the sons and daughters
> who died believing they carried
> a new world there in their hearts,
> but when the doctor was summoned
> and could not stop his wounds
> he forgot.

Remembering those victimized by systems political or economic is perhaps the cornerstone of Levine's poetry, the sacred act of memorializing upon which all of his art is built. If Durruti's failure to remember receives rebuke here, the speaker's real argument is with the system that violently snuffed out the anarchist's dream. But lest he too easily let himself off the hook, the speaker recalls his own forgotten vow:

> When old Nathan Pine
> gave two hands to a drop-forge
> at Chevy, my spit turned to gall
> and I swore I'd never forget.
> When the years turned to a gray mist
> and my sons grew away without faith,
> the memory slept, and I bowed
> my head so that I might live.

This fusing of the personal and the historical gives the poem emotional depth and historical sweep. It shows Levine's readiness to interpolate his own historical presence within the broader scope of history, a practice which, as we shall see, only intensifies as his work matures.

In *7 Years from Somewhere*, three years after the publication of "Gift to a Believer" in *The Names of the Lost* (1976), Levine still stubbornly mulls over the complex interrelationship of his own past and the broader movements of history, particularly the Spanish Civil War. If Levine broods, he does so not to satisfy some yearning for self-pity, or to feed the self-congratulatory conviction that he is indeed more sensitive than most. Instead, he ponders the past as a way to give proportion and perspective to the present, as a way to make sense of what it is to be human and caught up in the spiralling of larger forces against which our grandest designs have so little effect. Levine appears stolidly intent upon contradicting Heidegger's advice to the poet residing in a period such as ours, the "time of the world's night": "To be a poet in a destitute time means: to attend, singing, to the trace of the fugitive gods."[16] Levine purposefully neglects the godly in favor of the human. He turns his eyes not to heaven but to the dirt beneath his feet, to the horizon he moves through and which moves through him.

It's no wonder, then, that Levine throughout his career makes frequent pilgrimages to cemeteries, locales that hold the last physical traces of those whose lives have ended but whose influence may doggedly persist. For example, in "Francisco, I'll Bring You Red

Carnations," a poem addressed to the anarchist Ascaso, the speaker wanders the "great cemetery / behind the fortress of Barcelona," among the graves of poor and rich alike, all of them finally equal in the blank, earthly brotherhood of death.[17] The poem quickly moves to Levine's characteristic themes: poverty, economic and political oppression, and testing of the human spirit's will to endure. But the poem also marks a clear departure from the earlier "Gift for a Believer," for in it the speaker regains his confidence in himself and the greater cause:

> While the streets are echoing
> with victory and revolution,
> Francisco Ascaso will take up
> the hammered little blade
> of his spirit and enter for
> the last time the republics
> of death. I remember
> his words to a frightened
> comrade who questioned
> the wisdom of attack: "We
> have gathered here to die, but we
> don't have to die with dogs,
> so go."

There again is that knife blade, the knife of battle and of table, glinting with the promise for which Ascaso and P.L. and others gave their lives. There again is the dream of a "city / of God, where every man / and every woman gives / and receives the gifts of work / and care." This time, however, the speaker discovers that dream of social democracy "here / growing in our hearts, as / your comrade said." This time he asserts the dream will not end with their "last / breaths," for someone else will "gasp it home to their lives" and revivify its faltering spirit. This time, he vows to uphold that promise in word and deed:

> we will be back,
> across an ocean and a continent,
> to bring you red carnations,
> to celebrate the unbroken
> promise of your life that
> was once frail and flesh.

The startling transition that has taken place between *They Feed They Lion* (1972) and *7 Years from Somewhere* (1979) signals a transformation in Levine's attitude toward the persistence of the dream of social change. Just as remarkably, his personal horizon and the larger historical horizon have begun both to question and to define each other within these poems. It's arguable that the most compelling of these conversations with history appears in *One for the Rose* (1981), "To Cipriano, in the Wind," a piece that deftly conflates the personal and the historical.

Here, for the first time in these dialogic poems, the historical figure's own words take preeminence over the poet's, serving as both catalyst for the poem and object of the poet's need:

> Where did your words go,
> Cipriano, spoken to me 38 years
> ago in the back of Peerless Cleaners,
> where raised on a little wooden platform
> you bowed to the hissing press
> and under the glaring bulb the scars
> across your shoulders—'a gift
> of my country'—gleamed like wood.
> '*Dignidad*,' you said into my boy's
> wide eyes, 'without which is no riches.'
> And Ferrente, the dapper Sicilian
> coatmaker, laughed. What could
> a pants presser know of dignity?[18]

"*Dignidad.*" That which makes even the poorest human being rich. That which cannot be bought or stolen or wrenched by force from a man or woman who truly owns it. This, in a word, is the fullest expression of Levine's humanism. In the battle against political or economic oppression, Levine tells us, using Mera's words, we may be destroyed but never truly defeated if we retain our human dignity.[19] Later in the poem Mera says it more succinctly, in stately though broken English, with subtle Biblical overtones:

> . . . 'Some day the world
> is ours, someday you will see.'

And still later,

> 'Spring, spring, it always come after.'

After the winter's "worst snow," of course, when "within a week wild phlox leaped / in the open fields" surrounding Detroit. And after, Levine must also be thinking, P.L.'s death, after the old woman had liberated his boots, socks, and knife, soon came the spring and its "blood red poppies." Looking for a way to reaffirm his own beliefs, the speaker turns to Mera's words for emotional and intellectual succor. That out of apparent defeat, victory may come—this is what he sorely needs to be reminded of. He finds it not only in the person and words of Mera, but also in a host of personal memories that gain broader, historical perspective when associated with these remarks. Notice how the speaker personalizes the historical and, in turn, historicizes the personal:

> That was the winter of '41, it
> it would take my brother off to war,
> where you had come from, it would
> bring great snowfalls, graying
> in the streets, and the news of death
> racing through the halls of my school.
> I was growing . . . .
> That was the winter
> of '41, Bataan would fall
> to the Japanese and Sam Baghosian
> would make the long march
> with bayonet wounds in both legs,
> and somehow . . .
> he would return to us and eat
> the stale bread of victory.

This lesson of eventual "victory" in the long fight echoes the Biblical promise that the meek shall indeed inherit the earth. It is Mera's sustaining gift to Levine, a gift of belief equal to Costantini's and Ascaso's and more than enough to counter the ironic "gift" of scars Mera received from his country. Even more significant is what occurs near the close of the poem, when the poet, the supposed master of language, rejects his own words and instead appropriates Mera's. Levine speaks "Dignity" and "Some day this will all be ours" into the "winds" that surely blew across P.L., Ascaso, Durruti, his own dead Russian "cousins," as well as the inhabitants of Barcelona's cemetery, in the end imploring the past to enter his present:

> Come back, Cipriano Mera
> . . . . Enter my dreams
> or my life, Cipriano, come back
> out of the wind.

Levine's insistence on immersing himself in such dialogue with history brings with it a commensurate receptivity to the voice of the Other. By the publication of *A Walk with Tom Jefferson* (1988),

Levine's conversation becomes a true dialogue. Moreover, Levine shows a striking willingness to cede the remarkable lines of his poems, those lines most resonant of meaning and most memorable to the ear, to the voice of that Other. In the case of the title poem, it is Tom Jefferson, a black man scraping out a meager existence amidst a nearly abandoned neighborhood devastated by the 1967 riots in Levine's native Detroit. Levine offers a clue to the source of the poem, and a key to its manner, when he tells Mona Simpson: "I discovered in some of the areas that had been burned out back in '67 . . . almost a semi-rural life. . . . Lots of empty spaces, vacant lots, almost like the Detroit I knew during the war. . . . I met a guy who lived in one of these houses. He didn't own or rent it, and in fact he didn't even know who owned it. He described his life there, and the poem rose out of the conversation we had."[20]

By the time "A Walk with Tom Jefferson," a poem of nearly six hundred lines, appears in print, the "conversation" to which Levine alludes has grown considerably. It embraces not only the original two characters and their respective histories, but also the history of Detroit, as well as a broad gauge history of race relations in America. And clearly Levine ups the ante when he names the character Tom Jefferson, "[s]ame name as the other one," for this man carries with him the powerfully charged associations of the "other" Jefferson's conflicting roles as defender of individual rights, president, plantation owner, and slave holder.[21]

Given this range of characters, the poem's conversation with history can be expected to build and follow its own momentum, to veer off haphazardly in the manner such conversations take in the real world of late afternoon walks. In fact, the "walk" itself becomes a fitting metaphor for the process of dialogue, as the men amble over an ever-changing terrain, a wasteland, really, whose presence is both mental and physical. Gadamer recognizes this unpredictable quality of any conversation and clearly relishes it: "We say that we 'conduct' a conversation. . . . Rather, it is generally more correct to say that we fall into a conversation, or even that we become involved in it. The way in which one word follows another, with the conversation taking its own turnings and reaching its own conclusion, may well be conducted in some way, but the people conversing are far less the leaders of it than the led. No one knows what will 'come out' in a conversation."[22]

When the narrator discovers that Tom Jefferson was a schoolmate of the boxer Joe Louis, the conversation quickly accelerates. Louis, who knocked out Max Schmeling and thereby debunked at once the myths of Nazi superiority and black inferiority, serves as public symbol of the private fight for dignity Tom Jefferson and others like him have fought within our society. Like Louis, Tom's father was "up from Alabama" and its cotton fields, "lured" to the good life expressed piquantly by the delicious phrase, "the $5 day." Like so many African-Americans, his family came to Detroit to seek factory work, as others migrated north for the same reason to Cleveland, Gary, Indianapolis, Chicago, and a score of Midwestern industrial sites, changing, in the process, the literal and figurative complexion of these cities. Thomas, of Rita Dove's *Thomas and Beulah*, came to Akron for similar reasons, as we shall see in a later chapter.

Tom Jefferson embodies that transformation and its sullied promise. "We all come for $5 / a day and we got *this!*", Tom says, as he opens his arms, gesturing to both narrator and reader, upon a Whitmanian catalogue detailing the "dumping ground" of the broken and the lost. Here's a sampling:

> old couches and settees,
> burst open, the white innards
> gone grey, cracked
> and mangled chifforobes
> that long ago gave up
> their secrets, yellow wooden
> ice boxes yawning
> at the sky, their breath
> still fouled with years
> of eating garlic sausage
> and refried beans . . .

It's clear the narrator is touched by the sight of such desolation, especially in a neighborhood once familiar to him, and his choice of pronouns reveals his agitation and *angst*. He sails Tom's story amidst a heaving sea of pronouns, "he," "you," and "I" tossing on waves of emotion, sometimes allowing Tom to tell his story in his own words, sometimes paraphrasing him, and occasionally interjecting his own perspective on things, as he does below, when he links Tom, his readers, and himself in the inclusive embrace of "we":

> We feel it as iron
> in the wind. We could escape,
> each of us feels in
> his shuddering heart,
> take the bridge south to Canada,
> but we don't.

The narrator realizes "escape," whether real or imagined, remains impossible. Even though snow will soon transform the assembled junk into a strangely beautiful "new world," he refuses its easy enticements. More importantly, he again seems to refuse the larger possibility of the "new world" Durruti spoke of, the city Ascaso dreamed of where everyone receives "the gifts of work / and care." The narrator's previous sense of unity momentarily disintegrates as he recognizes what differentiates Tom from himself: While the narrator "won't believe" in such change, Tom Jefferson "is a believer. / You can't plant winter vegetables / if you aren't.'"

Not surprisingly, Jefferson's garden, planted out of the need to feed his family, then becomes the focus of conversation. It's one means of "making do" with diminished resources, of course, an expression of undaunted human will to survive, as the narrator smartly points out Tom was planting his "before the Victory Gardens" occasioned by World War II or those made popular among the genteel classes by the PBS television series. This garden, by necessity, values sustenance over beauty or hobby. But, as Gadamer remarks, "no one knows what will 'come out' in a conversation," and Jefferson's garden abruptly gains symbolic and Biblical overtones. Gradually the metaphor blossoms and spreads, entwining the narrator's and Jefferson's lives.

When Jefferson went off to World War II, his son "took over the garden," and later when his son went off to the Korean War and died there, Tom resumed his duties:

> 'That's Biblical,' he says,
>   'the son goes off,
> the father takes up the spade
>   again, that's Biblical.'

This sense of cycle and loss, as well as the corresponding need for someone to pick up the fallen flag and carry it forward, suddenly permeates the conversation. In Tom's eyes everything is "Biblical," and the word recurs, repeated like the chorus of a gospel hymn, each time more resonant and encompassing, each repetition more compelling. Tom relies on it to describe his relationship with his wife after their son's death, the story of David and Saul and Absalom, "[m]aybe even" war and the fighting of poor whites and poor blacks for the same "gray" jobs and housing. It's not clear in the poem whether the last two remarks are made by Tom or by the narrator, for as Richard Jackson points out, the narrator "seems to absorb some of Jefferson's vocabulary and images," so much so that a "gradual fusion of points of view" occurs in the poem.[23] Such fusion began fitfully, as I've noted, with the narrator's use of the pronoun "we," and it suggests a key to the poem's structure.

Levine's melding of viewpoints resembles the fusing of historical horizons Gadamer describes in *Truth and Method,* and the poet nicely gathers these perspectives into a complex but unified whole. Jefferson's belief that we "need / this season" of winter cold to fulfill Biblical and natural cycle persuades the narrator himself to believe that "the heart / of ice is fire waiting," that "the new seed / nestles in the old, / waiting, frozen, for the land to thaw." These sentiments surely echo Mera's belief in eventual "victory" in the long fight, in the coming birth of a moral state, in his conviction that "some day this will all be ours."

Here the poem's true dialogic structure reasserts itself. As a conversation can take unexpected swerves, so does the poem, for the dialogue sheers away to the narrator's memory of working, as a "kid," at Cadillac transmission (where Levine, it should be noted, once worked himself):

> When I worked nights
> on the milling machines
> at Cadillac transmission,
> another kid just up
> from West Virginia asked me
> what was we making,
> and I answered, I'm making
> 2.25 an hour,
> don't know what you're
> making, and he had
> to correct me, gently, what was
> we making out of
> this here metal, and I didn't know.
> Whatever it was we
> made, we made of earth. Amazing earth . . .

And with it the cycle continues, ineluctably, as another kid like Tom, "just up" from the South, sets to work in the factories. But if Tom knows what he makes out of earth, his beets and cabbages and tomatoes, these men have no idea what they are making on the assembly line. If ever the time were ripe for Levine to issue forth Marxist dogma, this is it. The dissociation of maker from the thing made begs the question of commodity reification, a process Fredric Jameson describes as the "way in which, under capitalism, the older forms of human activity are instrumentally reorganized and . . . re-constructed according to various rational models of efficiency."[24] The result, Jameson argues, is that "all forms of human labor" lose their qualitative differences as human acts of making and come to be judged solely "under the common denominator of money."[25]

Instead, through the voice of his narrator, Levine abjures such dogma, much as James Wright does, in favor of Jefferson's belief in the ultimate efficacy and dignity of human labor. Jefferson's example persuades the narrator to "half-believe" he was indeed making transmission parts all those years ago. Moreover, Jefferson's argument about the value of "making do," which pervades the poem, proves, in the end, more convincing than the fact it said "Chevrolet Gear & Axle / right on the checks they paid / us with." Through Jefferson's example, the narrator recognizes human dignity can endure, if not elude, enslavement by the "common denominator of money." He comes to understand that, no matter what he was in fact making on the assembly line, he was truly "making do"—the most blessed expression of human endeavor. Tom Jefferson's example bespeaks the full measure of Mera's "*Dignidad*," and as such, these two men (plus Jefferson's presidential namesake) blend race, nationality, and time in a kind of global/historical humanism.

One curious aspect of these conversations with history is the role of the reader, who has, for the most part, remained a passive witness to the proceedings. True enough, Levine occasionally refers to the reader as "you" in "A Walk with Tom Jefferson," and his use of the pronoun "we" further acknowledges the reader's presence. Still, the narrator's own ruminations and his interaction with Jefferson direct the poem's development through distance and time.

Many of Levine's most recent conversations with history change all of that. In *What Work Is,* winner of the 1991 National Book Award, Levine often reaches out to yank the reader into the poem, in the process decentering the speaker as the focus of attention and replacing him with the reader. One example of this is "Coming Close," where the speaker serves merely as guide for the reader's encounter with a brass polisher—one of those disempowered "historical" voices that Gadamer too conveniently overlooks. Once passive observer, the reader now becomes active participant, dirtied by the grimy reality of industrial labor. The poem's opening tugs its readers by the lapels into a dehumanizing factory setting that renders even gender questionable:

> Take this quiet woman, she has been
> standing before a polishing wheel

> for over three hours, and she lacks
> twenty minutes before she can take
> a lunch break. Is she a woman?[26]

The speaker asks the reader to consider what this kind of work has done to the woman, to note her "striated" triceps, the "dusting of dark brown" above her lip, even the sweat that spills beneath the "red / kerchief across the brow" and the "darkening" wrist band she uses to wipe it away. Everything is open to question, everything subject to debate, the speaker implies. What's more, when this distance proves too great to ascertain the facts, the speaker insists,

> You must come closer
> to find out, you must hang your tie
> and jacket in one of the lockers
> in favor of a black smock . . .

This merging of identities, this willingness to "experience the 'Thou' truly as 'Thou,'" as Gadamer argues, undergirds true historical consciousness: the ability to see, from our perspective in the present, the fusing of our personal horizon within the larger horizon of history. Precisely this understanding is available to the reader who grunts to lift heavy loads with the woman and who ferries her "new trays of dull, / unpolished tubes," experiencing, if only imaginatively, the bludgeoning repetitiveness of her work. To learn to see this woman as an individual, not as a nondescript face among masses of workers, this at once serves as the speaker's goal for the reader and the reader's unspoken, and perhaps unwilling, quest.

If in the past these conversations primarily involved the poet, history, the poem, and a reader whose role in the dialogue was rarely acknowledged, now this reader actively engages both text and history. Even though poetic form, of course, prevents the reader from actually speaking words within the text, that reader's response is what gives the poem its urgency and communion, its full historical vitality. Without the reader's active mental presence and rhetorically implied physical presence, the poem would falter. Its conversation would fall ineffectually silent. Similarly, although the reader cannot answer the woman when she asks "why" her life and work must be like this, that reader is marked for life by the encounter:

> Even if by some magic
> you knew, you wouldn't dare speak
> for fear of her laughter, which now
> you have anyway as she places the five

> tapering fingers of her filthy hand
> on the arm of your white shirt to mark
> you for your own, now and forever.

What's striking about the final gesture is the way the woman just as well marks the reader for *her* own, the dirt of her hand serving as outward sign of the reader's inward experience. Thus, Levine's rhetorical decision to engage the reader in the poem's dialogue introduces the reader to a person inhabiting a different historical circumstance. In the poem "What Work Is," as well as the poem above, that historical circumstance separating reader from Other has more to do with class than with temporal distance. If in "Coming Close" the reader merely assists the narrative's main figure, here the reader becomes the poem's central character. Note how the poem's opening pronouns forcefully merge speaker and reader, as the speaker's "we" pulls the reader's "you" into the line of men seeking work:

> We stand in the rain in a long line
> waiting at Ford Highland Park. For work.
> You know what work is—if you're
> old enough to read this you know what
> work is, although you may not do it.
> Forget you. This is about waiting,
> shifting from one foot to another.
> Feeling the light rain falling like mist
> into your hair, blurring your vision
> until you think you see your own brother
> ahead of you, maybe ten places.[27]

"Forget you," the speaker commands the reader. Forget you are reading poetry in an overstuffed chair and instead become the "you" standing in line, in light mist, "waiting" for an offer of work that odds say won't be forthcoming. Refocus your "vision" so radically that you see not a clump of men wearing flannel shirts and baseball caps but "your own brother" among those looking for work. Fuse your horizon with this "you" so as to become him, this Other "you."

Thereafter, the speaker's use of the word always carries a double meaning, so that the "you" experiencing the poem's narrative is joined with the "you" reading it. The effect is a compelling fusion of poem and reader, especially when "you" discover that, even though it is "someone else's brother" standing in line, that man shares your brother's "stubbornness, / the sad refusal to give in" to the cold reality of "No, / we're not hiring today" which awaits both of you. In fact, your brother is lucky; he has a job. He's home sleeping off "a miserable night shift" so he can awaken to study German and "can sing / Wagner . . . / the worst music ever invented."

The thought of your brother's refusal to be defeated by the economics of hard labor and thus his yearning for self-betterment, even through something as questionable as Wagnerian opera, floods "you" with an emotional torrent. In him, Mera's dream of *"Dignidad"* still breathes. Unlike so many of the workers Herbert Marcuse describes in *Eros and Civilization* (1955), your brother has not been psychologically victimized by mind-numbing factory labor, denuded of any individual qualities by the assembly line. But perhaps "you" have—not by work, but by the lack of it. The poem moves to climax as a result of this sudden recognition, which prompts an overwhelming urge to tell your brother you love him and "maybe" kiss his cheek:

> You've never
> done something so simple, so obvious,
> not because you're too young or too dumb,
> not because you're jealous or even mean
> or incapable of crying in
> the presence of another man, no,
> just because you don't know what work is.

The poem's final line *cleaves* the poem's "you" and the readerly "you," both unifies and separates them in keeping with the word's double meaning. On one hand, the line emphasizes the importance given to work in our culture, so much so that being without it strikes at the core of a man's sense of maleness, his acceptance of the stereotypical burden to support himself and his family. To "know what work is," to have a job, is to know one's place in the culture and thus to know one's self. On the other hand, the line carries an accusatory tone, particularly if one keeps in mind that the poem originally appeared in *The New Yorker.* Most of the magazine's up-scale readers, one assumes, have never known standing in line for work at "Ford Highland Park," or better, have never known the debilitating wound that lack of work can inflict upon one's psyche. Remember, also, that much of Levine's best work has appeared in *The New Yorker,* and he has been known to suggest at poetry readings that he frequently considers the response such a poem will generate among its readers.

One final poem, "On the Meeting of Garcia Lorca and Hart Crane," a poem which also appeared in *The New Yorker* and which opens Levine's 1995 Pulitzer Prize-winning *The Simple Truth,* ex-emplifies the tendencies discussed thus far. The poem concerns the speaker's cousin, Arthur Lieberman, a former "language student at Columbia" who, on his deathbed, told the speaker of his having brought together Lorca and Crane in Brooklyn in 1929. Not only does Arthur facilitate such historical dialogue, he also, because he "knows both Spanish and English," acts as its interpreter. He would therefore seem to be the perfect embodiment of Gadamer's "ef-fective-history."

Surprisingly, not a word of the conversation between the two "poetic geniuses" appears in the poem. Neither Arthur nor the speaker is "frivolous" enough to try to recapture it or to "pretend" it bore "wisdom." Neither is foolish enough to attempt to "invent a dia-logue of such eloquence / that even the ants in your own / house won't forget it." No doubt theirs was a conversation like all others, fraught with misunderstanding and peril and surprise. No doubt theirs was no better or worse than the conversations each of these poems has pursued. What does come to Arthur as a result of this en-counter is a "double vision" which fuses his historical horizon with theirs, shocking him with a premonition of the poets' untimely deaths: Crane's suicide from a ship at sea in 1932 and Lorca's at the hands of a firing squad during the Spanish Civil War (returning us to the wellspring of Levine's work). The speaker asks his reader:

> Have you ever
> had a vision? Have you ever shaken
> your head to pieces and jerked back
> at the image of your young son
> falling through open space, not
> from the stern of a ship bound
> from Vera Cruz to New York but from
> the roof of the building he works on?
> Have you risen from bed to pace
> until dawn to beg a merciless God
> to take these pictures away? Oh, yes,
> let's bless the imagination. It gives
> us the myths we live by. Let's bless
> the visionary power of the human
> (the only animal that's got it) . . .[28]

Levine acknowledges this perilous aspect of imagination, the way that we humans, by imagining the life of others, may come face to face with the "horror" as well as the beauty of our own existence.

This "double vision" issues from an assiduous attention to the intersection of our lives with that of the Other, and it orders our sense of place and value in a world divided along historical, social, and racial lines. Through their conversations with history, these poems seek to enlarge both the poet's and the reader's individual horizons, to extend what we can see from our "particular vantage point," as Gadamer puts it. These poems ask readers to chance a "vision" of ineffable loveliness and equal ugliness, a vision of what it is to be human. If we take Levine's word that "nothing is past," then we readers follow this vision toward a future always in dialogue with the past and the evanescent moment of our present.

Chapter Five

Vietnam and the "Voice Within"

Yusef Komunyakaa's *Dien Cai Dau*

The haunting locale of Yusef Komunyakaa's *Dien Cai Dau* (1988) is as much the domain of the human heart and mind as the jungles of Southeast Asia. Based on Komunyakaa's Vietnam War experiences, the book details an inward turning, "a way of dealing with the images inside my head," as Komunyakaa tells an interviewer, a means to put in order a private history that exists as much outside of history as within it.[1] Komunyakaa abjures the war's "objective" history that flickered in America's living rooms on the nightly news, objectivity figured most shockingly by the daily body count fulgurating behind Walter Cronkite's head like heat lightning on a steamy July evening. Instead, Komunyakaa's *Dien Cai Dau* operates within an essentially dialogic structure in which he carefully directs a dialogue between such communal history and the more personal accounts of those who took part in these events. As an African-American veteran, Komunyakaa exists on the margins of official war history, grouped with those Wallace Terry has called the forgotten "fact" of the war—the "Black Americans who fought there."[2] His collection provides a perspective on the war that other fine poetry collections by Vietnam vets—John Balaban's *After Our War* and Bruce Weigl's *The Monkey Wars* come to mind as perhaps the best—simply can't offer.[3] Komunyakaa creates a soldier's history of Vietnam from an African-American perspective, and not surprisingly, our view of what it was to be an American in Vietnam, particularly a Black American, alters considerably. Komunyakaa relies on elements of the very media we most closely associate with the war's communal experience—music, television, drama, and film—to reveal how these elements were perceived, often quite differently, by white and African-American soldiers.

Perhaps by virtue of this marginalization, Komunyakaa is acutely aware of the disparity between the history recorded in books and the history one immediately experiences. In fact, Komunyakaa's implicit recognition of the distinction between objective history and a personally felt history resembles Martin Heidegger's distinction between "Historie" and "Geschichte."[4] For Heidegger, in his study of temporality, *Being and Time,* "Historie" is roughly what is "recorded," the course of events that chronicles the rise and fall of nations, the wars these nations prosecute, the fate of civilizations on a large scale. It amounts to a "science" of history. On the other hand, "Geschichte" has more to do with the individual's own inward and "authentic" sense of life, the way what is recorded may pale in comparison to the individual's own immediate experience of those very outward events that shape "Historie." In "Geschichte," time becomes an ontological category, the historical-being of the individual. Thus, each individual must take responsibility for his/her own life and push ahead into the "possibilities" of a future not bound to historical time. In Komunyakaa's work, these two senses of the individual's place in history are often in dialogue, for while the actual events of history possess a real presence, the speaker nearly always subordinates them to a more intuited, felt, and existential sense of what it meant (and still means) to experience the Vietnam War.

Because his quest is inward and subjective, the war's actual events frequently serve as mere backdrop for Komunyakaa's obdurate, private search for meaning. As a result, time collapses and expands within the journey as the speaker moves from past to present to a tentative future. Thus, time itself attains a kind of mutability in Komunyakaa's work, for what we assume to be past, and therefore gone, feverishly reasserts itself in the speaker's mind. The past simply will not stay put. And neither will the dead—as the speaker of "The Dead at Quang Tri" laments when the Buddhist boy whose head he'd rubbed "for luck" comes floating by "like a white moon" one dark night, "He won't stay dead, dammit!"[5] Komunyakaa's goal is a careful thinking and rethinking that will simultaneously revivify such events and enable him to come to peace with them. He does so, as Heidegger believes all poets must, through the natural agent of memory, through the second "coming of what has been":

> . . . thinking holds to the
> coming of what has been, and
> is remembrance.[6]

This amalgam of public and private history, hauntingly persistent and deeply pooled in Komunyakaa's memory, spills out in these poems in sometimes unexpected effluences. Komunyakaa says as much when, in an interview, he describes his brain as "sort of like a reservoir," containing "all the frightening images and what have you" associated with the war. Komunyakaa realizes that writing the book was an actual process of "letting go" of those images, a release of the perilous waters of memory.[7] In the poetic process, Komunyakaa combines actual history and his own inward response to historical events, then subjects both to the filter of his artistic sensibility. What results is a different kind of history that makes use of external, historical events to produce an inward, aestheticized history flushed with personal values and interpretations. Jeffrey Walsh summarizes this process for any veteran who attempts to present an artistic "vision of Vietnam": "the writer needs to order and recreate his own memories, and then to communicate an aesthetic 'version' of the realities he faced."[8] Still, Komunyakaa's *Dien Cai Dau* differs considerably from earlier poetic texts devoted to the war. Because the book comes thirteen years after the war's close, its manner is more retrospective and ruminative than collections published while the war raged in Southeast Asia, volumes such as Michael Casey's *Obscenities* (1972), D. C. Berry's *saigon cemetery* (1972), and the anthology of poems by Vietnam veterans, *Winning Hearts and Minds* (1972).[9] It is less a book "against" the Vietnam War, the claimed purpose of much poetry published during the War, and more a book *about* the War and the experiences it held for soldiers and innocents alike.[10]

Like revenants returned from death, these ghostly images conspire in Komunyakaa's work to make the past discomfitingly present. A good example of the collapse and expansion of time in these poems is "Starlight Scope Myopia," which opens with a nearly surreal memory of an ambush aided by the nightscope's deft technology of death:

> Gray-blue shadows lift
> shadows onto an oxcart.
> Making night work for us,
> the starlight scope brings
> men into killing range.

Not only does the scope make the enemy visible in the dark night of that distant past, but it also serves as the agent of their return to the speaker in the present, as the ironic use of "[m]yopia" in the title indicates. If anything, the speaker's vision is farsighted, stretching from the past to the moment of his present.

Even though the speaker tells the story in past tense, he acknowledges, later in the poem, the event's continuing presence in his life
"years after" the war. In this way, the speaker alters the poem's radical of presentation, rhetorically shifting himself and his reader from
the past into the present. Moreover, he calls attention to himself as
speaker and storyteller, and thus breaks the willing suspension of
disbelief many poems demand of their readers:

> Viet Cong
> move under our eyelids,
> lords over loneliness
> winding like coral vine through
> sandalwood & lotus
>
> inside our lowered heads
> years after this scene
>
> ends.

The distance between poet and poem and between poet and reader
further collapses when the speaker suddenly begins to identify with
these "shadows" and begins painfully to see them as human beings
it is his job to kill. The essential dialogic structure of the poem, and
of much of the book, first manifests itself here, enabling the speaker
both to address his past "self" and to engage his reader in the
chilling scene. In the selection quoted below, the speaker's dialogue
between duty and moral humanism is expressed in his choice of the
pronoun "you," which enables the speaker to distance the self who
is speaking from the self who years ago experienced this incident in
Vietnam. At the same time, the pronoun "you" collapses the reader's
distance from the poem and entwines that reader in the scene's
moral ambivalence:

> You try reading ghost talk
> on their lips. They say
>
> 'up-up we go,' lifting as one.
> This one, old, bowlegged,
>
> you feel you could reach out
> & take him into your arms. You
>
> peer down the sights of your M-16,
> seeing the full moon
> loaded on an oxcart.

If violence against combatants brings moral questions to the fore, it's no wonder that the speaker finds violence against innocents especially disturbing. In "Re-creating the Scene," the speaker details the circumstances surrounding the rape of a Vietnamese woman by three American soldiers. Komunyakaa, who served as a journalist in Vietnam, uses those skills to narrate the incident with ostensibly detached, journalistic precision. This rhetorical strategy helps the reader understand that, while the speaker did not actually witness the incident firsthand, he recounts it much like a journalist whose job is to recreate "the scene" of a crime for his readers. The poem's speaker seems to understand, as must Komunyakaa, that the incident inheres with the potential for exploitative use of language as disturbing in its own way as were the government's obfuscations regarding "kill ratio," "protective reaction strikes," and "pacification." Such an understanding issues from what James Mersmann describes as the poet's "awareness that war (the ultimate insensibility and untruth) is itself an abuse of language (the ultimate vehicle of sensibility and truth), or at least an occasion for its abuse."[11] Here, the speaker pieces together a narrative replete with careful details that enlarge the context of the incident:

> The metal door groans
> & folds shut like an ancient turtle
> that won't let go
> of a finger till it thunders.
> The Confederate flag
> flaps from a radio antenna,
> & the woman's clothes
> come apart in their hands.
> Their mouths find hers
> in the titanic darkness
> of the steel grotto,
> as she counts the names of dead
> ancestors, shielding a baby
> in her arms.

The language, though restrained and measured, strikingly contrasts the relative condition of the empowered and disempowered characters it describes. Torn from her largely agrarian society, the woman is pulled through the "metal door" of an armored vehicle representing at once the best and worst of a powerfully mechanized culture. Not only is the woman desecrated by the men's actions, but so too are her past, in the figure of the ancestors she recalls, and her future, embodied by the child she protects in her arms—all of them simultaneously wounded inside "a machine / where men are gods." One subtle but telling detail enlarges the context of the woman's fate: the "Confederate flag" that flies above the vehicle. Given that the poem's speaker, one assumes, is African-American, this one enumeration evokes the implicit racism of the incident and makes it more than a discrete, if obscene, aspect of the spoils of war. Surely the speaker recognizes in the woman's plight a version of his own struggle for respect and equality, and just as surely he sees that skin color—black, white, yellow—silently undergirds much of the politics of this war.

This one detail—the Confederate flag flapping above the rape scene—offers a trenchant and disturbing irony which belies its nearly offhand inclusion. The flag itself is an emblem of an agrarian society similarly crushed in the nineteenth century by the North's powerful military-industrial complex. That war was ostensibly fought to free the oppressed African-American slave population of the South (notwithstanding Lincoln's desire to maintain the Union). However, no sooner than the war was concluded—the slaves freed and democratic principles upheld—did trouble begin to brew in the western United States. When miners violated treaties by moving into Sioux country looking for quick wealth, the same government which had fought for the human dignity of slaves now sent soldiers to subjugate the Sioux by lethal force. The Sioux responded violently by slaughtering Captain W. J. Fetterman's contingent of eighty-two soldiers near Fort Kearny in 1866. The Sioux War (1865–67) raged in the western territories, ending with the inauguration of a new governmental policy of "small reservations" meant to segregate Indians in out-of-the-way and often desolate areas spurned by whites.

White governmental policy toward those with red skin thus stood in stark contrast to its treatment of blacks. Although Congress had approved Radical Reconstruction in an attempt to assure equality and integration for black Southerners, at the same time it sanctioned inequality and segregation for Native Americans in the West. Gen. William T. Sherman, seen by many Northerners as the savior of Southern slaves, directed a decade-long war against Plains Indians who would not meekly accept the reservation system and forego their nomadic way of life. When Kiowa, Cheyenne, Sioux, and other tribes resisted, Sherman vehemently urged General Sheridan to "prosecute the war with vindictive earnestness against all hostile Indians, till they are obliterated or beg for mercy." Numerour pitched battles ensued over the following years, including Custer's infamous "last stand" and concluding with the horrific and misnamed "Battle of Wounded Knee," where U. S. troops killed two hundred Dakota men, women, and children. As a southern black man, Komunyakaa is surely familiar with how such brutal ironies complicate the history of race relations in America. That his poem would extend these ironies to Southeast Asia is therefore not surprising.

As with "Starlight Scope Myopia," time shrinks and swells in "Re-creating the Scene," both for the woman whose story has been told and for the speaker who tells it. Once released from the APC, the woman turns her attention to filing a complaint, and she's momentarily filled with the promise of justice as "for a moment the world's future tense." Here too the speaker enters the poem in his position as journalist, interrupting the narrative to claim his role in the incident he's retelling, "I inform *The Overseas Weekly*." Although he tells the story in present tense to increase the immediacy of the incident, the speaker, of course, knows the story's ending as well as he knows the previous events he's already related to his readers. Again the past- and present-self implicitly engage in dialogue, in this instance pitting the soldier-self's belief in justice against the present-day speaker's knowledge of what has become of such innocence. At the poem's close, he conflates time as a means to emphasize this dialogue between temporal versions of the self, both his and hers, in which a difference in time demarcates the line between innocence and experience:

> on the trial's second day
> she turns into mist—
> someone says money
> changed hands,
> & someone else swears
> she's buried at LZ Gator.
> But for now, the baby
> makes a fist & grabs at the air,
> searching for a breast.

Komunyakaa's poem makes disconcertingly apparent that the Vietnam War involved more than the all too familiar arguments about Communist expansionism that characterized America's "objective" history of the conflict. In fact, as early as 1968, political commentators such as George Liska haggled over the salient "domestic implications" of the war, asserting that the domino theory had real and pertinent influence over issues in the United States.[12] In *War and Order: Reflec-*

tions on Vietnam and History (1968), Liska asserts that the "key" domestic issue affected by the war at that time is quite simply America's "racial" turmoil, a situation he describes as a "crisis."[13] Liska explains at length why opposing camps of "interventionists" and "anti-interventionists" disagree vehemently on what is at stake domestically through America's foreign policy initiatives in Vietnam. He then offers this summary of the interventionist or "imperial" viewpoint, one which he shares:

> There is an interdependence between affirmation of American prestige and power vis-a-vis Hanoi and its allies and the prospect for semi-orderly integration of American society in the face of Black Power. In the last resort, whatever order exists in the United States depends on the government's known will and ability to deal firmly with hostile force. A collapse of this reputation abroad would strengthen the appeal and increase the credibility of domestic advocates of violence as a safe and profitable way to "racial equality." Any administration conspicuously threatened abroad would be bound to have the greatest difficulty in dealing with domestic crises. The consequence of default in the exercise of the imperial role might very well be a Second American Revolution for the "independence" of a hitherto "colonized" group.[14]

Liska's *War and Order* overtly defends, as the chilling oxymoron of its title implies, a relationship between the judicious prosecution of war and the maintenance of amenable social order. If America doesn't show the Viet Cong who's boss, Liska argues, America will never squash the Black Power movement for equality at home. Perhaps the "hostile force" Liska has rightfully in mind is the Black Panthers, who sought the violent overthrow of government structures they regarded as oppressive. Still, it's not difficult to see such an argument as a means both to justify the war and to maintain the then-current distribution of power at home, or to alter it only so much as not to disrupt its imbalance. Even the phrase "semi-orderly integration" implies the kind of glacial progress toward equal rights that contributed largely to the civil unrest Liska sought to forestall. For most Americans, this interrelationship between domestic and foreign policy remained well beyond the horizon of their attention, and equally beyond the periphery of their knowledge. Many of Komunyakaa's poems, to the contrary, address these larger ideological issues and their effects on Black Americans, whom Liska sarcastically refers to above as an internally "colonized" group seeking "independence." As a result, the social situation back in the States in the late sixties insistently reappears in the text of these poems, and, as one would expect, the issue often revolves around race. True enough, these poems refuse overt racial and political anger. Alvin Aubert, in fact, regards Komunyakaa as "cautious in dealing with his ethnicity."[15] But these poems' resolute will is the source of their rhetorical power. Komunyakaa's speaker looks his readers in the eye and does not blink. When Vicente Gotera argues, in an otherwise cogent essay, that the fact "Komunyakaa is black hardly matters in many of the poems in *Dien Cai Dau*," he diminishes a substantial number of poems that gain their ability to scald and instruct from the fact of Komunyakaa's being African-American.[16] Those poems offer a viewpoint attainable best, and perhaps only, from a source conversant with the politics of race in America.

In fact, Komunyakaa takes some of our easy assumptions about the war, oftentimes garnered from film and music, and turns them on ear. How frequently in films devoted to the war, for example, is music shown as a kind of unifying force among American soldiers? How many scenes out of a film such as *Good Morning, Vietnam,* for instance, use music as the common denominator linking our troops in a shared cultural heritage? While it's difficult to deny that music itself was a crucial part of the experience of the war, both in Vietnam and at home, notice how Komunyakaa's African-American experience illuminates incidents in the poem "Tu Do Street" where music is not the unifying element we might have thought it to be:

> Music divides the evening.
> I close my eyes & can see
> men drawing lines in the dust.
> America pushes through the membrane
> of mist & smoke, & I'm a small boy
> again in Bogalusa. White Only
> signs & Hank Snow. But tonight
> I walk into a place where bar girls
> fade like tropical birds. When
> I order a beer, the mama-san
> behind the counter acts as if she
> can't understand, while her eyes
> skirt each white face, as Hank Williams
> calls from the psychedelic jukebox.

In this instance, music, instead of unifying, "divides" as surely as those "lines" drawn in the dust by men behaving like schoolyard from another, and likewise dividing one country into separate and unequal parts. The irony proves to be trenchant for America, a country founded on the doctrine of equal rights to all, and especially poignant when that country has called its citizens, both black and white, to offer themselves in sacrifice at war. The speaker gives the betrayal of these political and moral dogma a Biblical context:

> We have played Judas where
> only machine gun fire brings us
> together.

And lest the reader miss the careful choice of the pronoun "we" above, the speaker clarifies and broadens the culpability for such racism:

> Down the street
> black GIs hold to their turf also.

Racism is answered, not surprisingly, by racism, though it's unarguable that one of these groups holds more power to act upon this prejudice. Still, and this illustrates Komunyakaa's tenacious will and intellectual honesty, the poem does not stop here, at this ironic sense of brothers-in-arms at war amongst themselves. To his credit, Komunyakaa pushes the poem further into the darkened recesses of human relationships, discovering in the Saigon brothel neighborhood an even greater irony:

> Back in the bush at Dak To
> & Khe Sanh, we fought
> the brothers of these women
> we now run to hold in our arms.
> There's more than a nation
> inside us, as black & white
> soldiers touch the same lovers
> minutes apart, tasting
> each other's breath,
> without knowing these rooms
> run into each other like tunnels
> leading to the underworld.

In this brothel scene, hardly the most promising site for such revelations, the poem's black speaker comes to an epiphanic understanding of "shared humanity" that, for the American combatants, runs

deeper than their skin color.[17] More importantly, the speaker recognizes a common humanity whose roots cross the superficial boundaries of nations, connecting those of black, white, yellow, and, re-
calling Komunyakaa's "Recreating the Scene," red skin. Surely the
Vietnamese women these soldiers "run to hold," as well as their
brothers who fight the Americans, understand what it is to be human
upon this green globe and what sentence awaits each of us in death's
"underworld." However, this revelation does not come without its
share of ominous undertones, for the figurative "tunnels" that link
these men and women in their humanity also have a literal reality
in the deadly maze of tunnels the Viet Cong used to ferry supplies,
to fight and quickly disappear, and into which many American
soldiers ventured never to return (as "Tunnels," the book's second
poem, memorably describes). Such ironies did not escape the attention of the Viet Cong, who employed every tactic available to them
to undermine the morale of the American troops. Vietnam's version
of Tokyo Rose is the spritely "Hanoi Hannah," who, in a poem
bearing her name, strives to induce homesickness among the American troops by playing their music and reminding them of women
left behind:

> Ray Charles! His voice
> calls from waist-high grass,
> & we duck behind gray sandbags.
> "Hello, Soul Brothers. Yeah,
> Georgia's also on my mind" . . . .
> "It's Saturday night in the States.
> Guess what your woman's doing tonight.
> I think I'll let Tina Turner
> tell you, you homesick GIs."

Hannah's tactics are predictable, as predictable as the American
soldiers' reaction to them: they unleash "a white arc" of artillery
fire in vain attempt to silence her. The poem might easily fall prey
to cliché if it ended here, but Komunyakaa surprises his readers by
presenting an account of these tactics that has, for the most part,
gone unnoticed in other poetic descriptions of the war. His poems
become politically charged, though always understated, as he offers
a Black American's perspective on psychological warfare strategies
that accentuate racial division. Here the racial undercurrents of the
war produce the unpleasant, dull shock of nine-volt batteries held to
the tongue, as Hannah, having used Ray Charles and Tina Turner to
attract the black soldiers' attention, then spews forth her cynical
punch line while lamely attempting to mimic black dialect:

"You know you're dead men,
don't you? You're dead
as King today in Memphis" . . . .
"Soul Brothers, what you dying for?"

The question, of course, preys upon African-American soldiers' ambiguous position in the war, for they know the "King" who has died in Memphis is not Elvis, as some of my culturally impaired students have suggested, but Martin Luther King, Jr., assassinated at the hands of a white man. The question also calls to mind Muhammad Ali's curt retort when asked his reasons, other than religious, for not fighting in Vietnam: "No Viet Cong ever called me *nigger*."

Komunyakaa seizes this issue and examines it via a wide variety of media, employing television, drama, and even painting as portals to the human psyche. What's most interesting about each of these examples is the location where these events take place—inside an individual soldier's, or ex-soldier's, mind. The paradoxical effect of this existential mode, rather surprisingly, is to interrogate the reader's own assumptions about the interplay of this war and racial politics, and its results are startling. One piece in particular, "The One-legged Stool," makes clear that the Viet Cong realized the potential value of America's own latent racism and used it with terrifying results. A rambling dramatic monologue set in prose and prefaced by stage directions, the poem reads like a one-man play invoking all of the racial politics and psychological warfare tactics the book alludes to elsewhere. Forced to squat all day on a one-legged stool and "partly hallucinating," as the stage directions indicate, a black soldier bravely attempts to subvert his captors' tactics by standing up, literally and figuratively, for himself and America:

Don't you know I'll never cooperate? No, don't care what you whisper into the darkness of this cage like it came out of my own head, I won't believe a word. Lies, lies, lies. You're lying. Those white prisoners didn't say what you say they said. They ain't laughing. Ain't cooperating. They ain't putting me down, calling me names like you say. Lies. Lies. It ain't the way you say it is. I'm American. (Pause.) Doctor King, he ain't dead like you say. Lies . . . . You didn't see that. I'm still sitting on my stool.

The piece moves at a frenetic pace, as the speaker himself lurches from reality to fantasy, from present to past, from Vietnam to home—all of it punctuated by the periodic appearance of a shadowy-faced Viet Cong at a peephole in the hut's only door. Near the breaking point, reduced to eating "dung beetles" pinched from the floor, the man repeats his name, rank, and serial number as if they are a mantra, a way to pull back so far inside of the self as to become unassailable. Defiantly, the speaker refuses to give in to the enemy's psychological manipulation, and in the end he sees it as a kind of racism even worse than that he experienced in the American South:

> Yeah, VC. I've been through Georgia. Yeah, been through 'Bama too. Mississippi, yeah. You know what? You eye me worse than those rednecks.

This sense of the perilous nature of American racial and national identity pervades the book. It appears in one form in "Communique," where African-American soldiers quickly tire of the dominant culture's offering of Bob Hope's shopworn routines and the Gold Diggers' "[w]hite legs." (They wait instead for "Aretha" Franklin, who never appears.) These black soldiers "don't wanna see no Miss America," no doubt because in the sixties she was sure to be white, and even reject "Lola" Falana because she "looks awful white" to them. Elsewhere, it serves as fulcrum in "Report from the Skull's Diorama," through which the poem's black GIs, back from night patrol "with five dead," confront both the reality of their loss and "red bordered / leaflets" printed with the reminder, "*VC didn't kill / Dr. Martin Luther King.*"

Balancing these expressions of ethnic isolation, several poems stitched throughout the collection insist that a shared cultural heritage does exist for the American soldier and that this heritage can bind rather than divide. A good example is "Eyeball Television," in which a captured soldier, whose race is never an issue, conjures up images from American television's more or less universal popular culture, lurching from "Spike Jones" to "Marilyn Monroe" as a way to endure his fate. One show the soldier replays in his head—Robert Culp and Bill Cosby's *I Spy*—carries particular cultural significance as American television's first to feature a black co-star:

> He sits crouched in a hole
> covered with slats of bamboo,
> recalling hundreds of faces
> from *I Love Lucy, Dragnet,*
> *I Spy, & The Ed Sullivan Show* . . . .
> When he can't stop laughing
> at *Roadrunner* on Channel 6
> the sharp pain goes away.

In the same fashion, these soldiers, once removed from the battle-field, are shown to share interests that blur lines of color, age, class. In "A Break from the Bush," for instance, a mixed-race platoon of men with names like "Clem," "Johnny," and "Frenchie" relax as a group on R & R. The men play volleyball together, get "high on Buddha grass," and jam to the great black guitarist Jimi Hendrix's "Purple Haze," a song which came to be regarded, among the drug culture anyway, as an anthem to LSD.[18] Another poem, "Seeing in the Dark," plays upon the serviceman's long-standing appreciation of "skin / flicks." Regardless of race, a randy mob of infantry men "just back from the boonies" gathers together to watch "washed-out images / thrown against a bed sheet." The image of the bed sheet provides a ghostly means to join two things that surely domi-nate these soldiers' thoughts: the poetic, figurative death found on the sex bed and the literal death had on the battlefield.

The core of this loose series and a key to its structure, as well as the clue to the existential mode of the entire book, lies in "Jungle Surrender," a poem based on Don Cooper's painting of the same name. In the poem, the speaker imagines himself in the place of the captured American soldier the painting portrays, and he wonders how he would have fared under such interrogation. Would he tell them of the ambush he sprung while "plugged into the Grateful Dead"? Would he suffer and break, only to return "almost whole"? In Cooper's painting, as within the human mind, the speaker recognizes:

> Love & hate
> flesh out the real man, how he wrestles
> himself through a hallucination of blues
> & deep purples that set the day on fire.
>
> He sleep walks a labyrinth of violet,
> measuring footsteps from one tree to the next,
>
> knowing somehow we're all connected.
> What would I have said?
>
> The real interrogator is a voice within.

Yeats once said that while rhetoric involves an argument with another person, true poetry requires an argument *with*—or perhaps, *against*—the self. Throughout the book, the poem's speaker has engaged in a lively debate with the self, invoking complex issues of morality and race and politics and basic humanity. In the process, the reader, be-cause "we're all connected" (a line which echoes the epiphany of

"Tu Do Street"), has necessarily been drawn into this dialogue between public and private history.

The book has at its core the quest for a personal and authentically
meaningful sense of history that, while acknowledging the presence
of "Historie," is not burdened by it. Perhaps the book seeks a concrete instance of Heidegger's "Geschichte" that enables an African-
American poet to deal with his past, accept the present, and forge
ahead into the possibilities of the future opening before him. It's
arguable that such a sense of history, once achieved, is actually *ahistorical,* bound more to an immediate experience of time than that
provided by objective history. One final poem in *Dien Cai Dau* best
delineates the dialogic process in Komunyakaa's work in which "Historie"
and "Geschichte" come to be juxtaposed. As such, the poem serves
as a good illustration of the Russian theorist M. M. Bakhtin's contention that an individual can indeed hold a "dialogic relationship"
with his/her own words: ". . . dialogic relationships are also possible toward one's own utterance as a whole, toward its separate
parts and toward an individual word within it, if we somehow de-
tach ourselves from them, speak with an inner reservation, if we
observe a certain distance from them, as if limiting our own authorship or dividing it in two."[19]

In "Facing It," the speaker appears to be very much in dialogue
with himself, intensely divided "in two." The speaker is torn between
the dialectics of power and powerlessness, racial difference and human
universality. Given the context of the book, its melding of personal
and collective history, it's difficult to see the speaker as anyone but
Komunyakaa himself. Here, the science of recorded history confronts
the poet's inward experience of "what happens," as the opening
lines reveal:

> My black face fades,
> hiding inside the black granite.
> I said I wouldn't,
> dammit: No tears.
> I'm stone, I'm flesh.
> My clouded reflection eyes me
> like a bird of prey, the profile of night
> slanted against morning. I turn
> this way—the stone lets me go.
> I turn that way—I'm inside
> the Vietnam Veterans Memorial
> again, depending on the light
> to make a difference.

The terms of Komunyakaa's dialectic are many and obvious: stone vs. flesh, night vs. morning, release from memory's cold cell vs. imprisonment inside the memorial which represents it. The most compelling expression of this dialogue, of course, is figured in the racial dialectic of the speaker's "black face, a "profile of night," fading and reappearing in the recurrent white "light" of "morning." It is a version of the argument which animates the book as a whole, extending beyond the mere question of race to larger and more fundamental questions of basic humanity that seek to know what we share, why, and to what end? Which ask what it means to be human and therefore intellectually capable of carrying forward a past, and yet willing to seize one's future? The poem demonstrates what the speaker of "Jungle Surrender" has already come to know, namely that the "real interrogator" is always the "voice within." Komunyakaa seems to understand, as does Heidegger, that our past is never truly gone until our future is complete, until the future has exhausted its endless possibilities to alter and realign the way we view the past which has led us to this present moment. That past, thus, must stay with him, ineluctably present. The book represents the poet's way of coming to terms with it, "a way of dealing with" its horrific images.

Curiously enough, "Facing It," the final poem in the collection, was the first poem written for this book, and it became the "standard" by which Komunyakaa judged those that followed.[20] It's not difficult to see why. The poem enacts the kind of transformations sought throughout the book and then coldly denies them, as when Komunyakaa touches the "name of Andrew Johnson," hoping to conjure up a vision of the man's face, his life, but instead sees only "the booby trap's white flash" of death. And later, when the names of the dead "shimmer on a woman's blouse," releasing them from the role of dead inscribed there, this release is short-lived, for "when she walks away / the names stay on the wall."

Near the poem's close, this same disenchanting pattern of promise followed by disappointment appears again:

> A white vet's image floats
> closer to me, then his pale eyes
> look through mine. I'm a window.

These lines promise the kind of mingling and transformation that the speaker has fervently sought through the book's interior dialogues. When the white vet comes "closer," his eyes momentarily "look through" those of the black speaker, unifying their presence and value. This, an uncautious reader might conclude, is just the point of the book, its ultimate achievement. Note, though, how Komunyakaa problematizes this scene of racial unity by following it immediately with the realization, "I'm a window." Two powerfully conflicting interpretations, held in juxtapose, result: that the white vet has indeed learned to see things empathetically "through" the black speaker's eyes, or more discomfitingly, that the white vet simply "looks through" the black speaker as if he were merely a window, an inhuman object hardly worth noticing.

If the poem were to end here, mired in ambivalence, the quest would barely seem worth the trouble, either for poet or reader. The speaker's dialogue with himself, with his reader, and with "Historie" is splendidly realized in the image of the window. He looks silently backward and forward in time, both toward his reader and away. He is at once visible and invisible, colorless as glass, neither black nor white. He serves as both sign and signified of the essential dialogic structure of the book, a window to history nailed in place, immovable and unmoved, both outside and inside of its margins—all of which, of course, refuses resolution in its ambiguity, in its very muteness.

However, the poem's (and the book's) closing image reverses the usual pattern and frees the speaker from his static, nearly deathlike trance:

> In the black mirror
> a woman is trying to erase names:
> No, she's brushing a boy's hair.

The woman's thoughtful, nurturing, thoroughly quotidian act of love closes the book on perhaps the most redemptive note imaginable for such a text. Her gesture focuses the book's ending on the future that young boy embodies, a future outside of the glass-like surface of the memorial and ahead of the faceless window the speaker has imagined himself to be. What's more, the question of whether this mother and son are black or white matters not at all. The touch of her hands is a kind of blessing, a simple but profound sacramental act enriching the lives of mother, son, and the poet who observes them. Komunyakaa's speaker comes to understand the existentialist Heidegger's concept of "*Dasein*," the "givenness" of human existence from which we cannot stand apart and of which the fabric of our lives is spun. His speaker discovers human existence is always founded on being-in-the-world, bound up with others in the beautiful and frightening relations that constitute our very lives. "Dasein" places the individual out in the world, connects his/her being to others' being. In such a view there is no retreat, no escape into the separate realms of "subject" and "object," for these categories overlap and contain each other. Thus immutably bound up with others and the material world through which he moves, Komunyakaa closes his dialogue between private and public history. In the end, the recognition that issues from this dialogue and enables him to move resolutely forward, neither erasing the "names" of the past nor failing to seize his future, proves to be fittingly "authentic" and revivifying.[21]

Chapter Six

Lives in Motion

Multiple Perspectives in
the Poetry of Rita Dove

In Rita Dove's poetry collections, *The Yellow House on the Corner* (1980), *Museum* (1983), and *Thomas and Beulah* (1986), history is figured as a continuum of ostensibly discrete and quiescent events that, in actuality, shudder against each other, thus quaking the solid ground of our present moment. For Dove, nothing about history is static, stitched in place like the pages of a high school history text-book; nothing about it is placidly "objective," dependable, and *real*. Dove envisions history as motion itself, something, like the stars, constantly in flux, always coming toward or receding from those of us who inhabit the evanescent present.[1] History, thus, necessarily produces multiple perspectives, various vantage points from which the same event can be seen and interpreted in vastly different ways. As a poet, Dove distrusts the complacency of Leopold Ranke's much-quoted remark that history can show a past event *"wie es eigentlich gewesen"*—"as it actually was," as it actually happened. She under-stands that historical accounts, whether written or oral, familial or public, are often undependable narrations of what happened to whom, for what reason, and to what end.[2] Those accounts contain the sub-tly encoded conscious and unconscious prejudices of the author, for as Jurij Lotman succinctly explains in *Universe of the Mind*, any "text is always created by someone for some purpose and events are presented in the text in encoded form."[3]

What then is left for a poet like Dove, one who openly admits to the allure of an "ultimate—and ultimately unanswerable" question regarding personal and communal origins: "How does where I come from determine where I've ended up?"[4] The answer lies in acknowl-edging one's essential connection to history's multiple perspectives and encodings, its constant flux, its reverberations. For a poet ena-moured of the point of intersection of public and private history, as

Dove clearly is, the poet's primary task becomes to attend to (and thus "decode") both the realm of public history, supposedly factual and objective, and that of private history, woven from the subjective thread of familial and individual memory. Just as importantly, Dove then re-encodes these accounts, using poetic imagination to infuse bare "fact" with the flash of insight and human emotion. In essence, Dove takes a "fact" and imagines a universe for it to inhabit. The result is a poem itself deeply encoded, as Lotman would have it, by the workings of poetic invention, a text which seeks poetic "truth" neither historical nor ahistorical, neither wholly true nor wholly invented.

That is why Dove's poems dealing with history show an equal interest in origins and endings; that is, she's as much concerned with how things began as with how events happened to end in, or lead to, the present. This mix of concerns creates a compelling tension in which her poetry borrows from forms as disparate as the historical novel and the mythological text. Here's how Lotman distinguishes between the orientation—and intentions—of these two forms: "Historical narrative and novels associated with it are subject to temporal and causal sequence and as such are oriented towards the end. The main structural meaning is concentrated at the end of the text. The question 'how did it end?' is typical of our perception both of the historical episode and of the novel. Mythological texts which tell of the act of creation and of legendary originators are oriented towards the beginning. We see this . . . in the persistent question 'where did it come from?'. . . ."[5] Dove balances these competing urges, seeking to examine both the origins of certain ideas or incidents and the repercussions they exert on present events—a condition perhaps most evident in *Thomas and Beulah* but prevalent in her other work as well. The poet's imagination continually moves backward from the present and forward from the past. The action is reflexive and restless, borne of the conviction that history is in flux and thus the poet must move with it.

It's no wonder, then, that so many of Dove's poems dealing with historical subjects show the subjects themselves in motion. Dove thus implies that life itself is choice in motion. "The Abduction," for example, recounts the story of freed slave Solomon Northrup, who, along with his "new friends Brown and Hamilton," travels the circuit playing fiddle while the other two dance and collect pennies from the audience. Restless, but enlivened by his freedom of travel, Northrup falls prey to the treachery of his new "friends" and awakens, after a night of drinking wine, to find himself "in darkness and in chains," sold downriver into slavery. Likewise, "Corduroy Road" uses historical fact to underscore the relative peril of any foray into the wild and uncharted. That death attends every step of those who clear a *"track two rods wide / From Prairie du Chien to Fort Howard at Green Bay"* elicits this revelation:

> The symbol of motion is static, finite,
> And kills by the coachload.

The most poignant of these poems is surely "The Transport of Slaves from Maryland to Mississippi." Dove opens the poem with a one-sentence summary of its narrative content, which would, were her intentions purely narrative, make the poem that follows almost unnecessary: "(On August 22, 1839, a wagonload of slaves broke their chains, killed two white men, and would have escaped, had not a slave woman helped the Negro driver mount his horse and ride for help.)"[6] But Dove is interested not so much in the incident as in the emotions and attitudes involved, those forces which have come to shape accounts of "what actually happened." Accentuating multiple perspectives, she divides the poem into three sections, based variously on historical fact or poetic invention. Dove recognizes the indeterminacy of historical fact, much as does Claude Lévi-Strauss in *The Savage Mind,* and includes in her poem conflicting versions of the incident which illustrate the disturbing distance among historial accounts of an event. Each of these is "biased," as Lévi-Strauss explains, "even when it claims not to be," simply for the reason that to answer the question, "Where did anything take place?", proves to be a knotty problem. Lévi-Strauss posits that one answer to this question must be simply "in the mind" of witness and participant, as well as in the mind of the historian who records and interprets these events. He makes his point by suggesting: "Each episode . . . resolves itself into a multitude of individual psychic moments. Each of these moments is the translation of unconscious development, and these resolve themselves into cerebral, hormonal, or nervous phenomena, which themselves have reference to the physical or chemical order. Consequently, historical facts are no more *given* than any other. It is the historian, or the agent of history, who constitutes them in abstraction. . . ."[7]

As both poet and "agent of history," Dove imagines the first section spoken in the voice of the slave woman. This section offers a rationale for the woman's behavior, as the following shows:

The skin across his cheek bones
burst open like baked yams—
deliberate, the eyelids came apart—
his eyes were my eyes in a yellower face.
Death and salvation—one accommodates the other.
I am no brute. I got feelings.
He might have been a son of mine.

Denied her humanity by slavery, she nonetheless displays it through her compassionate actions, though she fatefully dooms both her fellows and herself to further slavery. She sees in the driver's "yellower" face, its color perhaps testifying to sex between master and slave, a version of her own fate, of her own victimization.

The other two sections of the poem suggest entirely different perspectives on the incident, perspectives more in keeping with "traditional" historical texts and the presumed reaction of white victims. The second section suggests that Dove, for the sake of contrast, is drawing from a found text—a more historically "objective" account of the incident—that is, history written by those in power: white citizens. The entire five-line section, composed in elevated as opposed to spoken dialect, is enclosed within quotation marks. The text details how the "Negro Gordon, barely escaping with his life" alerted the plantation owners, led a search, and thus ended "this most shocking affray and murder." It's the final section, however, that demonstrates clearly the intellectual distance separating the attitudes of the participants that August day in 1839. Hearing the commotion, baggage man Petit rushes to the wagon, thinking, *"some nigger's laid on another one's leg,"* and is surprised to see the slaves loose. Petit believes the slaves will fall passive before the snap of his whip and screams, *"Hold it!"*: "but not even the wenches stopped. To his right Atkins dropped under a crown of clubs. They didn't even flinch. *Wait. You ain't supposed to act this way.*"

Tremors emanating from the kind of racial stereotyping evident in Petit's remarks confound communication between the races to this day. One group "knows" another largely through the shifting ground of suspicion and prejudice, denying in each other a shared humanity which the poem's slave woman tragically embodies. Clearly the idea of "transport" operative in the poem rises beyond the literal to a metaphorical notion of movement toward knowledge of Self and Other. The slave owners, and to curious extent the Negro driver, unquestionably regard their payload as chattel, as property no more accorded human rights than cattle or hogs bound for market. They

have been taught by law, custom, and social practice to consider
slaves as less then human—a misconception at root in Petit's surprised "You ain't supposed to act this way." Petit and Atkins are
instructed, though fatally so, in the confoundingly unpredictable
quality of human nature these slaves share with them. The slaves'
will to rise up, to refuse to "flinch" in the face of his whip teaches
Petit a belated and deadly lesson in respect. However, that the
slaves' response to their situation is not merely violent—witness
the old woman's selfless act—underscores the humane sensibility of
a people repressed by those held to be morally and intellectually
superior. Thus, on one level, the "transport" Dove's poem alludes to
involves movement toward greater understanding of what it means
to be human. Through public and historical fact long since fallen
silent, Dove reconnects her readers to the past and amplifies its message to the present.

Elsewhere in *Yellow House,* Dove's speaker herself becomes the
traveler, the one in "transport" whose quest for knowledge of origins and endings demands that she set out to see things for herself.
The result is a peripatetic poem, a walking tour of the fractured
world, during which the speaker ruminates on and then postulates
reasons for the unreasonable things she encounters. The best, "Sight-
seeing," concerns a speaker who has come upon a European church
and its inner courtyard of statues damaged during World War II.
The villagers have chosen to leave the dismembered statues exactly
as they found them after the Allies departed. "Come here," the
speaker asks the reader at the poem's beginning, "I want to show
you something":

> What a consort
> of broken dolls! Look, they were mounted
> at the four corners of the third floor terrace
> and the impact from the cobblestones
>
> snapped off wings and other appendages.
> The heads rolled the farthest.

Realizing the scene engenders strong but various reactions, the
speaker plays upon that ambiguity to establish a dialectic between
the mongers of despair and belief, distrusting either extreme. The
villagers who locked the gates in the face of this "terrible sign" overlook what the speaker does not: that good indeed did prevail over
evil in the war, that civilization did indeed reestablish order over
such chaos. To the speaker, heavenly intervention, or heavenly retri-
bution, seems hardly the point. To clarify these multiple perspec-

tives, the speaker first invokes Yeats' "The Second Coming" and then delineates the virtues of both remembering and forgetting:

> But all this palaver about symbols and
>
> "the ceremony of innocence drowned" is —
> as you and I know—civilization's way
> of manufacturing hope. Let's look
> at the facts. Forget they are children of angels
>
> and they become childish monsters.
> Remember, and an arm gracefully upraised
>
> is raised not in anger but a mockery of gesture.
> The hand will hold both of mine. . . .

This careful balancing of opposites, her playfulness with history's multiple perspectives, is characteristic of Dove's work. It accounts for why what is viewed by the speaker instructively as the "vulgarity / / of life in exemplary size" can be merely "a bunch of smashed statues" in the eyes of two drunks who take in the same scene at the poem's close.

The great distance between the levels of language cited above—the "smashed statues" and the "vulgarity / / of life in exemplary size"—emphasizes the role language has not only in expressing but also in ordering our lives. We come to know experience itself through language; we ponder and arrange and comprehend our lives through language. In other words, meaning is not just *reflected* in language but also something *produced* by it. Which is to say, we are forever confronting its enabling and limiting aspects. Moreover, one's sense of self, and implicitly the constraints and possibilities one finds in fashioning that self, are bound up in language. What we can—and cannot—say or think is a function of language, of having the words to say or think those things. Who cannot remember the elation of finding the word for a previously inarticulate idea or feeling, and the corollary rush of validation which accrued to that idea or feeling once there was a word for it? Or the sense of possibility one feels upon learning a new word, that door opening into a field abloom with flowers? To the contrary, who cannot remember the experience of having a word forced upon oneself, being "named" and thus having borders erected around the self which one may never escape.

As a poet examining public and private history, Dove must necessarily pay attention to language, the shared medium through which filter both public events and our private lives. It's not surprising that two of her most important poems focus on language's ability either to free or to enchain us. The first of these, "Ö," from *Yellow House,* begins:

Shape the lips to an o, say a.
That's island.

One word of Swedish has changed the whole neighborhood.
When I look up, the yellow house on the corner
is a galleon stranded in flowers.

The exotic sound and feel of the word on her lips, the sensual awareness of the Other transforms and intoxicates the speaker. It's almost as if, in that one word, she has also the *world* on her lips, lively as any lover's kiss, erotic as only words can be. Freed by language and thus no longer place bound, the speaker imagines a complementary world where motion is possibility and distance collapses before the power of language. Where historical time subsides in sea breezes, where the house on the corner might take off "over marshland" and neither the speaker nor her neighbor "would be amazed." In knowledge, in one word "so right / / it trembles," the speaker has found a way to alter her conception of her Self and the possibilities her life might bring—transforming equally the present and the future she imagines:

You start out with one thing, end
up with another, and nothing's
like it used to be, not even the future.

But if language can thus liberate and unify, Dove also acknowledges its counter ability to subjugate and divide. The haunting poem, "Parsley," from *Museum,* recounts the story of Rafael Trujillo (1891–1961), dictator of the Dominican Republic, who, Dove tells us in an endnote, "ordered 20,000 blacks killed because they could not pronounce the letter 'r' in *perejil,* the Spanish word for parsley."[8] The terrible associations of that one word counter the romantic exigency found in "Ö." Dove examines the abuses of power and violence that stem from the idea of a dominant language, a so-called pure language that demarcates the empowered from the disempowered. Surely Dove, as an African-American, is conversant with the tension existing between a culture's dominant language and its dialects, and with the ways language is used to exclude some from membership in the dominant culture.[9] Although history is not language itself, it comes to us—and thus we come to know it—through words, as Dove implies: ". . . the word [parsley], or the Haitians'

ability to pronounce it, was something that created history. But
history is also the way we perceive it, and we do perceive it through
words. . . . And language does shape our perceptions. . . . the
way we perceive things is, of course, circumscribed by our ability to
express those things."[10]

Again Dove employs multiple perspectives to juxtapose differing
ways to inhabit the historical reality of these events; one lense is
focused on experiences in the "Cane Fields" and the other on what
happens in the "Palace." The poem's first section—a melodious
villanelle—conveys the feelings of the field workers. Its horrific content seems to "smash," as Robert McDowell asserts, "against the
stark and beautiful container of the form."[11] Here's the opening
movement:

> There is a parrot imitating spring
> in the palace, its feathers parsley green.
> Out of the swamps the cane appears
>
> to haunt us, and we cut it down. El General
> searches for a word; he is all the world
> there is. Like a parrot imitating spring
>
> we lie down screaming as rain punches through
> and we come up green. We cannot speak an R . . .

On the other hand, the poem's second section, a third-person narrative, traces the general's warped thought processes in language
markedly different from that of the villanelle. The parrot, the green
cane fields, the rain, and other lyric elements of the first section
reappear, but this time they're couched in flat, declarative sentences
that highlight the surreal quality of the general's stream of consciousness:

> It is fall, when thoughts turn
> to love and death; the general thinks
> of his mother, how she died in the fall
> . . . . he stomps to
> her room in the palace, the one without
> curtains, the one with a parrot
> in a brass ring. As he paces he wonders
> Who can I kill today. . . .
>
> the general sees the fields of sugar
> cane, lashed by rain and streaming.
> He sees his mother's smile, the teeth

gnawed to arrowheads. He hears
the Haitians sing without R's . . .

Soon the general's love for his dead mother, who could "roll an R
like a queen," becomes linked with his "love in death" and the sprig
of parsley villagers wore to "honor the birth of a son." In name
of the dominant language, in memory of his neurotic (and incestu-
ous?) love for his mother, the general orders the killings "for a single, beautiful word." Thus, the poem offers a meditation on history
examined through the powers and permutations of language.

The balancing of perspectives I've identified in Dove's work operates also within some of her most personal narratives, as in "My
Father's Telescope," where her father fails in his attempt to make
the impossible become tangible:

> The oldest joke
> in the world,
> a chair on three legs. . . .
>
> After
> years of cupboards
> and end tables, after
>
> a plywood Santa
> and seven elves
> for the lawn in snow,
>
> he knows.
> He's failed, and
> in oak.

Balance is so important to Dove it's no wonder she would focus on
her father's efforts to level the chair's three legs; instead of achieving
balance, the chair simply "shrinks" beneath the father's saw.

The chair is an apt symbol for Dove's sense of historical perspective, the seeking of which is perhaps the world's "oldest joke." History, like the chair, can't offer a solid and unmoving foundation; it
shifts and lurches, tossing the unwary unceremoniously on their
backsides. Two of its legs—public and private history—are notor-
iously unreliable and perhaps unmeasurable. The third, one's sense
of self, much of which is necessarily intuitional and invented, requires
a balanced negotiation between the other two. History therefore
resides less in the physical event than in memory and language—
intangible things that hold but cannot be held. It cannot literally be
"made" like a chair. History, if made at all, is made only in the liv-

ing of it; we have no way of extracting ourselves or history from the swirling events around us. We are, as Heidegger believed, intimately wrapped up in being-in-the-world, inextricably tied to it through our relations with our fellows.

The father's Christmas present for himself and his son, a telescope, redeems him in the speaker's eyes, for implicitly he comes to see that historical perspective demands a restless searching outside of the self. One needs such a telescope to see what happened, what is, and providently, what will be. The telescope also figures prominently in "Anti-Father," a poem in which the now mature speaker dares to contradict both the Big Bang theory and her father's explanation that the "stars / are far apart":

> Rather
> they draw
>
> closer together
> with years. . . .
>
>   Stars
>
> speak to a child.
> The past
>
> is silent. . . .
> Just between
>
> me and you,
> woman to man,
>
> outer space is
> inconceivably
>
> intimate.

That physical and historical space outside the self should appear intimately connected to the self ought not to surprise any reader of Dove's work. But the notion that the past is "silent" hardly seems to be the case for Dove, especially given her achievement in imaginatively tracing the lives of her grandparents in *Thomas and Beulah*. In fact, *Thomas and Beulah* can be seen as the culmination of Dove's poetic interest in history as lives in motion, for she draws freely from both public and familial history, supplementing these accounts, where the fabric of fact frays, with the whole cloth of poetic invention.

Thomas and Beulah, as the title implies, is foremost the story of two lives caught amidst the cascading events of the early- to mid-

twentieth century United States. Dove organizes the book in keeping
with what by now ought to be her familiar devotion to multiple
perspectives, dividing it into two sections, each relating the life
and personal perspective of one title character. If one should doubt
the importance of these multiple perspectives, Dove opens the book
with the following invocation: "These poems tell two sides of a
story and are meant to be read in sequence." Two sides of a single
story, two angles which proceed ineluctably from the intersection of
lives in fact and happening; one story interwoven of two distinct
threads. It is tempting to consider such an arrangement dialogic, but
to do so is to elevate form over substance. Thomas and Beulah don't
so much as speak *to* each other as *about* each other, and their stories
are told in the third person, refusing the intimacy (and narrative
complications) of first person. True enough, their versions of one
event often diverge, and those differing views, as we shall see, reveal
much about one character's view of the other. Still, the dialogue is
implicit, restrained, and understated.

However, these two lives are placed in dialogue with larger historical reality. To emphasize this dialogic historical context, Dove ap-
pends a chronology that lists both familial and public events such as
the births of children and the 1963 Civil Rights March on Washington. In an aesthetic sense, it performs a necessary function, filling in
the gaps which the elliptical form of the poems often leaves unspoken. If there's a shortcoming to the book, it lies in the reliance
on slow accrual to gradually provide narrative facts omitted from individual poems. It's difficult to discern, for example, in the poem
"The Oriental Ballerina," that Beulah's blurred and nearly opaque
view of her bedroom results from glaucoma—unless one consults the
next to last item in the chronology. In another, largely historical
sense, Dove has other intentions for the chronology: "It's a very ec-
centric chronology, so you can see what was happening in the social
structure of midwest America at the time this couple was growing
up."[12] Just how thoroughly Dove envisions history as lives in motion
is made clear in the book's first poem. When we meet Thomas in
"The Event," he stands upon the deck of a riverboat heading north
from Tennessee. This initial "fact" of the book has its source in
familial oral history, handed down from one generation to the next
like a precious heirloom, as Dove explains: "My grandmother had
told me a story that had happened to my grandfather when he was
young, coming up on a riverboat to Akron, Ohio, my hometown.
But that was all I had basically. And the story so fascinated me that
I tried to write stories about it."[13] But this fact soon becomes insuffi-

cient. When family history evaporates, Dove discovers another wellspring to feed her story: ". . . because I ran out of real fact, in order
to keep going, I made up facts for this character, Thomas."[14] Through
the workings of imagination, through "made up facts," Dove's
grandfather becomes something larger than the reality of his life. He
becomes "this character, Thomas," embodying not only himself but
also others whose lives have gone unexamined and unrecounted.
George Garrett summarizes the difficulty and reward of thus imagining history: "To write imaginary history is to celebrate the human
imagination. Not one's own. . . . The subject is the larger imagination, the possibility of imagining lives and spirits of other human
beings, living or dead, without assaulting their essential and, anyway,
ineffable mystery, to dream again in recapitulation the dream of
Adam, knowing, as he did until he awoke, that it is true; for Adam
dreamed in innocence. We can only imagine that condition."[15]

This is especially true if one considers how Dove uses poetic invention to meld private and public history: Thomas, in his trip up river
to the North, takes part in this century's huge exodus of blacks from
America's southern states to those of the North.[16] Heading out in
hopes of work and the new life it might afford, Thomas partakes in
what has been called the "Great Migration," 1915–60, during which
nearly five million African-Americans from the rural South migrated
to the cities of the industrial North.[17] The movement's root cause
lies first in the failure of blacks to receive the "forty acres and a
mule" promised after the Civil War, but by the beginning of the
century a more insidious cause was to blame as racial violence often
culminated in lynchings. In addition to the usually cited wage differ-
entials and "expansion of employment opportunities in the North,"
and the general disenfranchisement of black voters in the South,
Stewart Tolnay and E. M. Beck point to a possible and surprising
"reciprocal relationship between black migration and racial violence,
that is, that violence induced migration, which in turn moderated
the level of violence."[18] What is clear is that blacks chose to leave
the South generally as last recourse, as is evident in an editorial published in the militant *Atlanta Independent* and addressed to white
Southerners in 1917: "This is our home and . . . we are not going
to leave, unless we are driven by want and lack of freedom." Elsewhere, the editorial asks that whites welcome blacks into the social
and economic infrastructure, arguing that whites ought to "open the
doors of the shops, of the industries and facilities for our children;
because we love them as they do their children."[19] Such social change,
history tells us, proceeded at a snail's pace.

Whatever the reason for his departure in 1919, Thomas's personal motives become part and parcel of historical fact when he leaves Tennessee and settles later in Akron. Thomas is one of those responsible for the North experiencing a net population gain of over 500,000 blacks in the decade of 1910–20, a rush of migration no doubt accelerated by the industrialization accompanying the country's war effort.

On the riverboat, drunk from the heady effects of both possibility and cheap wine, Thomas sings to the accompaniment of his "inseparable" friend Lem's mandolin. The scene is exotic with moonlight and "tarantulas" among the boat's cargo of bananas, and one "boast" leads to another. Lem dives overboard for chestnuts crowning a river delta island, but tragically

> the island slipped
> under, dissolved
> in the thickening steam.

Lem drowns, disappearing from the poem but not from Thomas's psyche. He looms large in Thomas's life, presiding like a revenant returning from death on numerous occasions—all of which lends itself to Dove's strategy to build the book's narrative in lyric pieces and thus by accrual. Thomas feels Lem's presence or hears his words when he and Beulah buy a new car ("Nothing Down"), when, after his working at the zeppelin factory, he sees the Goodyear blimp "Akron" float over ("The Zeppelin Factory"), and when in dream he imagines the dead Lem "naked and swollen / under the backyard tree" ("The Charm"). Lem evokes such strong presence in Thomas's sensibility that when a stroke threatens to end his life, Thomas believes the pain was simply "Lem's knuckles tapping his chest in passing" ("The Stroke").

Because Dove is, as I've suggested, a poet who envisions history as lives in motion, it's curious that in the midst of so much movement there is relatively little overt reference to great events in The Movement—black America's movement for racial and social equality. In fact, Arnold Rampersad, noting that Dove writes "few poems about racism today," argues that she "apparently declines to dwell on the links between past history and present history."[20] However, Dove's linking of past and present racial history is, as we've seen, implicit and understated. Admittedly, Dove's work lacks racial pungency, but much like Yusef Komunyakaa's poems of racial history, her poems work implicitly to link past and present grievances. It is precisely in the common and day-to-day experiences of African-Americans that Dove deals with racial bigotry, and often in subtle terms. Dove shows a fondness for "small" history as opposed to "big historical events," choosing, as she explains, to "talk about things which no one will remember but which are just as important in shaping our concept of ourselves and the world we live in as the biggies, so to speak."[21] Take, for example, "Nothing Down," in which Thomas and Beulah venture south to Tennessee in a new car, a "sky blue Chandler!", which ought to signal their success on the literal and figurative road to achieving the American Dream. The automobile is, of course, the American symbol of freedom and mobility as well). Instead, in an incident tart with irony, the car breaks down outside Murfreesboro and a jeering

> . . . carload of white men
> halloo past them on route 231.
> "You and your South!" she shouts
> above the radiator hiss.

And then there's "Roast Possum," a delightful poem showing Thomas reading to his grandchildren from the 1909 edition of the Werner encyclopedia, telling tales of possum hunting and embellishing the story of "Strolling Jim," a horse "who could balance / a glass of water on his back / and trot the village square / without spilling a drop." In the midst of this quaint domestic scene, Thomas considers telling the children another, more disturbing item from the Werner: "He could have gone on to tell them / that the Werner admitted Negro children / to be intelligent, though briskness / clouded over at puberty, bringing / indirection and laziness." Thomas says nothing of the above, choosing to continue his story of possum hunting, but Dove's poem says it for him—his silence speaking more loudly than her words.

These "small" events demarcate the pressures of "big" history on our lives, engraining its very texture into the day-to-day activities we often pass off with hardly a shrug. Occasionally, one of those events stands out in relief from the casual backdrop of our lives, and the light of our attention strikes at just the right angle to bring it forth into consciousness. We are then made suddenly aware of the strangeness of the apparently normal. Precisely this occurs in Dove's "Wingfoot Lake," where the pattern of Beulah's personal life on July Fourth 1964 becomes portentously intermingled with public history on a grand scale:

> Now this act of mercy: four daughters
> dragging her to their husband's company picnic,
> white families on one side and them
> on the other, unpacking the same
> squeeze bottles of Heinz, the same
> waxy beef patties and Salem potato chip bags.

The repetition of "the same," of course, accentuates what's simply not the same for the two groups, whites and blacks absurdly minding the color line while dishing out identical picnic lunches at Goodyear's Wingfoot Lake. Despite the similar menus, the two groups surely don't see themselves—their social lives as well—as equal, as "the same." Considering that the poem is set, perhaps none too subtly, on Independence Day, only emphasizes the point. In a rare gesture of overt acknowledgment of larger historical events, Dove allows Beulah to reflect on the scene in the context of the 1963 Civil Rights March on Washington:

> Last August she stood alone for hours
> in front of the T.V. set
> as a crow's wing moved slowly through
> the white streets of government.
> That brave swimming
> scared her, like Joanna saying
> *Mother, we're Afro-Americans now!*
> What did she know about Africa?
> Were there lakes like this one
> with a rowboat pushed under the pier?
> Or Thomas' Great Mississippi
> with its sullen silks?. . . .
>   Where she came from
> was the past, 12 miles into town
> where nobody locked their back door,
> and Goodyear hadn't begun to dream of a park
> under the company symbol, a white foot
> sprouting two small wings.

The poem's lines of demarcation between the races are apparent, though nonetheless compelling. The black "crow's wing" of marchers moving through the "white streets" of our federal government; the white wings and foot of the Goodyear symbol set alongside the segregated black picnickers. What's equally striking is the line marking sides of the black experience. The line between the terms "Negro" and "Afro-American" implies a disparate fashioning of self both invoked and embodied by language. In a nod to the powers of language reminiscent of "Ö" and "Parsley," the poem speaks to the ability of a people to rename and thus remake themselves.

Such change can be disquieting, even within the affected group itself. It implicitly strikes a line between old and new—between Beulah, the old woman of a rural "past" of unlocked back doors, and her children, inhabitants of an urban present. Inexorably, the movement for social equality, "slowly" as it's destined to move, has begun to evoke change in the lives of older blacks like Beulah, for whom new pride in her African heritage is understandably both exciting and somewhat unsettling. Beulah surely knows less of Africa than she does of the rural South she and her family fled in 1906 during the early stages of the Great Migration, less of the Nile than of "Thomas' Great Mississippi." Thus Beulah feels doubly uprooted, doubly removed from her origins. Where has the incessant movement of her race—and of history in general—brought her, and more importantly, to what has it delivered her children? Nearly fifty years after the *Atlanta Independent*'s call for whites to "open the doors" of industry to black children, Beulah's children have found that economic equality in the North. They have not, however, found social equality. It is the stubborn constancy of that fact, rooted in racial bigotry, that gives depth and measure to the kind of restless motion that permeates Dove's poetry. The poem suggests that in 1964, one year after the march on Washington, much marching remains to be done, much "transport" toward a goal still distant in 1996. For a poet not usually associated with pungent racial commentary, Dove has fashioned a poignant statement on the notion of social change.

If, as Helen Vendler argues, Dove's is poetry of the "disarticulated," it is in her presentation of the inchoate and unspoken histories of these individuals that Dove gives them voice.[22] It is almost painful to witness Thomas and Beulah, two people clearly devoted to each other, continually misinterpret each other's behavior. Even the intimate act of courting carries with it high stakes, a gamble in which one's acts or those of fate can be misread for good or ill, as "Courtship" examines when Thomas sets aside his mandolin and

> . . . wraps the yellow silk
> still warm from his throat
> around her shoulders. (He made
> good money; he could buy another.)
> A gnat flies
> in his eye and she thinks
> he's crying.

What follows reminds one, in both image and idea, of "Ö"; suddenly, the future's sail is taut with the intoxicating breezes of possibility:

> Then the parlor festooned
> like a ship and Thomas
> twirling his hat in his hands
> wondering how did I get here.

Still, the distance between Thomas's and Beulah's perspectives on this scene proves chilling; it sighs like an inarticulate gulf stretching between them. Beulah's version of these events, given in "Courtship, Diligence," takes the wind out of Thomas's solicitude:

> Cigar-box music!
> She'd much prefer a pianola
> and scent in a sky-colored flask.
>
> Not that scarf, bright as butter.
> Not his hands, cool as dimes.

Occasions such as these give Dove the opportunity to replay one of her favorite tunes: the unreliability of fact, whether historical or familial—and thus the daunting task of interpreting static truth from events fraught with multiple perspectives.

The restless motion that characterizes the subjects of Dove's poems animates Beulah's yearning to break free of her circumscribed roles of wife and mother. If Thomas continually yearns for a place to go fishing (see, for instance, "Lightnin' Blues" and "One Volume Missing"), Beulah fretfully wishes to escape to a more exotic location, namely, France. In "The Great Palaces of Versailles," she irons alterations in the "backroom of Charlotte's Dress Shoppe" while musing on what she'd once read in the library:

> how French ladies at court would tuck
> their fans in a sleeve
> and walk in the gardens for air. Swaying
> among the lilies, lifting shy layers of silk . . .

The agent of her travel is, of course, not literal but literary, and unsatisfyingly brief as well. Such travel requires a turn of mind, a "rehearsed deception," as the poem "Magic" refers to it. With concerted practice in evasions of reality, she convinces herself that a picture of the Eiffel Tower in the Sunday paper amounts to a "sign / / she would make it to Paris one day."

She makes it only as far as the backyard. In "Daystar," Beulah successfully creates space for herself, "a little room for thinking," by toting a chair out back "behind the garage" while the children nap. It is perhaps the most disconcerting of Dove's "travelogue" poems. On most days, Beulah's trip offers highlights as mundane as a "floating maple leaf" or a dead cricket; on others, she closes her eyes to see "her own vivid blood." Each day her flight ends with a violent crash:

> She had only an hour, at best, before Liza appeared
> pouting from the top of the stairs.
> and just what was mother doing
> out back with the field mice?

That coming and going, the frenetic fleeing of one moment into another is the very stuff of Dove's view of public and private life: history as lives in motion. The wish to still that ceaseless motion could well have been the impetus behind the mostly nostalgic and autobiographical poems of her recent collection *Grace Notes*, a book replete with memories of childhood summers, youthful math proficiency, and the animated behavior of parents, sisters and brother, and assorted aunts. I say *wish* because the book acknowledges the futility of that urge by its very celebration of times long gone. In the poem "Ozone," even the present lurches ineluctably into the past, into "history." One can detect both the momentary longing for stasis and an equal awareness of its unavailability in the conditional "If only" which opens the closing movement of the poem:

> If only we could lose ourselves
> in the wreckage of the moment! Forget
> where we stand, dead center, and
> look up, look up,
> track a falling star . . .
>   now you see it
>   now you don't

"Daystar" aptly suggests the goal of much of Dove's poetry: to recognize, within the vagaries of personal and communal history, our "own vivid blood." It is perhaps her best response to the "ultimately unanswerable" human question of "where I come from." Dove acknowledges history's multiple perspectives and encodings and its perpetual flux. If historical fact and family tale and even personal experience shudder with indeterminacy, if history "as it actually was" must elude her, she settles for what might have happened, how, and why—all from multiple vantage points. She searches equally for origins and endings and yet distrusts both. In the end, if indeterminacy is our only claim, she answers the unreliability of history with the "truth" of poetic imagination.

Chapter Seven

Manipulating Cultural Assumptions

Transgression and Obedience in
David Wojahn's Rock 'n' Roll Sonnets

One impetus for David Wojahn's series of poems about the cultural phenomenon of rock 'n' roll, published as the middle section of his third collection, *Mystery Train* (1990), can be fairly well traced to the issue of historical and poetic novelty. Simply put, almost no one else was doing it. Arguably one of the great cultural events of the last half century, rock had mostly eluded the interest—or the respect—of his generation as proper subject matter for poetry.[1] Wojahn was struck by this fact, slightly absurd on the face of it, as he explained in a 1991 interview: "A lot of people I knew as writers and thinkers were very, very influenced by rock 'n' roll music, rock 'n' roll culture, yet it never got into their poems . . . They were writing about their families, their love affairs, but they weren't writing about this particular kind of music that was a great passion in their lives."[2]

His description of the striking dissonance between communal experience and poets' private art implies that Wojahn sees his poems as a sort of rear-guard action meant to reacquaint poet (and public) with cultural history, even something as tawdry and undeniably glitzy as pop culture. Throughout the series, Wojahn's rock sonnets gesture off the printed page towards an attendant cultural / historical text shared by poet and reader by virtue of their being situated in a largely communal historical circumstance.

While this explanation tantalizes, taken alone it fails to satisfy, especially if we recall that Wojahn's clutch of rock 'n' roll poems is a sonnet series and that Wojahn is no New Formalist. To decide to write poems about pop culture as historical gloss says one thing, but to choose to write these poems as sonnets says quite another.

Which leads to another factor, an aesthetic one, inextricably bound to the cultural and historical context I've begun to delineate above.

Namely this, writing sonnets about rock 'n' roll fortuitously brings together expressions of what Van Wyck Brooks had dubbed, as early as the turn of the century, American "Highbrow" and "Lowbrow" culture.[3] This coming together, part collision and part embrace, enables the poet to work in an aesthetically charged field where breaking tradition often means simultaneously upholding it. Wojahn honors both the orthodoxy of the sonnet and the rebellion of rock— all the while breaking from their respective traditions as expressions of highbrow and lowbrow art.

What's important here is the way Wojahn manipulates cultural perceptions of the sonnet as decorous and of rock 'n' roll as rebellious. Never mind that the supposedly decorous sonnet has often been nothing more than a high-falutin invitation to sexual adventure (like much of rock). Never mind that supposedly counter-cultural rock 'n' roll has become an institution in itself, a multinational industry dominated as much by profit motives as by aesthetic principles. Never mind that the two forms share real and meaningful similarities. What matters most are readers' cultural perceptions—or better, misperceptions—which insist on viewing the forms as opposites. Wojahn uses the apparent tension between the two forms to imply that they have much more in common than many of us would readily admit. Through these rock 'n' roll sonnets, Wojahn, in his own words, seeks

> an uneasy balance—the sort of balance we all contrive in a world where the traditional boundaries that separate high culture from low don't exist. . . . I realized that a rigorously traditional form such as the sonnet is not unlike a great three-chord rock 'n' roll song. . . . When I reflect on the sonnet's wonderful symmetry and compression, and the delirious joy I experience when I read the 140-odd syllables of a good sonnet, it seems like the same sort of delight I experience listening to the Ramones do their cover version of "Needles and Pins." These two cultural poles have a highly subjective, deeply resonant linkage for me. In *Mystery Train* I found a method that would allow me to celebrate that.[4]

Probably to the displeasure of advocates of both forms, Wojahn understands the necessary and complementary relationship between them. On one hand, he negates the highbrow and yet negates his own negation by choosing the sonnet form. On the other, he honors the transgressiveness of lowbrow rock while co-opting that rebellion within the essentially orthodox sonnet form. One way to give perspective to what Wojahn does here is to recall Stephen Greenblatt's discussion of Marlowe's work. Marlowe's protagonists, Greenblatt argues in *Renaissance Self-Fashioning,* may indeed "rebel against authority," yet their various "acts of negation not only conjure up the order they would destroy, but seem at times to be themselves conjured up by that very order."[5] This suggests an answer to the question of why Wojahn might select the sonnet form to write about rock music. In my view, Wojahn's rock 'n' roll sonnet sequence underscores the notion that radical alternatives in music or poetry or other arts are inescapably tied to the orthodoxy they ostensibly reject. Rock's aesthetic revolution gains depth and texture mainly in relation to the authority it labors to overthrow. In essence, linking rock 'n' roll's rebelliousness with the sonnet's orthodoxy sustains and conveys that complementary relationship.

Of course, all poetic forms, even free verse, carry with them this tension. Each aesthetic choice to negate tradition carries with it the shadow of that tradition, ineluctably bound up in both the poet's choice and in the poem produced. As the Russian critic Jurij Lotman contends, every effort of "simplification" of an "original" form like the sonnet instead always makes it "more complicated," as those elements removed beyond the text still reside within it as "minus-devices" present, paradoxically, in their absence.[6] This plays on Newtonian physics where each action has an opposite and equal response—and yet both reside, in opposition, within the exclusive parameters of what's put in the text and what's left out.

One curious result is the way the series calls into question the nature of artistic transgression and obedience. The series, much like rock 'n' roll, may not be as wholly transgressive as one would first assume. Even if the poet were to compose his most brash sex, drugs, and rock 'n' roll sonnet, its rebelliousness would be mitigated by the sonnet's traditional rules governing internal and external form. In short, the question becomes just what aesthetic is being transgressed and what one being obeyed. For instance, is the sonnet scandalized by being tied to rock 'n' roll, or has rock been appropriated (and thus purified) by the highbrow sonnet form? Form and content, as a result, necessarily battle in full view of both poet and reader.

By choosing the sonnet, Wojahn is working with a form older and more rule-bound than the relatively new and malleable novel form. Taught in the schools and praised there—often naively—as the highest achievement of refined expression, the traditional sonnet form can be said to have been culturally inscripted. Those who write and those who read a sonnet have been trained by the culture to know a sonnet when they see one and further to identify its constitutive parts. Both writer and reader belong to what Stanley Fish, in *Is There a Text in This Class?*, has called an "interpretive community" who share common assumptions about what a sonnet looks like and what it is meant to do.[7]

Wojahn relies upon readers' shared cultural and literary assumptions. He subverts rules governing the sonnet's physical and intellectual design and steps over unspoken rules of content by focusing on rock music, a brash and impertinent popular art form whose root experiences music critic Peter Wicke describes as "completely different from those suggested by bourgeois artistic norms."[8] Wicke argues that rock music at once sets itself off from and claims equal value with the more "serious" arts aptly represented here by the sonnet. In fact, Wicke feels confident enough to cite the initial instance of rock music's arrival as alternative-but-equal art: Chuck Berry's 1956 hit "Roll Over Beethoven," and he assesses in broad cultural terms the song's effects as one of the "new experiences in art" challenging the acknowledged masters:[9] "Not without irony, while claiming the same status and cultural relevance, rock music appears self-consciously juxtaposed to an artistic appreciation, represented by the names of Beethoven and Tschaikowsky, for which we cannot imagine greater contrasts than a jukebox and a self-sufficient sensuousness."[10]

Wojahn himself, perhaps unwittingly, alluded to the rebellious nature of his writing poems about rock when he explained in our interview that his "notion was just to try to *break* that unwritten taboo" which had kept poets from writing about the music they had grown up with. Whatever his intentions, conscious or not, Wojahn's sonnets lie at the convergence of aesthetic, cultural, and historical lines, and as such they offer an intriguing look at the ways these forces intersect in the lives of writers and readers.

This collision of high and low culture has become a staple of recent avant-garde art. One need only point to the work of Robert Coover, Andy Warhol, Laurie Anderson, Vargas Llosa, and countless other pop artists to illustrate the manifest ways mass cultural forms have been exploited for artistic effect. True enough, high culture, while not wholly inured to such unorthodox content, is not so easily scandalized as it once was. A row of urinals, packaged and displayed as art by a hip young sculptor, is more likely to fetch a high price than to raise eyebrows. Still, the sonnet has remained largely untouched by these incursions of popular culture. In fact, perhaps the best precedent for Wojahn's rock 'n' roll sonnets can be found in the sonnets of Robert Lowell's *Notebook* (1970) and *History* (1973)—that deal with friends, politics, and the day-to-day events of his life, some of which we discussed earlier.

On the surface, rock music violates the sonnet sequence's acceptable subject matter of love, romance, intellectual inquiry, and emotional sensitivity. Better yet, it replaces that decorous subject matter with what William Matthews refers to on the book's dust jacket as the "sleazy heart" of popular culture. Viewed with suspicion by the status quo, rock culture is often regarded as destroying the moral fiber of America's youth through sexually suggestive lyrics and glorification of rebellion, violence, apathy, even suicide. Its outlaw status is confirmed by numerous publications like Al Menconi's *Should My Child Listen to Rock Music?* Menconi's book is meant to help parents to interpret the behavioral warning signals associated with listening to rock 'n' roll, for rock can be a "window" to a child's troubled soul.[11] Wojahn's simply choosing popular music as subject matter for a sonnet sequence will be seen by some as an impertinent act.

Nowhere is that more clear than in the third of the thirty-five sonnets in the series, "W.C.W. Watching Presley's Second Appearance on 'The Ed Sullivan Show': Mercy Hospital, Newark, 1956." One clue to Wojahn's estimation of his audience is clearly visible in the title; he assumes his readers will recognize W.C.W. as the poet William Carlos Williams, Presley as the one and only Elvis, and Ed Sullivan as the popular variety show host of the fifties and sixties. In other words, he presumes his readers will be literate, music-loving, and at least of baby boomer age. Thus a silent and invisible companion text, based on shared cultural and historical knowledge, necessarily resides alongside the poem. A simple way to illustrate this situation is to diagram what elements Wojahn's assumed ideal readers consider and manipulate when they read such a poem. On one side appears the poem itself; on the other, the companion text composed of shared historical knowledge:

The Poem—"W.C.W. Watching Presley's Second Appearance . . ."	+	Readers' knowledge of WCW's poetry, Presley's music, Sullivan's show, and the sonnet form

The poem's opener reinforces those assumptions, paraphrasing Williams' remarks on the sonnet form and including a partial quotation from his "To Elsie":

> The tube,
> > like a sonnet,
> > > is a fascist form.
> I read they refused
> > to show this kid's
> > > wriggling bum.
> "The pure products
> > of America. . . ."
> > > etc.[12]

"[G]o crazy," the quotation continues in Williams' poem, which could as easily be said of Presley as of Elsie, the mentally handicapped nursemaid of Williams' poem. It's also true that Williams called the sonnet a fascist form, an irony only deepened by Wojahn's presentation of Williams speaking a sonnet lineated in his trademark "triadic line," the three-foot line that falls down the page with a heartbeat's flurry and pause.

That sense of a triad extends beyond the characteristic line and is echoed in several elements of the poem. Its main figures compose a triad—Presley, Ed Sullivan, and W.C.W.—and its apparent subject matter represents another—music, television, and poetry. The latter triad juxtaposes examples of what Pat Brantlinger in his *Bread and Circuses* calls "positive classicism" (in this case poetry) with its sullied cousin "negative classicism" (exemplified here by rock 'n' roll and television). The upstart form, "negative classicism," promulgated by the mass media of television, radio, and film, is viewed as potentially destructive because, Brantlinger contends, it is thought to derive from Roman "imperial decadence," and we all know what happened to the glory of Rome.[13] The poem's triad weaves differently colored threads of culture within a complex tapestry composed of Sullivan's campy television show, Williams' poetry, and Elvis' popular song, "Don't Be Cruel," as the poem's closer shows:

> > > Mid-
> thought. Midwinter,
> > > and stalled
> > > > between the TV screen
> and window. . . .
> > > This pomped-up kid, who preens
> and tell us
> > > "Don't Be Cruel."

                                        Kid, forget it.
   You don't know
                        a fucking thing
                                        about cruelty yet.

   By 1956, Williams had endured a heart attack and the first of a
series of strokes. As a physician, he understood his condition and
what probably lay ahead for him. Perhaps more troubling was what
lay behind: his bitter artistic struggle for recognition of his largely
demotic art in an era given to adulation of T. S. Eliot's hieratic and
intellectual refinements. Williams once remarked that the 1922 publication of Eliot's "The Waste Land" had destroyed his "world like
an atom bomb." Ironically, his poetry in the "American grain"
faced the same sort of prejudice that rock music faced; it was viewed
by many as unsophisticated and unrefined, following, as it did, the
countertradition of the great American rough, Walt Whitman. While
poets such as Robert Creeley, Charles Olson, and Allen Ginsberg
were inspired by his work, at the time Williams must have felt very
much the odd man out, conversant with the kind of "cruelty" life
can bring to a man's art and his physical being. In 1956, Presley,
another "pure product of America," was just beginning to attract
the attention of the ruling orthodoxy and the fame that would eventually bankrupt his art and destroy his person. The rebelliousness of
his music would soon be packaged by mainstream corporations, co-
opted, and sold for a profit to the masses, despite its supposedly
scandalous qualities.
   In the book's notes, Wojahn warns his readers that some of the
events described are "apocryphal" or "wholly invented"; thus, the
"historical" reality of these poems is always tempered by the poet's
own personal, imaginative perspective on these lives and these events.[14]
Whether Williams said the above of Presley matters less than the
fact that, given their circumstances, he very well could have made
those remarks. The poem's irony, conceived and constructed by the
poet, proves to be as true as simple historical truth, and there's the
rub.
   That idea troubles many of my students, most of whom expect a
literal history of rock 'n' roll that nicely coincides with the rock histories gracing their bookshelves. And they may not be familiar with
the historical issues Wojahn manipulates—which makes his ideal
audience a rather select one. His rock 'n' roll sonnets take facts of
historical reality and often create invented incidents to surround and
thereby deepen them, to make, as it were, art out of mere fact.
Which is also to say that Wojahn takes characters some of us know

and places them in narrative contexts that, while faithful to the cultural and historical milieu of the time, may be more true in spirit than in fact. This may be the case with "Matins: James Brown and His Famous Flames Tour the South, 1958," which opens as follows:

'Please, Please, Please' on the charts permits
Four canary yellow sequined suits
And a hulking Coupe de Ville—bought on credit—
For the Alabama-Georgia roadhouse circuit.
Half last night they drove from Athens, taking turns
At the wheel. The radio hissed National Guards
In Little Rock, static filling Jackie Wilson's
'Lonely Teardrops.'

The poem's opening lines, composed in quatrains of approximate iambic pentameter and rhymed as a Shakespearean sonnet, make good use of fact to establish the period's *zeitgeist*. Brown and his Flames did record a hit titled "Please, Please, Please" and Wilson's "Lonely Teardrops" was popular radio play at the time. That the group would be surprisingly and momentarily flush with cash as a result of a song on the charts also makes perfect economic sense; that they would thus splurge on fancy outfits and a Cadillac portrays an equally believable act of human nature. But the poem's edge, and a key to its latent power, comes with the mention of the National Guard called to Little Rock, there to quell turmoil brought on by segregation and racial bigotry. This intertwining of musical and social history establishes a plausibility for the incident that follows, as well as underscores the significant link between early rock music and society's first timid efforts to cross the color line. Notice how the closing couplet, obedient to the Shakespearean sonnet's internal form, offers stark commentary on the racial/historical setting established earlier:

Parked near Macon in a soybean field,
They sleep with heads in towels to protect
Their kingly pompadours, and as the pre-dawn
Mist burns off, they wake to knocks against
The windshield. A cruiser with its siren on
Dyes the fog bright red, *Don't you niggers know your place?*
A billy club, a face, the windshield breaks.

The behavior of the police in this incident—real or invented—mirrors the actions of police throughout the South as white and black Americans tentatively began to dismantle segregation. The poem, a loose Shakespearean sonnet, expresses this *zeitgeist* quite successfully. Because white Americans, many safely ensconced in suburbs and country clubs, initially became familiar with aspects of black culture through the medium of rock and rhythm and blues, this music exerted a considerable influence on what Andrew Ross has called a "radical rearticulation of the color line."[15] One result was white America's sudden valuing of original rhythm and blues songs performed by black artists such as Fats Domino, Chuck Berry, Bo Diddley, Sam Cook, and The Drifters, and a commensurate devaluing of cover versions of these songs performed by whites. A brief comparison of, say, Little Richard's version of "Tutti Fruiti" and Pat Boone's lame cover version was enough to convince most white listeners of the superiority of the original performer and performance. By the end of the fifties, Ross argues, being white and "hip" to black R&B music took on the "political connotation" of support for black "social and political aspiration," as evident in songs such as Brown's later hit "Say It Loud, I'm Black and I'm Proud."[16]

Rock culture's general overstepping of boundaries, figured so admirably in this case by its social incursions over the color line, did not always produce such positive results. Wojahn, to his credit, pursues those less desirable subjects with fervor. He delves into rock subjects as various as Jerry Lee Lewis's secret but soon discovered marriage to his thirteen-year-old first cousin, to the general dissipation of several of rock's most shining lights. Readers are treated to scenes of Janis Joplin slurping Four Roses whiskey on the train departing Port Arthur for "Points West"; the Beach Boys' Brian Wilson, having grown incredibly long manchu nails, at play in his living room "sandbox" with his "live-in shrink"; and the petulant behavior of the Rolling Stones demanding that their jet avoid air turbulence because it's "the *Stones* in here." Indeed it's the Stones' late Brian Jones whose excessive and self-destructive behavior serves as a gloss for all the fallen icons the book treats individually or collectively. In "Necromancy: The Last Days of Brian Jones," his case seems representative of how the laudable disregard for boundaries can sometimes lead to drowning in the blue waters of self:

Hair fanning out, he'll float upside down
Like the end, and beginning, of Sunset Boulevard.
Kicked out of the band, he's come home
To his manor in St. John's Wood—acid,

Hard drugs, delivered by minions to poolside,
Where for months on the nod he strums his National Steel,

> Sprawled on a Day-Glo deck chair, lavender strobes
> Festooning the water. He'll drown on his last meal. . .

Central to the series' allure are these acts of "necromancy," conjuring up spirits of the dead to tell their stories and foretell the future, seancelike encounters that also speak versions of our story and our future. This melding of personal and collective history, of cultural and social milieu perhaps finds its best expression in sonnets about Presley. From the relatively "pure" version of Elvis that readers encounter in "W.C.W. Watching Presley's Second Appearance . . ." to the rhinestoned and bloated Presley of later sonnets in the series, his rise and fall manifests our culture's fascination with innocence and its inevitable doom.

Several of these sonnets, by mingling fact, imagination, and a rhetorical trick or two, insist that we see in these figures versions of our collective history, as the poem "The Assassination of Robert Goulet as Performed by Elvis Presley: Memphis, 1968" demonstrates first with humor and then with subtle politics. Presley, as his Graceland den confirms, was fond of watching three televisions simultaneously, and the poem turns on that quaint fact. It opens with an epigraph, supposedly spoken by Presley, assessing Goulet's stiff musical delivery, "That jerk's got no heart." The poem than proceeds down the page in nattily rhymed couplets, doubly breaking the sonnet's usual outer form:

> He dies vicariously on "Carol Burnett,"
> Exploding to glass and tubes while singing "Camelot."
>
> Arms outstretched, he dies Las Vegas-ed in a tux,
> As the King, frenzied in his Graceland den, untucks
>
> His .38 and pumps a bullet in the set.
> (There are three on his wall, placed side by side.)
>
> The room goes dark with the shot, but he gets the Boys
> To change the fuses. By candlelight he toys
>
> With his pearl-handled beauty. Lights go back on,
> But Goulet's vanished, replaced by downtown Saigon:
>
> Satellite footage, the Tet offensive,
> Bodies strewn along Ky's palace fences.
>
> Above a boy whose head he's calmly blown apart,
> An ARVN colonel smokes a cigarette.

A brutal irony permeates the poem, built and directed by the speaker's making use of what his audience already knows about Elvis. The speaker assumes, quite rightly, that readers share his knowledge of Elvis's eventual fate: that Presley died "Las Vegas-ed" in his own inimitable style, purportedly of a "heart" attack precipitated by excessive use of prescription drugs. Even more striking is the crucial juxtapositioning of historical images at the poem's close. Having just witnessed Presley's figurative "assassination" of Goulet, readers now are presented with the reality of heartless wartime violence; the image conjures up the famous wire photo of an ARVN officer putting a bullet through the head of a suspected Viet Cong. This common cultural knowledge functions as an unseen historical companion text which accompanies and enhances the poem that appears on the page. In some ways, the ARVN officer's deadly imposition of order on chaos and rebellion mirrors what Wojahn risks doing in this sonnet series. He risks shooting his rebellious subject in the head with the bullet of prescribed form, and conversely takes the chance that he might detonate the form by filling it with explosive subject matter. However, chaos and order need each other; each carries in opposition the necessary image and definition of the other. In this instance, although the sonnet's outer form is rebellious, its internal form resembles that of a Petrarchan sonnet; roughly the poem's final six lines offer a surprising historical commentary enlarging the violent context featured in its octave.

Wojahn has taken two historically accurate facts and invented an artistically true representation, but to do so he has most probably played fast and free with the truth. It's unlikely that mundane reality, even for the King himself, would accommodate the aesthetic juxtapositioning of Goulet's symbolic death with "satellite footage" of real wartime carnage. Some readers may resent the sense of their having lost sight of the pea of truth beneath paper cups the poet dexterously manipulates before them. Still, the mode and mood of the poem are honest to the spirit of the time. The Tet offensive shattered some of America's vestigial innocence as explosively as Presley destroyed the televised image of Goulet. Tet made evident that America was not on the verge of quick victory in Vietnam, that the enemy was formidable and resourceful even in defeat, and that our allies, represented by the ARVN colonel, were not altogether saintly warriors in the battle against Communist expansion. It brought home—literally, through the medium of television—the disturbing reality that Kennedy's, and America's, "Camelot" had indeed ended with JFK's assassination. Presley's figurative murder of Goulet and the ARVN colonel's killing the boy, of course, bring to mind Kennedy's death in Dallas, prefiguring as well the later assassinations of Robert Kennedy and Martin Luther King.

Infusing politics into the realm of cultural history emphasizes rock's significance as contemporary America's epic of innocence and experience, where innocence, if it exists at all, is delusional or quickly destroyed. Instructively, the series begins with "Homage: Light from the Hall," in which a thirteen-year-old listens in bed, "beneath the midnight covers," to rock 'n' roll through "the single earphone" of a fifties-style transistor. The operative word is "Homage," for the teenager listens, thoroughly "rapt," to New Orleans' WKED broadcast songs he envisions "spinning" a musical and spiritual "alchemy" within the hallway light's "stammering glow." Unlike the miller's daughter of the folk tale, this child encounters no Rumpelstiltskin willing to spin these gold records into something redemptive, not even for the price of a firstborn, for it's precisely that childhood innocence the teenager must give up forever on the trip to adulthood. It's not difficult to imagine this teenager to be the grown-up and now jaded speaker of "At Graceland with a Six Year Old, 1985," the thirtieth poem of the series. Look what the space of twenty-nine of these sonnets has done to him. While the six-year-old he has brought to Graceland wholly admires its exquisite "kitch," including the living room wall mirrored to give the illusion of a "Pipsqueak Versailles," the speaker reduces the entire larger-than-life spectacle to something much more petty: the bald quest for money. The speaker acidly conjectures that Presley's death mattered little to Presley's manager, himself a fake Southerner, compared to the cash to be had from feeding off the public's memory of the dead singer:

> Colonel Parker was asked, after Elvis's death,
> What he'd do now to occupy his time:
>   "Ah guess
> Ah'll jus' keep awn managin' him." He's really Dutch.
> The accent, like the colonel tag, a ruse . . .

Thus one surprising aspect of the series is its vital questioning of the aesthetic and cultural assumptions that inform both it and rock 'n' roll. Readers hardly get the anthem of praise for rock which they reasonably could have expected and into which the series easily could have degenerated. Even those who rejected rock music's supposedly bankrupt artistic values and profit-greedy intentions have their clay feet revealed. For instance, in "Malcom McClaren Signs the Sex Pistols, London, 1976," the punk rockers are shown on the occasion of their contract signing to be crass, rude, degenerate fools "throwing up / Into a pail." Though the band may have thought they were offering an anti-art response to standard anti-art rock 'n' roll, their brief and self-destructive career was shrewdly designed by their manager Malcom McLaren to earn bundles of money, mainly for himself.[17] Such poems violate some of the assumptions upon which the series is ostensibly built by suggesting that rock 'n' roll itself is not as transgressive or countercultural as many of us would believe. In fact, one could argue that rock 'n' roll and other sixties countercultural forms of expression (like the rhetoric of so-called free love) simply acknowledge a rhetoric of "expenditure" that resides at the core of capitalism. One great irony of the countercultural intentions of rock is that many of those whose music protests the evils of capitalism and the deadening values of the status quo also turn a tidy profit from doing so. Also it's no secret that rock 'n' roll has been handily commercialized by the record companies and MTV, so much so that even those who set out to dismantle the realms of power, such as Nirvana's late Kurt Cobain, are scandalized by their own success and the flood of cash it brings. Another, perhaps more ominous angle of looking at this is to suggest that powerful authoritarian forces actually allow these rebellions to take place as a way to control and direct them, and eventually to co-opt them within the general orthodoxy. In this fashion, rebellion, as Greenblatt suggests, may indeed become "a tribute to authority."[18]

This irony accounts for the manner in which Wojahn, while disparaging orthodoxy, also seems to undercut its radical alternative. First, Wojahn chooses rock music as the outlaw subject of a sonnet series, then he presents few heroes among the anti-art artists of rock, and finally, even those who attempt to trespass the "standards" of rock anti-art he shows to be driven less by aesthetic than by monetary impulses.

Indeed, Wojahn works assiduously, through the series' careful chronological presentation of rock history, to isolate elements of rock 'n' roll's descent. The seeds of that decline lay not only in the allure of wealth and fame but also in the self-destructiveness of the form and its participants. Expressions of those self-destructive tendencies came to show themselves in rock 'n' roll both through the already discussed offstage behavior of its stars and through increasingly wild and tempestuous onstage performances. The Who, for example, frantically destroyed their instruments after each performance in what Pete Townsend referred to as "Pop Art Auto-Destruction." Jimi Hendrix enflamed the crowd at the 1967 Monterey International Pop Festival at the conclusion of the song "Wild Thing," splashing his guitar with lighter fluid, and then, John Fuller tells us, igniting the guitar while holding it "inches from his crotch."[19] This mix of creation and destruction, of making and unmaking underscores the perilous connection between self-definition and self-negation. The fire that creates, symbolized by the burning crotch, becomes dangerously identified with the fire that consumes and destroys. The very idea of self becomes mingled with its negation, as if a statement of oppositional identity demands a corollary consumption of that identity and everything proposed in opposition to the dominant order. This crescendo of self-destructive music and violence somehow eluded the 1969 Woodstock concert but reached fatal levels later that year at Altamont, a stock car track near San Francisco where 300,000 gathered to hear the Stones give the performance they hoped would rival Woodstock. Crowd control was the job of the Hell's Angels motorcycle gang, who Fuller contends were "hired at the rate of $500 worth of beer" and were "roaring drunk before the first chord sounded and high on cocaine and hash."[20] Not surprisingly, disaster broke out while Mick Jaggar strutted through "Sympathy for the Devil": within clear view of the stage, a young black man was stabbed and beaten to death by the Hell's Angels. While the broken formal metrics and lineation of Wojahn's "Photographer at Altamont: The Morning After 1969" physically express the incident's violence, note how the poem's content focuses not on the event itself but on its aftermath:

A dog sleeps with a frisbee in its mouth.

A lotus-sitting girl plays flute:

She's wearing a Confederate cap. Sleeping bag rolled out,
Her friends eat breakfast, orange juice

And jug wine. Flute joins with harmonica,
Invisible but somewhere, in a slovenly duet.
A paper bag, twisting its slow veronicas,

Plummets—that's the shot he wants—

Beside the flute-girl and a broken doll.
Dried blood, abstract, sinews the dirt
Before the stage,
                          though he's sorry that its details,
Earth tones and siennas, will be lost in his prints.

The girl lights a joint for him. He grins—

Matthew Brady posing corpses in the Devil's Den.

Even the "Morning After" of the title implies that speaker and reader share a common knowledge of what occurred the day before, so much so that any actual rendering of the killing is unnecessary. For a generation weaned on rock 'n' roll, just the word "Altamont" invokes images of chaos, frenzy, and violent death. Speaker and audience, the poem presumes, are part and parcel of the same generational myth, for both to some extent have been shaped by similar historical circumstances—a fact which makes possible a kind of historical/cultural shorthand where single words or phrases carry immense cultural baggage. This poem, as is the case with so many others in the series, gestures off the page towards an invisible companion text, historical and cultural in nature, upon which the poem depends for historical grounding and from which it derives the aesthetic freedom to interpret those facts artistically. Jean-Paul Sartre explains the basis of this phenomenon succinctly: ". . . people of the same period and community, who have lived through the same events, who have raised or avoided the same questions, have the same taste in their mouth; they have the same complicity, and there are the same corpses among them."[21]

One result is to increase the poem's compression, the poet's license to leave out most of the story and to focus exclusively on well-chosen and provocative details. Most of the sonnets amount to highly compressed narratives, telling stories, part truth and part lie, about characters often familiar to the reader. In fact, Wojahn himself admitted during our radio interview that, despite his intentions to the contrary, these were mostly "narrative sonnets." This is why the poet can train his (and the poem's) eye on the "lotus-sitting," flute-playing, dope-smoking flower child among the wreckage, assured that readers will recognize the disparity between this scene and the previous day's brutality. Her marijuana joint, the drug of choice for many of our generation seeking safe passage to peace, love, and a mellowed-out sense of well-being, cannot ameliorate the bitter taste of bitter reality. On their own, most readers no doubt enlarge the picture to include an ominous historical backdrop portraying the rock generation's idealistic values, at least as those values were threatened at Altamont. There, the revolution came to a violent, crashing halt. Worse yet, what came after the revolution was discomfitingly similar to what came before—despair in values and beliefs, failure of the will to change, a nod to the generally unredemptive state of humankind. Most of us still love rock's energy and rebellion; many of us also still cherish its celebration of promise. Probably few of us, however, retain a vision of rock as the dynamic engine for social change we once imagined—or hoped—it would be.

Much of this information exists outside of the poem and within the realm of shared cultural knowledge. Still, Wojahn's rhetorical and imagistic manipulations contribute to this effect. Much like the Civil War's Matthew Brady and this poem's Altamont photographer, Wojahn evocatively points his lense towards his culture's shared "corpses," a host of fallen stars such as Jones, Joplin, and Presley. He too stands guilty of "posing" historical facts in service of artistic truth. One figure in "'It's Only Rock and Roll But I Like It': The Fall of Saigon, 1975," fairly well embodies Wojahn's task and method. As the final helicopter rises above the desperate crowd storming the U.S. Embassy grounds, a Marine guard bangs the fists of a Vietnamese citizen until the man falls from the copter's landing gear. An inspired CBS cameraman, poised in the chopper door, recognizes an aesthetic angle in the chaos:

> One chopper left, and a CBS cameraman leans
> From inside its door, exploiting the artful
> Mayhem.

Which is not to say Wojahn's poems are exploitative, but only to say that in the "[m]ayhem" of rock 'n' roll he has attentively noted an "artful" quality that reveals much about ourselves and our culture. He "exploits" that quality by posing, arranging, and manipulating bare fact in aesthetically inventive ways, which may, of course, include a touch of the "apocryphal." What enables Wojahn to do so is the reality that this series was clearly written with an image of a particular reader who shares the poet's contemporary historical circumstance and his knowledge of rock history. Such common heritage enables a presumption of audience awareness that heightens the series' appeal both as art and as cultural document.

It's telling to note that many readers consider the success of *Mystery Train* to hinge on the appeal of its middle section of rock 'n' roll sonnets, notwithstanding the fact that the book's first and third sections contain a number of long narrative poems which, in many ways, aesthetically surpass the achievement of these sonnets. The rock 'n' roll series has clearly taken on a life of its own. That the book has been assigned reading in a required poetry survey course taken by 1,500 second year cadets at West Point Military Academy indicates its surprisingly wide appeal. Despite the rebellious nature of the subject matter, or perhaps because of it, the sonnet series' traditional appeal issues from the complex intersection of aesthetic, cultural, and historical lines.

Because the series relies on shared cultural and historical circumstances, the reader's role in these sonnets is an especially active one. Just as importantly, however, this reader must also know what a sonnet is and isn't and thus recognize violations of the form crucial to the series' unity. Nearly all of the sonnets are fourteenliners; nearly all follow iambic pentameter fairly closely; nearly all of them exhibit a determinate rhyme pattern. Just the same, the sonnets' rhyme pattern and lineation frequently violate standard sonnet fare, and their internal logic only occasionally accedes to the sonnet's demands. Those traditional elements missing from Wojahn's sonnets, say, the determinate rhyme pattern, invisibly accompany the printed poem by virtue of the reader's awareness of these elements' absence, or their paradoxical presence in the poem through what Lotman calls "minus-devices."

This makes perfect sense in the charged realm of aesthetic transgression and obedience, where breaking rules matters as much as keeping them. Lotman summarizes this basic tenet: "An artistic text does not merely represent the implementation of structural norms, but their violation as well. It functions in a dual structural field consisting of the tendency to establish order and to violate it. Although each tendency tries to dominate and destroy the opposing one, the victory of either would prove fatal to art. The life of an artistic text depends on their mutual tension."[22] Manipulating readers' (mis)perceptions of artistic orthodoxy and rebellion, Wojahn's rock sonnets operate in the volatile locale where tradition and readerly expectations converge with poetic experimentation. On one hand, the climate is enlivened by the poet's urge to transgress—and thereby extend—the boundaries of a form. On the other, while readers delight in surprise, they are just as prone to reject a sonnet that so radically alters the form's structure as to make the poet appear unskilled, foolish, or merely audacious. Wojahn successfully negotiates this tension between violating and minding the rules, reaching an "uneasy balance" between high art and low. His work celebrates at once something like the initial, surging riff of the Stones' "Start Me Up" and the taut, delicious tempo of a Shakespearean sonnet. We can, and should, be glad for both.

Chapter Eight

"The Hour Farthest From God"

Ethical Matters in Carolyn Forché's Poetry

> What we cannot speak about
> we must pass over in silence.
> —Ludwig Wittgenstein
> *Tractatus*

W hat cannot be said fascinates Carolyn Forché as much as what can be said. Such a statement reduces itself to separate but related issues circumscribing the boundaries of what a poet can and indeed might be able to say in a poem. The first of these involves the unspoken prohibitions that a culture places upon its writers and that writers curiously place upon themselves—the limits of acceptable subject matter and poetic intent. The second and more fundamental of these issues concerns the inevitable limitations of language and its inability to express the apparently inexpressible ideas and emotions of our lives—the lacunae that result, those vacuous white spaces of silence.

Comfortable with neither, Forché insistently seeks to trespass these boundaries, to stretch language beyond its conceived limitations to address both the mystical and the real, and their intersection in public and private history. She implicitly, and in more recent work, explicitly engages Ludwig Wittgenstein's philosophical and linguistic theories, especially those of his ponderous *Tractatus*. There Wittgenstein places, by virtue of his doctrine in pure logic, the whole arena of ethical dialogue beyond the realm of language. What most interests me about Forché's work is the way it transgresses this notion of "what we cannot speak about," often using dialogic form as means to challenge at once the boundaries of language as an expressive medium and the boundaries of acceptable poetic subject matter. Those issues most compelling to Forché are our century's multitude of ethical and moral questions—the very issues that Wittgenstein proposes reside beyond the veil of language. Simply put, Forché is a poet of morals and ethics who uses dialogic form to test the limits of language Wittgenstein describes.

In his *Tractatus,* Wittgenstein reduces the problematic nature of ethical discussion to its essentials, boldly stating: "It is clear that ethics cannot be put into words. Ethics is transcendental. (Ethics and aesthetics are one and the same.)"[1] After delegating ethics and aesthetics to the realm beyond language, and in many ways thus equating the two as the highest expressions of our humanity, Wittgenstein makes clear how these matters which cannot be spoken paradoxically show themselves to us: "There are, indeed, things that cannot be put into words. They *make themselves manifest.* They are what is mystical."[2] Any skeptical reader of the *Tractatus* will note that Wittgenstein is able to go on at some length about matters that supposedly remain in the mystical, inexpressible region beyond language. About matters of ethics, for example, Bertrand Russell concludes that in the *Tractatus* Wittgenstein shows himself quite "capable of conveying his ethical opinions" and "manages to say a good deal about what cannot be said."[3] In response, Wittgenstein might suggest these matters can be *shown* in action but not spoken of. His argument, in sum, is rooted in belief that the boundaries of language effectively preclude any useful discussion of these issues. In the *Tractatus,* Wittgenstein describes the transformational rules that govern communication in which the thought of one person is conveyed to another through language, since no one can perceive another's thoughts directly. First comes the speaker's idea or thought—itself an imperceptible structure in which meaning is determined by the structure of that thought, a meaning locus. Next the speaker necessarily encodes this thought in language by use of perceptible signs that connect to his/her idea or meaning in a specific way. Then the listener (or reader) must connect the perceptible signs to the imperceptible thought in the identical way. Essentially, for understanding to exist, the listener must *decode* what the speaker has *encoded* in precisely the same manner. Thus participants in a linguistic community must share the same rules for encoding/decoding, or understanding will remain elusive.

For Wittgenstein, this issue of encoding/decoding is the core of the problem in philosophical communication. Unlike statements of fact, philosophical and ethical matters are not simply about the physical structure of the world and their significance cannot be con-

veyed in an underlying thought structure, a meaning locus. Thus
there is no dependable set of transformational rules to enable a person to reconstruct another's imperceptible philosophical/ethical
meanings encoded in signs—largely because there is no systematic
connection between philosophical/ethical signs and their significance.
Wittgenstein conjectures that the boundaries of language preclude
such understanding. In his only public lecture, presented to a society
of scholars known as "The Heretics," Wittgenstein reveals his own
exasperation with these limits of language: "My whole tendency and
I believe the tendency of all men who ever tried to write or talk
about Ethics or Religion was to run against the boundaries of language. This running against the walls of our cage is perfectly, absolutely hopeless. Ethics so far as it springs from the desire to say
something about the ultimate meaning of life, the absolute good,
the absolute value, can be no science. What it says does not add to
our knowledge in any sense." However frustrated by these constraints,
Wittgenstein clearly admires the improbable human propensity to
engage such issues: ". . . it is a tendency in the human mind which
I personally cannot help respecting deeply and I would not for my
life ridicule it."[4]

Although frustrated by what he saw as the futility of *talking*
about ethics, Wittgenstein was said to be quite concerned with ethical matters as they were exhibited in a person's right action or conduct. He valued very little what people said on matters of ethical
behavior but instead valued highly what they actually did in their relations with their fellows. He measured his friends and colleagues by
the yardstick of right conduct, and in turn measured himself by the
same. This fierce insistence on moral behavior did not go unnoticed
among his friends and peers. Wittgenstein, for instance, was said to
have the remarkable effect of making a "better person" of those
who knew him.[5]

This review of Wittgenstein's theory of ethics bears largely on our
discussion of Forché's poetry. Clearly her work deals with issues of
ethical behavior germane to Wittgenstein. Any reader familiar with
her collection *The Country Between Us* (1981) is well aware of its
emphasis on matters of "the absolute good" and right conduct as
they relate to the tangible reality of how human beings treat each
other. More to the point, her recent poetry reveals the deep influence
of his thinking on the limits and efficacy of language, as evidenced
by references to Wittgenstein which crop up in *The Angel of History*
(1993). Throughout her work, Forché uses dialogic form to test,
perhaps extend, the walls of the language cage Wittgenstein de-

scribes. For Forché, the very attempt to speak about ethical matters is itself an ethical act.

Forché noticed early on that there were some things fenced off beyond the realm of poetic discourse. Not all of these were, in fact, strictly matters of ethics. She remarks in an interview that she once noticed a "kind of self-censorship operative among American poets and writers that seemed to preclude writing about contemporary events or historical events when those events were still unsafe"; the risk of breaking such taboo was, of course, to acquire inadvertently the label of "political" poet.[6]

Forché herself is partly responsible for the manner in which discussion of politics has infiltrated the critical reception of her work. Attempting to explain—and perhaps defend—those poems in *The Country Between Us* that deal with Salvadoran political oppression, in the text of what has now become a much-quoted article printed in *The American Poetry Review*, Forché pronounces a few common tenets of current language and cultural theory: "All language then is political; vision is always ideologically charged; perceptions are shaped *a priori* by our assumptions and sensibility formed by consciousness at once social, historical, and esthetic."[7] She then makes a pronouncement that has brought garlands of praise or shovelfuls of censure from poets as various as Robert Pinsky and Jonathan Holden:[8] "There is no such thing as non-political poetry."[9] Here Forché does not mean to advocate a slew of what she calls "propagandistic hackwork [that] has no independent life as poetry," but means merely to state what she sees as obvious: that poetry is both *pure* and *sullied*, composed of language aspiring *beyond* this world and yet still firmly *of* it.[10] As Philip Levine has remarked, even a poem with the ostensibly innocuous aesthetic goal of describing a tree's beauty can be perceived as a political statement by someone wishing to convert that tree to so many board feet of kiln-dried lumber. In essence, to argue that one's poem refuses politics in favor of eternal aesthetic values is, by definition, a political statement, one that inheres with assumptions of poetic value. To do so is also to ignore the political reality that there are those who would just as soon poetry kept its nose out of overtly social discourse, those who don't want poets meddling in the social arena where political values are debated. Hans Magnus Enzenberger summarizes the matter succinctly: ". . . a political quarantine placed on poetry in the name of eternal values, itself serves political ends."[11]

Making a distinction between ethics and politics in Forché's poetry is perhaps somewhat misleading on face value, for the two are often intertwined in serpentine fashion in her work. Still, accentuating the importance of ethical issues in Forché's work, I believe, both clarifies its focus and answers the spate of current criticism that views her work in merely political terms. Much of Forché's poetry mutes lines that distinguish between ethical, moral, aesthetic, and political matters. *The Country Between Us,* for instance, directs attention to ethical and moral issues inhering in the human rights abuses of El Salvador's ruling military junta. Her recent *The Angel of History* brushes an expansive portrait of twentieth-century moral failure evoked in collage images of the Holocaust, Salvadoran mass graves, and the Hiroshima bombing. Although Forché describes her poetic intentions in terms that intend to de-emphasize politics, "I am most compelled by moral and ethical questions, the aesthetic nature of morality, and the moral aspect of aesthetics, but . . . was never concerned, explicitly, with politics in the narrow sense of the term."[12] She cannot escape the fact that these very aesthetic and moral issues are subject to appropriation by others preferring the "narrow sense" of politics she abjures. The "narrow" sense of politics Forché wishes to avoid relegates the poet to propagandist for the left or the right, a poet whose artfulness is buried beneath ideological debate and the byzantine machinations of party affiliation. Forché admires a poet like Pablo Neruda, for whom individuals and their ethics matter more than political affiliations. Such a poet cares less about the identity of the torturer's political party than about the ethical violation this act of torture inflicts against all humanity. Such a poet resists becoming merely an unthinking mouthpiece of socialist, Marxist, or capitalist values. Nonetheless, she has become —it would appear, unwillingly—mainstream American poetry's foremost "political poet." Sharon Doubiago, for example, in defending *The Country Between Us* against Katha Pollit's complaints (*The Nation,* 8 May 1982), praises Forché as a feminist, the "female voice in many ways of my generation, representative of a vast number of women who are living outside of . . . the lives we were programmed for, the lives of mothers."[13] (Forché has since given birth to a son.) Doubiago contends, using thinly masked sexual imagery, that Forché took the insular, prettified, romantic "aesthetic jammed into her as a young woman gone to college and jamm[ed] it right back into the real, the political."[14] Choosing a similar approach, Michael Greer makes full use of Marxist theories of history to assert that Forché's poems manifest the notion that all poems are at root political. Greer contends that defining as acceptable only those poems which profess to be above politics "marginalizes those poems regarded as political without having explored the social and political constitution of all literary discourse."[15] Larry Levis, to the contrary, labors to placate defenders of traditional literary values by emphasizing the conventional humanism of *The Country Between Us* and downplaying the admittedly "partisan" political slant of the book as not "Leftist so much as simply decent, and human."[16] The result, Levis argues, is that Forché's poems show the "process of human psyche learning and becoming more openly human and vulnerable."[17]

Intentionally or not, these critics wall off exclusive preserves for Forché's poems to inhabit, a feminist or Marxist or humanist locale protected from the larger and inclusive domain of poetic discourse. For her part, Forché will have none of it. She proposes her own term, "poetry of witness," to describe poetry not inordinately bound to the overly simplified and mutually exclusive poles many critics use to categorize poetry:

> Poetry of witness presents the reader with an interesting interpretive problem. We are accustomed to rather easy categories: we distinguish between 'personal' and 'political' poems—the former calling to mind lyrics of love and emotional loss, the latter indicating a public partisanship that is considered divisive, even when necessary. The distinction between the personal and the political gives the political realm too much and too little scope; at the same time it renders the personal too important and not important enough. . . .
>
> We need a third term, one that can describe the space between the state and the supposedly safe havens of the personal. Let us call this space the 'social.'[18]

In my view, the intersection of public and private lives, as well as the intersection of communal politics and personal ethics, resides within this "social" space. Such locale has served as the site of our study of O'Hara, Lowell, Rich, Wright, Levine, Komunyakaa, Dove, and Wojahn. Each poet pursues within that charged field a personal and often idiosyncratic quest to situate the self within the complexities of communal life. Each refuses, in essence, to accept one popular version of Romanticism that pits the robust but isolated individual against the deadening impingements of society. Perhaps the very nature of the dialectic has encouraged these poets often to rely upon a similar rhetorical strategy—dialogic form—to convey the competing pressures active within this "social" space.

Forché employs several of the dialogic forms described by M. M. Bakhtin, doing so most strikingly in poems of *The Country Between*

Us which are rife with what may be viewed, superficially, as "political" content. While on a Guggenheim Fellowship between 1978 and 1980, Forché spent two years in El Salvador investigating human rights abuses for Amnesty International and other human rights organizations.[19] She went there, during a period in which El Salvador was experiencing an almost unfathomable flood of political torture and murder, to "further" her "education in the twentieth-century human condition," an education which has only intensified in her recent work.

Most striking is the way Forché explores a dialogic relationship with her readers regarding the moral and ethical dimensions of what it means to be human, those issues, as I've said, that Wittgenstein believes to be beyond the reach of language. If she cannot truly "speak about" these matters, cannot escape the "cage" of language, she can "show" examples of human behavior which interrogate readers' understanding of human morality and ethics. Using modes of dialogic form, Forché can present to her readers incidents that have inherent in them moral and ethical concerns—all the while trusting, as Wittgenstein conjectured, that these ethical matters will "make themselves manifest" in her readers' minds.

In this fashion, the give and take of that interchange, and its implicit acts of questioning and reappraisal, resemble the dialogic relationship M. M. Bakhtin ascribes in *The Dialogic Imagination* to "the actual life of speech." This interaction manifests Bakhtin's theory of "heteroglossia," which, reduced to its fundamental application, holds each spoken or written word to be in constant dialogue with each previous usage of that and other words. Thus for Bakhtin, no actual monologues are possible. Every word, each utterance, converses with a panoply of its own competing meanings.[21] Bakhtin relishes the dialogic basis of all speech, including the implicit conversation between writer and reader. In such an interchange, every "concrete act of understanding is active" because its value as a conversation is "indissolubly merged with the response, with a motivated agreement or disagreement" of the listener. Here the arena of "encounter" lies within the "subjective belief system of the listener,"[22] and thus the speaker's words enter into a dialogical relationship with the attitudes, values, and ideologies inherent in the listener's understanding of these words.

Given Wittgenstein's belief in the futility of talking about ethics, what results from such dialogism can appear, at first glance, to offer humans more frustration than promise. True enough, competing dialogic readings bounce back and forth between writer and reader, each straining against the cage walls of language. However, in the very act of straining against these limits lies the source of our humanity, the wellspring of human ethical concerns. What choice do we have? To refuse this quest, to abdicate the beautiful lost cause of ethical discussion, is to deny our humanity. As if to settle the matter, Wittgenstein goes as far as to equate the redemptive futility of such a "thrust" against the cage with the whole notion of ethics: "Anything we can say must, a priori, be only nonsense. Nevertheless, we thrust against the limits of language. . . . This thrust against the limits of language is ethics."[23] The point is this: If the poet's "thrust" against the limits of language is itself an ethical act, dialogism makes it doubly so as the reader responds to and thus engages in this thrust. Dialogue between poet and reader on ethical matters becomes itself an ethical act.

Forché's "San Onofre, California" begins that ethical dialogue with her audience. Simply put, the speaker of Forché's poems, as in conversation, partly determines what she says and how she says it by bearing in mind readers' preconceptions regarding what she says of the situation in El Salvador. The poem opens the section of *The Country Between Us* dealing with events in El Salvador with the inclusive embrace of the third person pronoun, "We have come far south." That gesture, of course, enables Forché both to refer to the party with which she literally travels to El Salvador and to address the reader who now figuratively embarks on the same journey. As if sensing both her own and her readers' hesitancy to travel further into the hellish "far south," the speaker acknowledges the risks of this quest to face ethical questions head on:

> If we go on, we might stop
> in the street in the very place
> where someone disappeared
> and the words Come with us! we might
> hear them. If that happened, we would
> lead our lives with our hands
> tied together.[24]

That final image evokes the fate of those who have "disappeared" in the midst of El Salvador's political turmoil, as well as the enduring sense of frustration and helplessness of those who venture south to give "witness" to these events. To do so is to be forever bound by them. The speaker therefore understands her own, and her readers', reluctance to get involved, especially when staying put up "north" affords North Americans the protection of time and distance:

the cries of those who vanish
might take years to get up here.

Having decided to surrender that armor, Forché arrives in El Salvador as an innocent prepared to be tutored firsthand in the specif-
ics of our "twentieth-century condition." Her conversations with
women whose husbands have "disappeared" or been imprisoned for
political reasons produce striking poems. In "The Memory of Elena," for example, a woman whose husband has been murdered by
the authorities remains so haunted by his loss that simple events of
daily life conjure terrible images of his death. Even lunch becomes
horribly transmogrified by her grief:

> The *paella*, comes, a bed of rice
> and *camarones*, fingers and shells,
> the lips of those whose lips
> have been removed, mussels
> the soft blue of a leg socket.
>
> This is not *paella*. . . .
>   This is the ring
> of a rifle report on the stones,
> her hand over her mouth,
> her husband falling against her.

Outside the obvious risk of politicizing the horror, and thus putting off readers disinclined to see the issues as anything but ideological battles, these poems take an equally compelling aesthetic risk.
They risk sensationalizing—and thus trivializing—human grief and
suffering. Moreover, anyone familiar with the evening news or the
daily newspaper has encountered a bevy of similar accounts by the age
of majority. We have become inured even to graphic displays of
inhumanity toward our fellows. How then to engage this reader in
dialogue? One prose poem, "The Colonel" offers some insight into
the process.

In some ways the most unpresupposing of these pieces, "The Colonel" describes, with ostensible journalistic precision and objectivity reminiscent of Komunyakaa's "Recreating the Scene," the
speaker's dinner with a member of El Salvador's military:

> What you have heard is true. I was in his house. His wife car-
> ried a tray of coffee and sugar. His daughter filed her nails, his
> son went out for the night. There were daily papers, pet dogs, a
> pistol on the cushion beside him. The moon swung bare on its
> black cord over the house. On the television was a cop show. It

was in English. Broken bottles were embedded in the walls around the house to scoop the kneecaps from a man's legs or cut his hands to lace. On the windows there were gratings like those in liquor stores. We had dinner, rack of lamb, good wine, a gold bell was on the table for calling the maid. The maid brought green mangoes, salt, a type of bread. I was asked how I enjoyed the country. There was a brief commercial in Spanish. His wife took everything away. There was some talk then of how difficult it had become to govern. The parrot said hello on the terrace. The colonel told it to shut up, and pushed himself from the table. My friend said to me with his eyes: say nothing. The colonel returned with a sack used to bring groceries home. He spilled human ears on the table. They were like dried peach halves. There is no other way to say this. He took one of them in his hands, shook it in our faces, dropped in into a water glass. It came alive there. I am tired of fooling around he said. As for the rights of anyone, tell your people they can go fuck themselves. He swept the ears to the floor with his arm and held the last of his wine in the air. Something for your poetry, no? he said. Some of the ears on the floor caught this scrap of his voice. Some of the ears on the floor were pressed to the ground.

At first reading, most of the prose seems almost unartfully composed. Laconic and understated, the speaker hardly varies her syntax beyond short declarative sentences. The prose poem lacks definitive rhythm, lurching forward from sentence to sentence without the adornments of musical phrase or elegant diction. It appears, despite its horrific subject matter, to be one of those occasions where, as Larry Levis puts it, "life imitates art . . . a realistic, reportorial account of a dinner party."[25] Forché herself lends credibility to this reading through her own remarks on the poem's source: "One evening I dined with a military officer who toasted America, private enterprise, Las Vegas, and the 'fatherland' until his wife excused herself and in a drape of cigar smoke the events of 'The Colonel' took place. Almost a *poeme trouve*, I had only to pare down the memory and render it whole, unlined and as precise as recollection would have it. I did not wish to endanger myself by the act of poeticizing such a necessary reportage."[26]

A closer look at the piece, however, shows it to be deftly arranged and rhetorically situated. No matter how much Forché wishes it to be otherwise, "recollection" is itself a poetic act in which what one remembers and how one arranges those details account for the prose poem's rhetorical presentation, its appeal as art. It is no accident, for example, that the "pistol" on the cushion nicely parallels the "gold bell" on the table, invoking both power and privilege and their cynical interrelationship. Likewise, the quotidian nature of "pet dogs," "daily papers," dutiful wife and daughter, and American television clashes to poetic effect with the "gratings" on the windows and the surreal grocery bag full of severed human ears. When Forché says "There is no other way to say this" after describing the ears as resembling "dried peach halves," she apologizes, on one hand, for resorting to metaphor. On the other, she does just that—resorts to metaphor—to offer a chillingly accurate image of that scene and the one that follows when the ears come "alive" in a water glass.

Moreover, that Forché sets out to avoid such "poeticizing" provides the basis for the piece's very aesthetic—a prose poem whose anti-poetic gestures are precisely those aspects which define its poetics. This refusal, as we have seen earlier by applying Jurij Lotman's theory of the "minus-device" to Frank O'Hara's and David Wojahn's poetry, predicates the work's artful qualities. In large part, the poem's breaking of the rules governing what a poem *ought to be* gives depth and relevance to its appeal as a poem, a fundamental matter of rhetoric that can be attributed even to the seemingly rebellious decision to present the piece as a prose poem. In laboring to avoid poetically "prettifying" the subject, in simplifying its syntax and diction, even in attempting to disguise its poetic qualities within an ostensibly reportorial prose form, Forché has paradoxically made the piece more poetic, more aesthetically complex. To say that "The Colonel" is a highly rhetorical piece is no denigration. To the contrary, such a statement simply acknowledges the implicit rhetorical basis of all art, even that which aspires—or pretends to aspire—to inhabit some unattainable zone free of rhetoric.

In fact, the speaker's initial sentence acknowledges her rhetorical dialogue with the reader: "What you have heard is true." The speaker, whom her readers reasonably assume is Forché herself, directly addresses the sum of those readers' moral and ethical knowledge, opinions, misconceptions, etc., related to political oppression in El Salvador. She knows that the value of her utterance will depend greatly upon a dialogical relationship with what Bakhtin calls the "background of other concrete utterances on the same theme, a background made up of contradictory opinions, points of view and value judgments" which reside in the "consciousness of the listener . . . pregnant with responses and objections."[27] In much the same fashion as Wojahn's rock 'n' roll sonnets, Forché's poem relies on an attendant companion text, replete with historical and social reverberations:

"The Colonel"	+	"What you [readers] have heard" about Salvadoran political oppression

That companion text, in essence, resides within the reader, offering a culturally shared experience bound in historical time. Similar to Wojahn's work, Forché's poems also assume a particular reader. Without the assumption of shared experience on the part of the reader—essentially, "What you have heard"—her poem lacks both the purpose and direction that phrase assumes for the poem.

In brief, Forché's goal is to convince the reader, who may harbor doubts as to the veracity of accounts of oppression and human rights abuses in El Salvador, that what she says is "true," if only because she literally was "in [the] house" of such oppressors. Thus Forché predicates, albeit subtly, her "[a]lmost found poem" upon the rhetorical contract implicit in such dialogue. Even more noteworthy is Forché's choice to highlight the colonel's own recognition of the poetic and rhetorical power inhering in his sack full of ears, an awareness made particularly evident when he remarks, "Something for your poetry, no?" Forché's including the comment in the poem has several curious rhetorical effects, not the least of which is to enable the colonel to insult both poet and readers and to make them compatriots in the struggle against the kind of inhumanity the colonel embodies. Finally, Forché trusts that merely presenting the image of the sack of ears—without guiding commentary—will enable the resonant ethical issues to echo in her readers' minds, to "make themselves manifest" in the manner Wittgenstein suggests these things become known to us. In this way, her effort simply to "report" what she saw rather than to engage in ethical discussion demonstrates how keenly Forché acknowledges the limits of language in ethical matters and how subtly she tries to extend them. Note, though, how difficult it is to avoid overt "poeticizing" in favor of simple reporting. Surely the images of the prose poem's last two sentences—the ears which magically heard the colonel's obscene words and those which were pressed to the ground to hear the silent cry of the dead—offer a poetic mix of emotion and political commentary meant to sway readers' response to these events and to honor struggle against oppression. Although clearly aware of limits, Forché imbues her work with something equally heartfelt and feisty, something that refuses to give in.

Another poem from *The Country Between Us,* "Return," illustrates how effectively Forché employs dialogic form to converse with her reader. In this instance, the reader is never directly addressed, although that reader is allowed to "overhear"—and thus made privy to and participant in—a conversation between the speaker and Josephine Crum, to whom the poem is dedicated, upon the speaker's "return to America." The speaker opens the poem by relating to Josephine the strangeness of her return to America's "iced drinks and paper umbrellas, clean / toilets." Josephine, familiar with the intricacies of Salvadoran politics, listens intently to the speaker's "stories" of brutality.

Burdened by what she has seen, and feeling helpless to alter the situation, Forché admits the inefficacy of words when she tries to lecture Americans, privileged Safeway shoppers who greedily benefit from El Salvador's "lettuce, papayas and sugar, pineapples / and coffee, especially the coffee." The speaker's discussion of co-op farms and Central American political figures merely bores her audience, especially American men, in whom "there is some absence of recognition." Forché suggests something few of us like to admit, that our attention is not drawn to abstract discussions of politics and human rights, especially when the "cries" of the dead will "take years to get here," as she says in "San Onofre." North Americans are not fond of abstractions; they prefer the tangible reality of fresh fruit and coffee. The question then remains: How to reach her readers? Josephine knows the answer lies in another haunting reality: that "men and women of good will read / torture reports with fascination," as she explains:

> Go try on
> Americans your long, dull story
> of corruption, but better to give
> them what they want: Lil Milagro Ramirez,
> who after years of confinement did not
> know what year it was, how she walked
> with help and was forced to shit in public.
> Tell them about the razor, the live wire,
> dry ice and concrete, grey rats and above all
> who fucked her, how many times and when.
> Tell them about retaliation: José lying
> on the flat bed truck, waving his stumps
> in your face, his hands cut off by his
> captors. . . .
>   many children strung
> together, as if they were cut from paper

and all in a delicate chain. And that people
who rescue physicists, lawyers and poets
lie in their beds at night with reports
of mice introduced into women, of men
whose testicles are crushed like eggs.

Josephine understands, as Forché must, that boatloads of abstraction
sink silently in the presence of one horrific detail. That comparing a
"delicate chain" of dead children, for example, to a string of paper
dolls forcefully arrests readers' attention and interrogates their assumptions about Central American politics.

The poem's subtle rhetorical gestures warrant closer attention, especially as they relate to the poet's speaking of the unspeakable.
That Forché and Josephine admit in the poem the difficulties they've
encountered talking with others about these incidents indicates both
of them have "run against the boundaries of language" Wittgenstein
laments. As the poem's two speakers crash against the walls of the
cage, so do the poem's readers "thrust" against these same boundaries, bound up as they are in the poem's dialogic act and its implicit
ethical concerns. Note also how the poem's fundamental dialogic
structure enables Forché to say many of these things without *really*
saying them. She cedes the poem's most startling lines to Josephine,
a strategy similar to that we've already identified in Philip Levine's
poems about Cipriano Mera and Tom Jefferson. One effect, of
course, is to permit Forché to avoid deftly the image of overt political stridency that surely accrues to one who speaks of such things. A
corollary effect is to increase readers' trust of Forché as speaker, for
in the poem she is as much a listener as her readers are. Forché can
dialogically engage readers' "subjective beliefs" about Salvadoran
political oppression without appearing to preach to—and thus risk
losing—those readers. Through Josephine's voice, and the essential
dialogic form, Forché can appear to be much more the one instructed
rather than the instructor, therefore forging a strong bond of mutual
vulnerability with her readers. If, in the end, Forché's readers are indeed chastised for their political naiveté and shameful inaction, she
is made to appear one of them, equally culpable:

Your problem is not your life as it is
in America, not that your hands, as you
tell me, are tied to do something. It is
that you were born to an island of greed
and grace where you have this sense
of yourself as apart from others.

In many ways Josephine's excoriating remarks undergird Forché's ruminations in the recent collection, *The Angel of History*. What it means to regard oneself as safely and protectively "apart from others," and the folly of such belief, serves as the book's fulcrum. Moreover, the basic dialogic structure of *The Country Between Us* gives way to a more complex dialogic rendering of historical voices. The poet's experience and the lyrical expression of that experience are no longer the focal points of her poems. Gone is the first-person poet-speaker engaged in dialogue with reader or select other. She has been replaced with a chorus of individuals speaking a swirl of competing voices, voices framed within snatches of narrative torn whole from others' historical experience. As early as the 1986 publication of the pointedly titled essay, "A Lesson in Commitment," Forché gave indication that the mode of her work was undergoing change due to the pressures of her "education in the twentieth-century human condition": "I am no longer able to focus my imagination to the exclusion of all that haunts and distracts me. No single voice lifts pure from the cacophony of voices and each image is one of horror, with no single image burned more deeply than others and all seeming to be fragments of a vague and larger horror . . . that we are, as a species, now careening toward our complete destruction . . ."[28] Forché's remarks seem those of someone who has discovered evil, its patent and interminable horror.

The Angel of History embodies the collective angst of a century known less for its civility than for its inventiveness in producing new forms of cruelty and inhumanity. The book's litany of human offenses against our fellows is as compelling as it is lengthy, including the Holocaust, the horrors of both World Wars and localized political oppression in El Salvador, the Czechoslovakian freedom protests against Soviet occupation, and the aftermath of the Hiroshima bombing. The book emphasizes the redemptive ethical courage of humans in the face of oppression, and just as importantly, the ethical questions these incidents must, implicitly, pose of God.

In a note to the collection, Forché describes it as a "gathering of utterances," and later as a "work which has desired its own bodying forth: polyphonic, broken, haunted, and in ruins, with no possibility of restoration."[29] Forché's "gathering of utterances" is indeed "polyphonic," admitting of her own and that of countless others, all of whom are given voice in these poems. Even a partial list of those authors whose quoted works appear in the text includes René Char, Walter Benjamin, Martin Heidegger, Paul Valéry, Georg Trakl, Elie Weisel, and Ludwig Wittgenstein, as well as a welter of unknowns, survivors of the Holocaust or the Hiroshima bombing, whose conversations sift through the poem like voices heard through a hotel wall. That sense of the reader, and indeed the poet, *overhearing* a conversation among this century's most plangent voices best describes the effect of reading *The Angel of History*. It is a rhetorical strategy reminiscent of the overheard conversation of Forché's earlier poem "Return." It is also on this basis that the book largely succeeds or fails. Readers who sense no overall design amidst its quick cuts are likely to feel they've experienced this sensation before—while standing on a busy street corner, for instance, isolated and confused amongst a slurry of disparate, partial voices. Those, on the other hand, who hear, within its cacophony, echoes of their own internal dialogues will find themselves actively participating in Forché's fragmented recapitulation of twentieth-century turmoil.

The book's stylized collage effect, as well as its summary of shabby human behavior, can't help but bring to mind T. S. Eliot's "The Waste Land." To mention that text in the same breath as Forché's is to open her book to summary praise or condemnation, depending on whether one views "The Waste Land" as the zenith or the nadir of twentieth-century American poetry. However different their particulars, both texts tend to see human beings fitfully in the process of, to reiterate Forché's remark, "careening toward our complete destruction." Forché herself invokes Eliot's hulking shadow by echoing the phrase many have cited from "The Waste Land" to describe its mode of development: "These fragments I have shored against my ruins." In "Book Codes: II," Forché fairly well describes her own work's aesthetic using similar terms: "fragments together into a story before the shape of the whole."

Divided into five parts—three containing long poems, one of relatively short pieces, and the last a group of fragments called "Book Codes"—the collection opens with an epigraph from section X of Walter Benjamin's "Theses on the Philosophy of History," itself a reflection on Paul Klee's painting "Angelus Novus." Benjamin's angel sees, from a perspective not available to us, the apparently discrete events of history in their true form, compressed into a single and contiguous "catastrophe": "This is how one pictures the angel of history. His face is turned toward the past. Where we perceive a chain of events, he sees one single catastrophe which keeps piling wreckage and hurls it in front of his feet. The angel would like to stay, awaken the dead, and make whole what has been smashed. But a storm is blowing in from Paradise; it has caught in his wings with such violence that the angel can no longer close them. The storm irresistibly propels him into the future to which his back is turned, while the pile of debris before him grows skyward."[31]

Benjamin's voice appropriately serves to reopen the dialogue begun by Josephine Crum in Forché's "The Return." His vision of history makes clear the interconnectedness of human lives and events and makes absurd the belief one might live "apart from others." Benjamin, as well, tragically embodies the nature of this "catastrophe." A refugee from Nazi Germany, Benjamin continued to write in Paris until the Gestapo confiscated the portion of his library he'd been able to bring with him in exile. He later committed suicide at the Franco-Spanish border, partly in despair of having been refused passage at the border, which would have brought escape to Spain on route to America through Portugal.[31]

Part I of the book, "The Angel of History," introduces a flurry of voices interspersed in dialogue with a speaker loosely associated with the poet herself. In the first few lines of the poem, that speaker sets high stakes for the conversations to follow, indicting both herself and her culture:

> In the world it was the language of the agreed-upon
>   lie, and it bound me to
>   itself, demanding of my life an explanation.[32]

At root, the "agreed-upon lie" wrongly assumes the separateness of human life and activity we've already discussed. It also presumes an enthusiastic belief in the upward spiral of human progress and a conversely quiescent relationship to events of the past which might threaten this naiveté. Against it, Forché quickly juxtaposes a farmhouse in the French village of Izieu, where during World War II forty-four Jewish children were successfully "hidden April to April." Forché quite rightly assumes that ethical and moral issues will "make themselves manifest" simply by her reporting the children were taken to "Auschwitz"—the word invoking, in terrible verbal shorthand, a slew of ethical questions surrounding the Holocaust:

> Within the house, the silence of God. Forty-four
>   bedrolls, forty-four metal cups.
> And *the silence of God is God* . . . .
>
> The children were taken to Poland.
> The children were taken to Auschwitz in Poland
>   singing *Vous n'aurez pas L'Alsace et la Loraine.*

> In a farmhouse still standing in Izieu, *le silence de*
> *Dieu est Dieu.*

Forché's use of Holocaust survivor Elie Weisel's phrase "the silence of God is God" drapes a curtain of held breath over the scene. What can words accomplish against the terrible silence of God in such a matter? Here again, Forché has "run against the boundaries of language," the "wall" of the "cage" that Wittgenstein argues circumscribes any meaningful discussion of ethics. In *Real Presences*, George Steiner contends that the very experience of aesthetic meaning in literature and the arts issues from the "necessary possibility" of God's presence.[33] Forché, to the contrary, implies that the terrible irony of this presence, given God's immutable silence, is what puts into doubt meaning of any kind—aesthetic, moral, or ethical.[34] It's no wonder that the Jewish deportee Ellie, another of the poem's disparate voices, later remarks:

> *Le Dieu? Le Dieu is un feu. A psychopath. Le Dieu*
> *est feu.*

That God is "a fire," made of hungry flames making rubble of the present and consuming the past.

Flames provide a symbolic refrain for the collection, no doubt partly in metaphorical reference to the Holocaust. Things are continually beset by fire wishing to transform or erase. For example, Ellie, whose skin peels from her arms in great sheaths, is afflicted with a disease called "St. Anthony's Fire." Her body thus seems fiercely intent upon erasing itself, with nothingness and silence its sole reward. One horrific dream sequence in Part I recounts how the speaker awakened to a room *"filled with vultures . / . . . hopping about . . . belching and vomiting flesh , / as you saw them at Puerto Diablo and El Playon,"* two of El Salvador's surreal body dumps where the bodies of political prisoners who had "disappeared" from their homes literally disappeared beneath vultures' beaks. In Part II's "The Notebook of the Uprising," another figure associated with fire looms large: Jan Palach, the young student who immolated himself in protest of the Soviet and Warsaw Pact invasion of Czechoslovakia. In fact, one of the book's primary dialectics pits the insistent forces of erasure against those of memory and will, or as this poem puts it:

> An erasure of everything destroyed yet left
>   intact . . . .
> What was here before imperfectly erased
>   and memory a reliquary in a wall of silence.

"The Notebook of the Uprising" is a particularly important poem for our purposes. The poem extends the ethical basis of remembering and speaking of history to a jointly personal and communal act, for "memory barely retrieved from a fire is (the past) in its hiding place." Against the "wall of silence" built by God and much of humanity, against the fires of forgetting, the poem's multiple voices speak to ensure that forces which would erase the past do so only "imperfectly." Their testimony, muffled by time and others' forgetfulness, murmurs like the ghost voices that haunt an "imperfectly" re-recorded cassette tape, voices most audible in the hissing margins between songs, most noticeable in what otherwise would be silence. In the process, their words perform the most fundamental dialogic act of this or any text; they

> Put into question others, put into question God.

The blessing and curse attending an awareness that it is impossible to live "apart from others" is to live always "as if someone not alive were watching," as the speaker remarks in the poem "The Angel of History." Moreover, when that same speaker looks in the mirror, she doesn't simply see familiar crags and creases, but instead witnesses how "my face would become hers, yours, and hers, the other's, facing / each other through days, pain, the prisoner's visiting window." Elsewhere, Forché underscores this belief in one of the more brutal images of the collection, section IX of "The Recording Angel":

> It isn't necessary to explain
> The girl was thought to be with child
> Until it was discovered that her belly had been
>   cut open
> And a man's head placed where the child would have
>   been
> The tanks dug ladders in the earth no one was able
>   to climb
> In every war someone puts a cigarette in the
>   corpse's mouth
> And the corpse
> The corpse is never mentioned
> In the hours before the body was found
> It was this, this life that he longed for, this
>   that he wrote of desiring . . .

What's most curious is the way this act of butchery offers a startling metaphor for the very interconnectedness of human life that the act would seem ferociously to deny. The dead woman offers a brutal metaphor for the manner in which we all carry our fellows inside of us. She emphasizes, as well, the common inheritance of those who share an historical era, who witness and partake of its sullen rituals. Sartre contends we are inextricably bound by our historical milieu, applying, in fact, an uncomfortably appropriate metaphor to argue that we therefore "share the same corpses."[35] Elsewhere in "The Recording Angel," Forché compares this "matter of shared history" to having "lived the same lie."

The book's disparate chorus of voices offers a dialogic response to the forces of erasure and forgetting. The poet who listens to them, and for that matter the reader who overhears, refuse to despair in spite of the "silence of God." This is the essence of Forché's "poetry of witness," as a survivor of the Hiroshima bombing asserts in "The Garden Shukkei-en":

> And in the silence surrounding what happened to us
> it is the bell to awaken God that we've heard ringing.

This bell rings in the words of those who speak and in the ears of those who listen. Each person understands full well that nothing that can be said "will be enough" ("The Garden Shukkei-en"). Each recognizes the boundaries of language, the "cage" Wittgenstein believes humans brush up against in the effort to speak of the mystical, the ethical, the moral—those subjects which most define the human condition. Each endures the hopelessness attending the act of trying to speak of absolute good and right conduct. Still, within their attempt to express the inexpressible, however preordained to failure, lies their fundamental humanity.

Much of what Forché reaches for in the complex structures of *The Angel of History,* her "gathering of utterances," is a dialogic relationship with her culture and her readers, as well as with the larger forces of history. She does so because she has lost faith in the ability of the solitary lyric voice to counter silence—that of God and of the collective human race. In short, she has sought to do the very thing Wittgenstein thought most impossible in language, to speak of matters of ethics and morality. Through her poems, she challenges the limits of language and thus manages, as Russell said of Wittgenstein, "to say a good deal about what cannot be said." In doing so, she has been in explicit dialogue with Wittgenstein's *Tractatus.* It's no surprise, therefore, to see that "Book Codes: I," a found poem composed of citational fragments from Wittgenstein's writings, is concerned with how the limits of language indicate the boundaries of one's world. Wittgenstein believed the very possibility of understanding is dependent on shared rules for encoding and decoding language structure; here, Forché offers her readers "codes" meant to help them decode the book's thematic and aesthetic structure and thereby understand it. As a way to situate the general overstepping of boundaries in *The Angel of History*, "Book Codes: I" closes with direct reference to the issue that began our discussion—the matter of what can be spoken of in language. The piece also suggests Wittgenstein's view that the metaphysical subject does not belong to this world but is rather a boundary of it:

> We must know *whether*
> *And if not:* then what is the task
> very much on the surface
> by means of finite signs
> when one is frightened of the truth
> "Are there simple things?"
>   What depends on my life?
> would be possible for me to write
> like the film on deep water
> over too wide chasms of thought
> the world does not change
> the visual field has not a form like this
> so many graces of fate
> the boundary (not a part) of the world
> mirrored in its use
> nothing except what can be said[36]

Part of Forché's challenge in *The Angel of History* is to stretch the boundaries of her personal and cultural language, to extend, in a fashion, the boundaries of the metaphysical subject. The concluding poem, "Book Codes: III," alludes to this struggle and to the inevitable collision with the "walls" of the cage Wittgenstein considered language to be:

> for our having tried to cross the river caught between walls
> one could hear a voice "Bear the unbearable"
> and the broadcast was at an end

Catching the overheard voice, "broadcast" through "walls" of time and space and language, serves as Forché's mission in *Angel*. No doubt that has something to do with her inclusion of so many excerpts from French and German, as well as those from other authors and historical figures of varying significance. The bigger the language, the bigger the "cage." The bigger the "cage," the bigger the human metaphysical subject. It is a challenge Wittgenstein would have respected, for it engages the essential ethical act of human language—our perhaps doomed but redemptive "thrust against the limits of language." If, as Forché suggests in the poem "Message," we now inhabit "the hour farthest from God," this struggle is both blessing and curse. To hear the muffled voices nearly lost amongst the furious rush of history and to engage them with our own is to refuse silence in favor of possibility—our most solemn obligation.

Notes

Introduction

1. R. G. Collingwood, *The Idea of History* (New York: Oxford University Press, 1956), pp. 17–18.

2. Ibid., 18.

3. Robert Penn Warren, *Brother to Dragons* (New York: Random House, 1979), p. xiii.

4. Benedetto Croce, *Aesthetic: As Science of Expression and General Linguistic,* trans. Douglas Ainslie (New York: Macmillan, 1922), p. 26.

5. Ibid., 27.

6. Hayden White, *Tropics of Discourse: Essays in Cultural Criticism* (Baltimore: Johns Hopkins University Press, 1978), p. 51.

7. Ibid., 31.

8. Ibid., 62.

9. Roland Barthes, "The Discourse of History," trans. Stephen Bann, in *Comparative Criticism: A Year Book,* vol. 3, ed. E. S. Schaffer (Cambridge: Cambridge University Press, 1981), p. 7.

10. Claude Lévi-Strauss, *The Savage Mind* (Chicago: University of Chicago Press, 1966), p. 257.

11. Northrup Frye, "New Directions from Old," in *Fables of Identity* (New York: Harcourt, Brace, & World, 1963), pp. 53–54.

12. Hayden White suggests much of this, as well as Hegel's theories on writing about history, in *Tropics of Discourse.* White singles out Hegel's *Vorlesungen uber die Asthetik, Dritter Teil, Drittes Kapitel,* particularly "Die Poesie" as a useful source. See especially *Topics of Discourse,* p. 76, n. 10.

13. Friedrich Nietzsche, *The Use and Abuse of History,* trans. Adrian Collins (New York: Liberal Arts Press, 1949), p. 45.

14. Ibid.

15. Ibid., 44.

16. Ibid., 45.

17. Ibid., 11.

18. Ibid., 38.

19. Fernand Braudel, *On History,* trans. Sarah Matthews (Chicago: University of Chicago Press, 1980), p. 11.

20. See Harold Bloom, *The Anxiety of Influence: A Theory of Poetry* (New York: Oxford University Press, 1973). For a complementary reading of the power of poetic influence, see Walter Jackson Bate, *The Burden of the Past and the English Poet* (New York: Belknap Press, 1970).

21. Michel Foucault, "Truth and Power," in *The Foucault Reader,* ed. Paul Rabinow (New York: Pantheon, 1984), p. 56.

22. See Foucault's "Nietzsche, Genealogy, History," in *Language, Counter-Memory, Practice,* ed. and intro. Donald F. Bouchard, trans. Donald F. Bouchard and

Sherry Simon (Ithaca: Cornell University Press, 1977), for a discussion of "effective" history.

23. White, 31.

24. Graham Hough, "The Modernist Lyric," in *Modernism: 1890–1930,* ed. M. Bradbury and Jay McFarlane (Harmondsworth, U.K.: Penguin, 1976), p. 318.

25. Roger Mitchell, "Modernism Comes to America: 1908–1920," in *A Profile of Twentieth-Century American Poetry,* ed. Jack Meyers and David Wojahn (Carbondale: Southern Illinois University Press, 1991), p. 33.

26. Ibid., 32–33.

27. Irving Howe, "The Idea of the Modern," in *The Idea of the Modern in Literature and the Arts,* ed. Irving Howe (New York: Horizon, 1967), pp. 11–40.

28. Walter Sutton, *American Free Verse: The Modern Revolution in Poetry* (New York: New Directions, 1973), p. 60.

29. Allen Tate, *Reason in Madness* (New York: Putnam's 1941), p. 136.

30. Ibid.

31. George Williamson, "Donne and the Poetry of Today," in *A Garland for John Donne,* ed. Theodore Spencer (Gloucester, Mass.: Peter Smith, 1958), pp. 153–54.

32. John Crowe Ransom, *The World's Body* (New York: Scribner's, 1938), p. 29.

33. Robert Kelly, "Notes on the Poetry of the Deep Image," *Trobar 2* (1961): 16.

34. Paul Breslin, *The Psycho-Political Muse* (Chicago: University of Chicago Press, 1987), p. 157.

35. See Robert Bly, "A Wrong Turning in American Poetry," *Choice 3* (1963): 33–47.

36. Ibid., 38.

37. Robert Bly, *Silence in the Snowy Fields* (Middletown, Conn: Wesleyan University Press, 1962), p. 38.

38. See Charles Altieri, *Self and Sensibility in Contemporary American Poetry* (Cambridge: Cambridge University Press, 1984), especially the book's first chapter.

39. Ibid., 15.

40. Ibid., 14.

41. Ibid., 16.

42. Dana Gioia, "Can Poetry Matter?" *The Atlantic Monthly* (May 1991): 94. Accepting responsibility for expanding poetry's audience, Gioia offers six "modest proposals" for helping poetry "again become a part of American public culture" (106). Although too lengthy to detail here, in general Gioia's suggestions have to do with asking poets to read some work by other poets at their own public readings, combining poetry with other arts at readings, encouraging poets to write prose about poetry, asking editors who compile anthologies to accept only poems they truly admire, suggesting that high school and undergraduate teachers spend more time on performance and less on analysis of poetry in the classroom, and using radio to enlarge poetry's audience.

43. Though Epstein's essay first appeared in the August 1988 issue of *Commentary,* its largest, and most engaged audience, came with its reprinting in the *AWP Chronicle* 21 (May 1989): 1–5, 16–17.

44. Donald Hall, "Death to the Death of Poetry," *Harper's* 279 (September 1989): 72–76.

45. Ibid., 74.

46. The "New Formalism" received its first book-length consideration in *Ex-*

pansive Poetry, ed. Frederick Feirstein, (Santa Cruz: Story Line Press, 1989), an anthology of essays of which half were devoted to New Formalism and half to New Narrative. Before then, essays such as Brad Leithauser's "Metrical Illiteracy," *The New Criterion* 1 (January 1983): 41–46, cleared the way for renewed appreciation of formal verse.

47. Now defunct, *The Reaper* offered a piquant sampling of poetry and polemics which advocated a return to narrative poetry. The magazine lives on, transmogrified into the Story Line Press, which McDowell directs. See also *Expansive Poetry* noted above.

48. Jonathan Holden, *The Fate of American Poetry* (Athens: University of Georgia Press, 1991), p. 105.

49. Donald Hall, introduction to *Contemporary American Poetry,* ed. Donald Hall (Baltimore: Penguin, 1962), p. 23.

50. Bruce Andrews, "Poetry as Explanation, Poetry as Praxis," in *The Politics of Poetic Form: Poetry and Public Policy,* ed. Charles Bernstein (New York: Roof Books, 1989).

51. See Charles Bernstein, *Rough Trades* (Los Angeles: Sun & Moon Press, 1991), p. 25.

52. Since much of an appreciation for L-A-N-G-U-A-G-E poetry depends upon knowledge of those sources cited in the text, a good place to begin one's study of its theoretical foundation would be Ron Silliman's *The New Sentence* (New York: Roof Books, 1989) and Charles Bernstein's *Content's Dream: Essays 1975–1984* (Los Angeles: Sun & Moon Press, 1986). Add to those *The L-A-N-G-U-A-G-E Book,* edited by Bruce Andrews and Charles Bernstein (Carbondale: Southern Illinois University Press, 1984).

53. Christopher Dewdney, "Fractal Diffusion," in the *L-A-N-G-U-A-G-E Book,* ed. Bruce Andrews and Charles Bernstein, p. 109.

54. Gerald Graff, *Literature Against Itself* (Chicago: University of Chicago Press, 1979), p. 139.

55. See Foucault's "What is an Author?" trans. Josue V. Harari, in *The Foucault Reader,* ed. Paul Rabinow, pp. 101–20.

56. Bernstein, *Content's Dream,* p. 49.

57. Robert Pinsky, "Responsibilities of the Poet," in *Poetry and the World* (New York: Ecco Press, 1988), p. 86–89.

58. Benedetto Croce, *History: Theory and Practice,* trans. Douglas Ainslie (New York: Russell & Russell, 1960), p. 12.

Chapter One

1. Alan Williamson, *Pity the Monsters: The Political Vision of Robert Lowell* (New York: Yale, 1974), p. 3.

2. Adrienne Rich, "When We Dead Awaken: Writing as Revision," in *On Lies, Secrets, and Silence: Selected Prose, 1966–1978* (New York: Norton, 1979), p. 35.

3. Frank O'Hara, "Statement for *The New American Poetry*" and "Statement for Paterson Society," in *The Collected Poems of Frank O'Hara,* ed. Donald Allen (New York: Knopf, 1971), pp. 500, 510 respectively.

4. See M. L. Rosenthal, "Poetry as Confession," *Nation* 189 (19 September 1959): 154–55. See also Rosenthal's chapter on Lowell's *Life Studies* in *The New Poets* (New York: Oxford University Press, 1967).

5. Stanley Kunitz, "Telling the Time," *Salmagundi* 1.4 (1966–67): 22. Lowell's

rise to literary stardom began as early as 1947, when *Lord Weary's Castle* won the Pulitzer. *Time* called him the year's "most rewarded poet" (19 May 1947, 44), and *Life* pronounced that Lowell had already achieved "the status of a major poet" (19 May 1947, 91).

6. Robert Lowell, "On 'Skunk Hour'" in *Robert Lowell: A Collection of Critical Essays*, ed. Thomas Parkinson (New York: Prentice-Hall, 1968), p. 132.

7. Robert Lowell, *Life Studies* (New York: Farrar, Straus, and Cudahy, 1959), p. 85.

8. Robert Lowell, *For the Union Dead* (New York: Farrar, Straus, and Giroux, 1964), p. 70.

9. Robert Lowell, in *Writers at Work: The Paris Review Interviews—Second Series*, (New York: Viking, 1965), p. 347.

10. Richard Poirer, "Our Truest Historian," *Book Week*, 11 October 1964: 1.

11. Alan Williamson has remarked, quite rightly, that there is "no dividing Lowell into a 'public' and a 'private' poet. . . . the same categories of human experience preoccupy Lowell in both and constantly overflow from one to the other" (*Pity the Monsters*, 6). On the other hand, Patrick Cosgrave labors, with mixed results, to do just that—separate Lowell's private and public verse—in his *The Public Poetry of Robert Lowell* (New York: Taplinger, 1972).

12. Randall Jarrell, *Poetry and the Age* (1953: reprint, New York: Random House, Vintage, 1959), p. 193.

13. Robert Lowell, *History* (New York: Farrar, Straus, and Giroux, 1973). All references to the book are to this edition.

14. Ibid., vii.

15. Stephen Yenser identifies a "circular form" at work in the organization of *History:* "That form is to be expected partly because for Lowell every discovery is a 'discovery to be repeated many times,' or because for him past and present form one whole—which is no doubt one reason that the simple chronological structure was so long in coming" (314). See *Circle to Circle* (Berkeley: University of California Press, 1975).

16. In a cogent essay, James Sullivan makes much of Lowell's publishing a version of this poem for RFK in broadside format, arguing for Lowell's assiduous use of his literary and political capital. See "Investing the Cultural Capital of Robert Lowell," *Twentieth Century Literature* 38 (Summer 1992): 194–213.

17. Adrienne Rich, "When We Dead Awaken: Writing as Re-Vision," in *On Lies, Secrets, and Silence*, p. 35.

18. Rich, "The Anti-Feminist Woman," in *Lies, Secrets, and Silence*, p. 79.

19. Adrienne Rich, foreword to *Blood, Bread, and Poetry: Selected Prose, 1979–1985* (New York: Norton, 1986), pp. vii–viii.

20. W. H. Auden, introduction to *A Change of World* by Adrienne Rich (New Haven: Yale University Press, 1951), p. 11.

21. Adrienne Rich, *The Fact of a Door Frame* (New York: Norton), p. 3. Where not indicated otherwise, cited poems are from this edition.

22. Rich, "When We Dead Awaken," 40–41.

23. Ibid., 38–39.

24. Rich, "Husband-Right and Father-Right," in *On Lies, Secrets, and Silence*, 215.

25. Michel Foucault, "Truth and Power," in *The Foucault Reader*, ed. Paul Rabinow (New York: Pantheon, 1984), p. 56.

26. Michel Foucault, "Nietzsche, Genealogy, History," in *Language, Counter-Memory, Practice: Selected Essays and Interviews*, ed. and intro. Donald F. Bou-

chard, trans. Donald F. Bouchard and Sherry Simon (Ithaca: Cornell University Press, 1977), p. 154.

27. Alicia Ostriker, *Writing Like a Woman* (Ann Arbor: University of Michigan Press, 1984), p. 117.

28. Helen Vendler, *Part of Nature, Part of Us* (Cambridge: Harvard University Press, 1980), p. 243.

29. Adrian Oktenberg, " 'Disloyal to Civilization': *The Twenty-One Love Poems* of Adrienne Rich," in *Reading Adrienne Rich: Reviews and Re-Visions, 1951–81,* ed. Jane Roberta Cooper (Ann Arbor: University of Michigan Press, 1984), pp. 73–74. For those seeking a helpful overview of the critical reception of Rich's work, this anthology is a good place to start.

30. Adrienne Rich, *The Dream of Common Language* (New York: Norton, 1978), p. 30.

31. David Kalstone argues persuasively that "Rich's engagement with the American past has always been different from Lowell's. Rather than providing the materials for elegy, it has licensed a fierce optimism. . . . interested in American life as registered and suffered by those not in power, those not directly responsible for it, and especially women . . ." (137). See *Five Temperaments* (New York: Oxford University Press, 1977).

32. Marianne Whelchel, "Mining the 'Earth-Deposits': Women's History in Adrienne Rich's Poetry," in *Reading Adrienne Rich,* 52.

33. Adrienne Rich, *Of Women Born: Motherhood as Experience and Institution* (New York: Norton, 1986), p. x.

Chapter Two

1. Using a word popular in the fifties, James Wright defines the mode and shape of the decade's typical poem in "An Interview with Michael Andre," *Collected Prose,* ed. Anne Wright (Ann Arbor: University of Michigan Press, 1984), p. 142.

2. John Ashbery, introduction to *The Collected Poems of Frank O'Hara,* ed. Donald Allen (New York: Knopf, 1971), p. vii.

3. Jurij Lotman, *The Structure of the Artistic Text,* trans. Ronald Vroon, Michigan Slavic Contribution, no. 7 (Ann Arbor: University of Michigan Press, 1977), pp. 51, 95. In his preface to this volume, Ronald Vroon, who translates Lotman's text from Russian to English, offers this assessment of how Lotman's "controversial" structuralist theories have been received in Russia: "The comments made are, for the most part, disparaging. While most Soviet critics admit, somewhat begrudgingly, that Lotman has some very interesting things to say about literature, almost all agree that his approach suffers from the same 'errors' that the formalists committed." Obviously, Vroon would dispute that Lotman's structuralist theories are erroneous, and he maintains that the science of semiotics "continues to flourish in the Soviet Union." He offers Lotman's theories, much as I do here, in the hope of encouraging a discussion of them.

4. Ibid., 99.

5. Ibid., 95.

6. Ibid.

7. Frank O'Hara, "Statement for *The New American Poetry,*" *The Collected Poems of Frank O'Hara,* p. 500.

8. O'Hara, "Statement for Paterson Society," *The Collected Poems of Frank O'Hara*, p. 510. As a note in *The Collected Poems* indicates, the statement, dated March 16, 1961, was never sent to the Paterson Society (p. 558).

9. Ashbery, vii.

10. Robert Hass, *Twentieth Century Pleasures* (New York: Ecco Press, 1984), p. 40.

11. O'Hara, "Statement for *The New American Poetry*," 500.

12. Frank O'Hara, *Lunch Poems* (San Francisco: City Lights Books, 1964), p. 44. All further references to the text are to this edition.

13. Helen Vendler, *Part of Nature, Part of Us* (Cambridge: Harvard University Press, 1980), p. 183.

14. O'Hara, "Statement for *The New American Poetry*," 500.

15. O'Hara, "Larry Rivers: A Memoir," *The Collected Poems of Frank O'Hara*, p. 513. In the same memoir, O'Hara clarifies his own conception of himself as a poet doing "everything the opposite" and indicates the importance of painters as an audience for his work: "An interesting sidelight . . . was that for most of us non-Academic and indeed non-literary poets in the sense of the American scene at the time, the painters were the only generous audience for our poetry, and most of us first read publicly in art galleries" (p. 512).

16. Paul Carroll praises O'Hara's poem as "impure" for the way the poet mentions Bastille Day then never returns to it and for devoting only four lines to Holiday in a poem ostensibly an elegy to her. Carroll cites how these—and other elements—show the poem's rebellion against New Critical notions of organic wholeness. See *The Poem in Its Skin* (Chicago: Follett, 1968), pp. 157–64.

17. O'Hara, "Statement for Paterson Society," 510.

18. Adrienne Rich, "When We Dead Awaken: Writing as Re-Vision," *On Lies, Secrets, and Silence: Selected Prose, 1966–1978* (New York: W. W. Norton, 1979), pp. 40–41.

19. Frank O'Hara, "Personism: A Manifesto," *The Collected Poems of Frank O'Hara*, p. 499.

20. Ibid.

21. Frank O'Hara, "About Zhivago and His Poems," *The Collected Poems of Frank O'Hara*, p. 502.

22. James Wright, "The Stiff Smile of Mr. Warren," *Collected Prose*, p. 242. In his 1958 review of Warren's *Promises,* Wright excoriates the output of many poets then writing, castigating even his own work among the "ten thousand safe and competent versifyings produced by our current crop of punks in America. . . . we all know who we are . . . us safe boys."

23. O'Hara, "About Zhivago and His Poems," 503.

24. Ibid.

25. Richard Howard, *Alone with America* (New York: Atheneum, 1969), p. 397. Howard examines O'Hara's poetry in light of O'Hara's early death and his repeated references to dying, concluding that O'Hara "obliged himself to see life as an ensemble of impulses not for resisting but for bearing us toward death."

26. Frank O'Hara, "Notes on Second Avenue," *The Collected Poems of Frank O'Hara*, p. 497. Donald Allen, the editor of *The Collected Poems,* speculates that O'Hara's piece was "written in 1953 or later, apparently as a letter to an editor of a literary magazine," p. 558.

27. Ibid., 497.

Chapter Three

1. W. H. Auden, introduction to *The Green Wall* (New Haven: Yale University Press, 1957), reprinted in *James Wright: The Heart of the Light,* ed. Peter Stitt and Frank Graziano (Ann Arbor: University of Michigan Press, 1990), p. 24.

2. See Wright's "The Minneapolis Poem," *Shall We Gather at the River* (Middletown, Conn.: Wesleyan University Press, 1968). Other editions cited include: *The Branch Will Not Break* (Middletown, Conn.: Wesleyan University Press, 1963), *Two Citizens* (New York: Farrar, Straus, and Giroux, 1973), *To a Blossoming Pear Tree* (Farrar, Straus, and Giroux, 1977), and *This Journey* (New York: Vintage Books, 1982).

3. James Scully, *Line Break: Poetry as Social Practice* (Seattle: Bay Press, 1988), p. 5.

4. C. K. Williams, "The Poet and History," *TriQuarterly* 72 (Spring/Summer 1988): 196.

5. James Wright, in "James Wright: The Pure Clear Word, an Interview with Dave Smith," *American Poetry Review* 9, No. 3 (1980): 19–30; reprinted in *James Wright: Collected Prose* (Ann Arbor: University of Michigan Press, 1983), p. 192.

6. Paul Breslin argues that the "notion that conditions of work in industrial America repress sexuality is . . . commonplace in the radical social criticism of the late fifties and early sixties, especially in the work of Marcuse," in his own fine book *The Psycho-Political Muse* (Chicago: University of Chicago Press, 1987), p. 168. As Breslin suggests, see Herbert Marcuse, *Eros and Civilization: A Philosophical Inquiry Into Freud* (1955; reprint, New York: Vintage, 1962), pp. 77–78.

7. Wright, interview with Smith, p. 195. Wright talks at length about Martins Ferry, football in the Ohio River Valley, the importance of "place" to good writing, and his family background. "All of my relatives were working people," he remarks. "Back in the thirties I would have called them working class" (199). Except for one "distant cousin," Wright was the first of his family to attend college, and only the second to graduate from high school.

8. See Ron Fimrite, "The Valley Boys," *Sports Illustrated* 68, 23 May 1988, 78–90.

9. Ibid., 80.

10. Rebecca Harding Davis' *Life in the Iron Mills: or the Korl Woman* (Old Westbury, N.Y.: The Feminist Press, 1972), originally published in 1861, portrays the brutally hard lives of nineteenth-century America's working poor. The story was set in Wheeling, West Virginia, just across the Ohio River from Martins Ferry. Here is her description of the area in the early 1860s: "A cloudy day: do you know what that is in a town of iron-works? The sky sank down before dawn, muddy, flat, immovable. The air is thick, clammy with the breath of crowded human beings. . . . The idiosyncrasy of this town is smoke. It rolls sullenly in slow folds from the great chimneys of the iron-foundaries, and settles down in black, slimy pools on the muddy streets. Smoke on the wharves, smoke on the dingy boats, on the yellow river,—clinging in a coating of greasy soot to the house-front, the two faded poplars, the faces of passersby" (11).

11. Lou Groza, as quoted in "The Valley Boys," 81.

12. Phil Niekro, as quoted in "The Valley Boys," 84.

13. Alex Groza, as quoted in "The Valley Boys," 83.

14. Jason Ellis, as quoted in "The Valley Boys," 90.

15. As always, I thank Anne Wright for permission to quote these poems. Some

unpublished, some retitled, revised, and later published, the poems are gathered in the 5 March 1961 version of Wright's *Amenities of Stone*. For a discussion of the manuscript, see my *James Wright: The Poetry of a Grown Man* (Athens: Ohio University Press, 1989). See also the James Wright Papers, Literary Manuscripts Collection, Manuscripts Division, University of Minnesota Libraries, St. Paul, Minnesota.

16. Wright's comments appear in a letter to Knoepfle, dated 19 April 1961, quoted here with permission. The occasion was Wright's seeking Knoepfle's signature on a $10 check, made out to both men, received from *The Nation* for a published translation of Cesar Vallejo. Knoepfle's river poems and accompanying commentary appeared in *Audit*, 1, No. 10 (March 1961): 9–11. Knoepfle's interest in Midwestern rivers, and the men and women who consort with them, is evident throughout his work. See especially *Rivers into Islands* (University of Chicago Press), published just four years following Wright's letter, and *poems from the sangamon* (University of Illinois Press, 1985).

17. See James Wright Papers. As far as I can detect, no typescript of this unpublished poem exists, only the handwritten version scribbled beneath a draft of the poem "Rain." Wright's characteristically pinched handwriting here has the look of someone writing under a rush of emotion. Next to the poem's title, and separated by a slash, Wright has written what appears to be "Bulbs like a thunderhead trying to / snuff out / whole cities." A marginal note in Wright's handwriting and an arrow pointing roughly to the middle of the poem indicate: "This material used in *3 Letters*." Thirteen lines of "Continental Can" thus mysteriously reappear, somewhat revised, elsewhere in *Amenities*. Wright includes them in "Three Letters in One Evening," a long, unpublished poem offering a narrative on the death of Jenny, the dead lover/muse and ethereal spirit of place frequenting many of his poems. In this instance, each "car-hood is a dark sloop bearing / Living men *under* water" (my emphasis). For an extended discussion of that poem, see my *James Wright: The Poetry of a Grown Man*, pp. 113–17.

18. See Donald Hall, introduction to *Above the River: The Complete Poems* by James Wright (New York: Farrar, Straus and Giroux and University Presses of New England, a Wesleyan University Press Edition, 1990), xxxi, xxv. Hall also cites an incident, late at night, when Wright, obviously agitated, remarked angrily that ". . . *they* wanted him to go back to the mills. He made a speech about how he would never go back to the mills, no matter how much *they* tried to push him there; he had fought *them* all his life."

19. See Philip Levine, *They Feed They Lion* (New York: Atheneum, 1972), and *One for the Rose* (New York: Atheneum, 1981), respectively.

20. A good deal of irony surrounds Wright's mentioning that his "portrait hangs" in the Martins Ferry Public Library. That irony extends and deepens the local, social context of Wright's poem. In 1977—when "The Flying Eagles" appeared in *To a Blossoming Pear Tree*—Wright's portrait did *not* hang there, according to John Storck, director of the Martins Ferry Public Library. Storck postulates that the poet may have been referring to painter Ken Koehnlein's portrait of Wright which, though never on permanent display in the library, may have hung there once in exhibition. Either partial (and thus mis-) information or mere poetic licence may have prompted Wright to make his claim. Someone down home, perhaps a family member or old friend, may have seen the portrait, mistakenly assumed it was on permanent display, and then passed the word to Wright. Or Wright may have simply meant the present tense "hangs" to indicate that the por-

trait was hanging there when he heard the news and at the moment of his writing the poem. Then again, Wright may have purposely employed poetic licence, to honest effect, in the poem. Wright's widow, Anne, was aware of this distance between poetic and actual fact and resolved to rectify the situation. In 1990, at the James Wright Poetry Festival held yearly in Martins Ferry since Wright's death, Anne Wright unveiled—to the applause of the festival audience—a photo portrait of her husband. On permanent display in the library, the color photo portrait is an enlargement of one taken by Wright's brother, Ted, a photographer in Zanesville, Ohio.

Chapter Four

1. See Philip Levine, *Sweet Will* (New York: Atheneum, 1985), p. 15.

2. Hans-Georg Gadamer, *Truth and Method,* ed. and trans. Garrett Barden and John Cumming (New York: Seabury Press, 1975), p. 324. Gadamer's conception of how one relates to history and its texts is predicated on this notion of a conversation, and he returns to the metaphor repeatedly to illustrate his arguments. This instance, for my purposes, offers a splendid example.

3. Ibid., 273.

4. Ibid., 269, 271.

5. Ibid., 273.

6. Ibid., 267. Gadamer is adamant that this process requires the individual to retain a sense of his/her own historical presence when dealing with an historical subject: "True historical thinking must be aware of its own historicality. . . . The true historical object is not an object at all, but the unity of the one and the other, a relationship in which exist both the reality of history and the reality of historical understanding" (267).

7. Ibid., 273.

8. Calvin Bedient, "An Interview with Philip Levine," in *Don't Ask* by Philip Levine (Ann Arbor: University of Michigan Press, 1981), p. 92.

9. Ibid., 93.

10. Studs Terkel, "An Interview with Philip Levine," in *Don't Ask,* 82.

11. M. M. Bakhtin, *Problems of Dostoevsky's Poetics,* ed. and trans. Caryl Emerson (Minneapolis: University of Minnesota Press, 1984), p. 197.

12. Philip Levine, *New Selected Poems* (New York: Knopf, 1991), p. 86.

13. Terkel, 82.

14. Ibid., 83.

15. Levine, *New Selected Poems,* 137.

16. Martin Heidegger, *Poetry, Language, Thought,* trans. and intro. Albert Hofstadter (New York: Harper & Row, 1971), p. 94.

17. Levine, *New Selected Poems,* p. 180.

18. Ibid., 218.

19. Mera may very well have been one of two Italian anarchists "who ran a cleaning and dyeing operation down on" Levine's corner in Detroit, as Levine tells Calvin Bedient (92). The name Cipriano Mera may also refer, as Fred Marchant points out, to an anarchist militia leader of the same name who commanded a unit in Barcelona in 1936. See Marchant, "Cipriano Mera and the Lion: A Reading of Philip Levine," in *On the Poetry of Philip Levine: Stranger to Nothing,* ed. Christopher Buckley (Ann Arbor: University of Michigan Press, 1991), pp. 303–10. The two figures may have been merged, enabling Levine to link again the personal and

the historical, or as Marchant puts it, to make of the men "two faces of the same volatile spirit" (309).

20. Mona Simpson, "An Interview with Philip Levine," in *Don't Ask,* 185–86.

21. Philip Levine, *A Walk with Tom Jefferson* (New York: Knopf, 1991), p. 51.

22. Gadamer, p. 345.

23. In an intelligent essay, Jackson traces the structural evolution of Levine's longer poems in achieving a sense of "larger unity" (325). He argues that Levine chooses to "accommodate . . . discordant elements" rather than trying "to create a false and homogenous unit" (325). See Jackson's "The Long Embrace: Philip Levine's Longer Poems," in *On the Poetry of Philip Levine,* p. 335.

24. Fredric Jameson, "Reification and Utopia in Mass Culture," *Social Text* 1 (Winter 1979): 130.

25. Jameson, 131.

26. Philip Levine, *What Work Is* (New York: Knopf, 1991), p. 5.

27. Ibid., 18.

28. Levine's "On the Meeting of Garcia Lorca and Hart Crane" appeared in *The New Yorker,* 19 October 1992, 79. It serves as the opening poem of his *The Simple Truth* (New York: Knopf, 1994), p. 3. Levine's new book extends his interest in the convergence of private and public history, especially as this convergence shows itself in the lives of industrial workers, incidents set in World War II years, and his own experiences as a Jew.

Chapter Five

1. Yusef Komunyakaa, quoted from David Houghtaling, "A Radio Interview with Yusef Komunyakaa," WCBU, Peoria, IL: 24 February 1989.

2. Terry provocatively suggests that, much like the contribution of black soldiers in World War II, African-American soldiers' role in Vietnam will be diminished to the point of invisibility by the year 2000. See *Reading the Wind: The Literature of the Vietnam War,* an interpretive critique by Timothy J. Lomperis, with bibliographic commentary by John Clark Pratt (Durham: Duke University Press, 1987).

3. These books represent the broad range of soldier-poets' interpretations of their experiences in Vietnam; at least, they represent my favorites. For a helpful appraisal of these and other collections by soldier-poets, as well as a measured reading of *Hearts and Minds,* see W. D. Ehrhart, "Soldier-Poets of the Vietnam War," in *America Rediscovered: Critical Essays on Literature and Film of the Vietnam War,* ed. Owen W. Gilman, Jr. and Lorrie Smith (New York: Garland, 1990), pp. 313–31. A recent issue of *Journal of American Culture* 16 (fall 1993) is devoted to the topic "Poetry and the Vietnam War." In addition to the usual critical essays, it contains a section of new Vietnam War poetry by poets such as Komunyakaa, Bruce Weigl, and W. D. Ehrhart.

4. The distinction is crucial to Heidegger's discussions and it appears, in various forms, throughout the text. As usual with Heidegger, he makes much of small distinctions in word choice and etymology, and he carries through the distinction with the corresponding adjectives "historich" and "geschichtlich." "Historie" seems to refer to what Heidegger considers a "science of history." See pages 375 and 378 in Heidegger's pagination. For discussion of "Geschichte," the kind of history that "happens" and is authentically felt, see especially Sections 6 and 76 of *Being and Time.*

5. Yusef Komunyakaa, *Dien Cai Dau* (Middletown: Wesleyan University Press, 1988), p. 12. All further references to the text are to this edition.

6. Heidegger, "The Poet as Thinker," in *Poetry, Language, Thought,* trans. and intro. Albert Hofstadter (New York: Harper and Row, 1971), p. 10. The piece, itself a poetic rumination on the why and how and what of a poet's thinking, elsewhere describes the process of this interior dialogue: "We never come to thoughts. They come / to us. / / That is the proper hour of discourse" (6).

7. Komunyakaa, quoted from Houghtaling, 24 February 1989.

8. Jeffrey Walsh, *American War Literature: 1914 to Vietnam* (New York: St. Martin's, 1982), p. 203.

9. *Winning Hearts and Minds: War Poems by Vietnam Veterans* (New York: McGraw-Hill, 1972), ed. Larry Rottmann, Jan Barry, and Basil Paquet, drew a fair amount of attention in the United States. Although the work was honest and often poignant, critics have noted its lack of aesthetic sophistication (a consideration surely not paramount for most of the poets whose work was gathered there). Negative critical views of *Hearts and Minds* are offered, for example, by John Felsteiner in "American Poetry and the War in Vietnam," *Stand,* 19.2 (1978): 4–11, and Jeffrey Walsh, *American War Literature 1914 to Vietnam.* Walsh's somewhat brutal judgment is fairly summarized by these remarks: ". . . the war is, in general, presented in a rather repetitive, stereotyped, ahistorical and conventionally 'realistic' way. . . . What clearly is lacking is an available artistic mode of a sustained kind, an extended formal utterance or discourse in which the war's distinctive technical nature as well as its moral nature can be realised" (204).

10. I have in mind here the slew of protest poetry published during the war by a plethora of well-known poets. Their goal, admirable in most views, was to alert the American public to the senselessness of the war and to hasten its end. A partial list would surely include poets such as Robert Bly, James Wright, Denise Levertov, Robert Duncan, Allen Ginsberg, Galway Kinnell, William Stafford, and Marge Piercy. Although not meant to be inclusive, the list gives indication of the widespread vitality of a movement which came to be known as "Poets and Writers against the Vietnam War."

11. James Mersmann, *Out of the Vietnam Vortex: A Study of Poets and Poetry Against the War* (Lawrence: University Press of Kansas, 1974), p. 207.

12. George Liska, *War and Order: Reflections on Vietnam and History, Studies in International Affairs No. 11* (Baltimore: Johns Hopkins University Press, 1968), p. 87.

13. Ibid.

14. Ibid. Liska's *War and Order,* according to its foreword by Robert E. Osgood, then Director of the Washington Center of Foreign Policy Research, "elaborates the imperial conception, refines the scope and limits of its practical application, and relates it more specifically to America's involvement in the Vietnamese war" (vii). Liska's work appeared as Number 11 in the Studies in International Affairs series published by Johns Hopkins University Press. For a view opposing Liska's, see Number 10 in the same Johns Hopkins series, Robert W. Tucker, *Nation or Empire? The Debate over American Foreign Policy* (1968), which Mr. Osgood characterizes, quite correctly, as reaching "fundamentally different conclusions" from those reached in Liska's *War and Order* (vii).

15. Alvin Aubert, "Rare Instances of Reconciliation," *Epoch* 38 (spring 1989): 67.

16. Vicente Gotera, "Depending on the Light: Yusef Komunyakaa's *Dien Cai Dau,*" in *America Rediscovered: Critical Essays on Literature and Film of the Viet-*

nam War, ed. Owen W. Gilman, Jr. and Lorrie Smith (New York: Garland, 1990), p. 296.

17. Alvin Aubert, "Yusef Komunyakaa: The Unified Vision, Canonization, and Humanity," *African American Review* 27 (spring 1993): 122.

18. Hendrix himself described the song's source and content in terms more than vaguely related to war: "I had the thing on my mind about a dream I had that I was walking under the sea. It's linked to a story I read in a science fiction magazine about a purple death ray." These remarks appear, most recently, in the liner notes of the compact disc *Jimi Hendrix: The Ultimate Experience,* MCA Records, 1993.

19. M. M. Bakhtin, *Problems of Dostoevsky's Poetics,* ed. and trans. Caryl Emerson. *Theory and History of Literature, Volume 8* (Minneapolis: University of Minnesota Press, 1984), p. 184.

20. Komunyakaa, quoted from Houghtaling, 24 February 1989.

21. Evidence that Komunyakaa's dialogue with history was both enabled and extended by his work in *Dien Cai Dau* is everywhere present in his most recent collections, *Magic City* (1992) and *Neon Vernacular: New and Selected Poems* (1993), both published by Wesleyan University Press. *Neon Vernacular* won the 1994 Pulitzer Prize for Poetry. To my mind *Magic City* most clearly extends Komunyakaa's focus on the intersection of public and private history. Much of the book details his youth in Bogalusa, Louisiana, which was, as the book jacket describes, both "a center of Klan activity, and later a focus of Civil Rights efforts." Although beyond the scope of this essay, one poem from *Magic City,* "History Lesson," serves to illustrate my point. In the poem, a young black man is given instruction in the violent past of local racial "history." An older black woman, perhaps the youth's mother, points out the "Tassel of wind-whipped hemp knotted around a limb" where a black man was lynched twenty-five years earlier. She also tells him the story of an innocent black prizefighter tarred and feathered when mistakenly accused of raping a white woman. A white man, in black face, was the actual attacker. When a white man from Bogalusa Dry Cleaners explains away the racially charged killing of Emmett Till by suggesting Till "had begged for it / with his damn wolf whistle," the speaker reacts without thinking of the possible consequences:

> The hot words
> Swarmed out of my mouth like African bees
> & my fists were cocked,
> Hammers in the air. He popped
> The clutch when he turned the corner,
> As she pulled me into her arms
> & whispered, *Son, you ain't gonna live long.*

The poem is representative of the collection's—and Komunyakaa's—relentless search into public and private history.

Chapter Six

1. Should anyone doubt Rita Dove's devotion to historical subjects, witness her new verse play, *The Darker Face of the Earth* (Brownsville, Ore: Story Line Press, 1994). A Story Line Press flier provides this synopsis: "Amalia, a plantation's strong-willed white mistress, gives birth to a black son, much to the horror of her

husband. The child is auctioned into slavery. From that day, Amalia 'gets eviler by the hour' and takes to running the plantation with an iron will. Twenty years later, as a challenge, she buys Augustus, a 'bright-skinned' slave with a reputation for rebelliousness. Augustus, filled with hate toward the white man who raped his black mother, cannot resist the advances of Amalia—master and slave become lovers, unaware of their blood connection."

2. The idea that history is thus a construct has enjoyed notoriety for at least a couple of hundred years, as this book's introduction describes. Frank Kermode, in addition, argues in *History and Value* (Oxford: Clarendon Press, 1988) that as early as 1789, Johan Christoph Friedrich von Schiller, in his inaugural lecture at Jena, "distinguished between events and their history" (109). He also cites Lionel Gossman's paraphrase of Schiller's remarks: "The historian's perception is determined by his own situation, so that events are often torn out of the dense and complex web of their contemporary relations in order to be set in a pattern constructed retrospectively by the historian" (19). See Gossman, "History and Literature," in eds., *The Writing of History: Literary Form and Historical Understanding*, ed. R. H. Canary and H. Kozicki (Madison: University of Wisconsin Press, 1978): 3–39. In *Universe of the Mind,* Yuri Lotman adds simply that the historian "predicts backwards" (236) from the present to the past historical moment, that, in effect, "the historian reconstructs the events in the opposite direction" (237). See *Universe of the Mind: A Semiotic Theory of Culture,* trans. Ann Shukman (Bloomington: Indiana University Press, 1990).

3. Lotman, 217.

4. This remark appears in Dove's introduction to *Selected Poems* (New York, Vintage, 1993), xxi, in which she hazards an answer to the question,"What made you want to be a writer?"

5. Lotman, 240.

6. Quotations from Dove's poems, except for one sampling from *Grace Notes,* refer to the *Selected Poems.*

7. Claude Lévi-Strauss, *The Savage Mind* (Chicago: University of Chicago Press, 1966), p. 257.

8. Dove, *Selected Poems,* 136.

9. For a sensible study of the forces of language and culture operating in current poetry by American minority women, see Patricia Wallace's essay, "Divided Loyalties: Literal and Literary in the Work of Lorna Dee Cervantes, Cathy Song, and Rita Dove," *Mellus* 18, no. 3 (fall 1993): 3–19. Discussing the interaction of "literary" convention and imagination and "literal" fact in these poets' work, she summarizes the idea in these terms: "We call what is distinct from the poet's power 'history' or 'the actual' or 'the real,' and it acts as a gravitational field through and against which the poems move and have their life" (17).

10. Dove, as quoted in Stan Sanvel Rubin and Earl G. Ingersoll, "A Conversation with Rita Dove," *Black American Literature Forum* 20 (fall 1986): 229.

11. Robert McDowell, "The Assembling Vision of Rita Dove," *Callaloo* 9 (winter 1986): 66. In a feisty essay, McDowell compares Dove's "assembling vision" and her devotion to history against what he calls the typical fare of most literary magazines. Those poems, he argues, show that most young writers have been persuaded to "renounce realistic depiction and offer it up to the province of prose," thereby promoting "subjectivity and imagination-as-image." McDowell concludes, not without some justification, that this situation has "strangled a generation of poems" (61).

12. Rubin and Ingersoll, 236.

13. Ibid., 235–36.

14. Ibid., 236.

15. George Garrett, "Dreaming with Adam: Notes on Imaginary History," in *New Directions in Literary History,* ed. Ralph Cohen (Baltimore: Johns Hopkins University Press, 1974), p. 262.

16. In a recent interview Dove explicitly connects Thomas and her family with this social movement: "I grew up as a first-generation middle-class black child—which means that my grandparents were blue-collar workers who moved north from the South in this century, during the Great Migration; and my parents were the first generation to make it into the professional world. My father was a chemist; he's retired now. He was the first black chemist in the rubber industry, which is the only industry in Akron, Ohio. My mom is a housewife . . ." (145). See William Walsh, "Isn't Reality Magic?: An Interview with Rita Dove." *The Kenyon Review* 16 (summer 1994): 142–154. In addition, Dove's interest in the interplay of "History with a capital H" and its "underside," small history at work in the lives of ordinary folks, is evident in Steven Bellin's, "An Interview with Rita Dove," *Mississippi Review* 23, No. 3 (1995): 10–34. Working with small history, Dove says, is like "larding the roast: you stick in a little garlic and add some fat, and the meat tastes better" (19).

17. Alferdteen Harrison cites this figure in the preface to *Black Exodus: The Great Migration from the American South* (Jackson: University Press of Mississippi, (1991), p. vii. Other essays in this anthology edited by Harrison address issues such as the social and economic life of blacks, the call for black labor, and social change during the Great Migration.

18. Stewart E. Tolnay and E. M. Beck, "Rethinking the Role of Racial Violence in the Great Migration," in *Black Exodus,* p. 21.

19. *Atlanta Independent,* 26 May 1917, typescript copy in Carter G. Woodson Collection, Migration Papers, box 11, folder 148, Library of Congress. William Cohen quotes from this piece in "The Great Migration as a Lever for Social Change," *Black Exodus,* p. 73.

20. Arnold Rampersad, "The Poems of Rita Dove," *Callaloo* 9 (winter 1986), p. 55. In remarks both provocative and enlightening, Rampersad astutely situates Dove within the movement of twentieth-century African-American poets to a degree far beyond the intentions of my essay.

21. Rubin and Ingersoll, 232.

22. Helen Vendler, "In the Zoo of the New," *New York Review of Books,* 23 October 1986, 51.

Chapter Seven

1. Although perhaps no other poet has devoted a sonnet series to the subject of rock 'n' roll, numerous others have written individual poems touching, at least partly, on the cultural, historical, and personal significance of rock music. An anthology has for the first time gathered together many of those poems. Look for *Sweet Nothings: An Anthology of Rock and Roll in American Poetry,* ed. Jim Elledge (Bloomington: Indiana University Press, 1994). In addition, Wojahn's interest in the intersection of public and private history, present throughout his work, is evident in his *Late Empire* (Pittsburgh: University of Pittsburgh Press, 1994).

2. On 25 April 1991, I conducted a radio interview of David Wojahn, broadcast on WCBU, Peoria, IL.

3. Van Wyck Brooks, *America's Coming of Age* (1915; reprinted in *Van Wyck Brooks: The Early Years*, ed. Claire Sprague, New York: Harper, 1968, p. 82).

4. Wojahn's remarks appear in Jonathan Veitch's "An Interview with David Wojahn," *Contemporary Literature* 36, no. 3 (fall 1995): 392–412. Throughout the interview, Wojahn speaks compellingly of his efforts "to explore the links between the personal and the historical . . . to explore the possibilities of their juxtaposition. . . . I wouldn't call myself a social poet, any more than I would call myself exclusively a poet of autobiographical concerns. My poems are often about the cusp or borderline which divides these two poles." Wojahn delineates his own efforts in "describing a personal history and finding the ways that history is linked to the culture."

5. Stephen Greenblatt, *Renaissance Self-Fashioning: From More to Shakespeare* (Chicago: University of Chicago Press, 1980), pp. 210, 222.

6. Jurij Lotman, *The Structure of the Artistic Text*, trans. Ronald Vroon, Michigan Slavic Contributions No. 7 (Ann Arbor: University of Michigan Press, 1977), p. 99.

7. Stanley Fish, *Is There a Text in This Class?: The Authority of Interpretative Communities* (Cambridge: Harvard University Press, 1980), p. 326. Fish contends that "shared ways of seeing" exist within an interpretative community, and thus, this accounts for the way that poems are "constituted in unison" by the group's individual members (326).

8. Peter Wicke, *Rock Music: Culture, Aesthetics, and Sociology*, trans. Rachel Fogg (Cambridge: Cambridge University Press, 1990), p. 12.

9. Ibid., p. 10.

10. Ibid., p. 3.

11. Al Menconi, *Should My Child Listen to Rock Music?* (Elgin, Ill.: LifeJourney Books, 1991), p. 7. Menconi divides rock music into four primary categories: Dark Music, Hard Rock / Heavy Metal, Rap Music, and Pop / Dance Music. For each of these forms, Menconi theorizes the kind of teenager drawn to that music and the kinds of problems they are most likely to possess. The analysis is often dangerously simplistic. For instance, "metal fans," Menconi contends, "are often looking for validation, excitement, and acceptance by their peers because they don't believe it lies within themselves. . . . They frequently admit to not liking or trusting their present circumstances or environment. These young people will learn that the party always ends and there are always dues to pay" (9). Of course, Christian Fundamentalists have identified even more dire consequences for those who listen to rock 'n' roll: the loss of their eternal souls. Robert Fuller argues that many Christian Fundamentalists regard rock as the voice of the Antichrist—thus the "perfect vehicle for disseminating apostasy and anarchy" among America's youth (174). These Christian groups, Fuller contends, frequently demonize rock as source of both apocalyptic revolution and Communist propaganda, and worse, as means for the Antichrist to recruit new members into the fold of darkness. See his incisive study, *Naming the Antichrist: The History of an American Obsession* (New York: Oxford University Press, 1995).

12. David Wojahn, *Mystery Train* (Pittsburgh: University of Pittsburgh Press, 1990), p. 27. All further references to the text are to this edition.

13. Pat Brantlinger, *Bread and Circuses: Theories of Mass Culture as Social Decay* (Ithaca: Cornell University Press, 1983), p. 17.

14. Wojahn, *Mystery Train*, p. 85.

15. Andrew Ross, *No Respect: Intellectuals & Popular Culture* (New York and London: Routledge, 1989), p. 95.

16. Ibid., 96.

17. Wicke describes the band's first performance on 6 November 1975, at St. Martin's School of Art in London, as exhibiting "wild noise from the stage mixed with graphic insults of the audience . . . accompanied with a careful dramaturgy of aggression and force. . . . It was the concept of the band's manager, Malcom McLaren, for whom this represented the carefully prepared conversion of an avant-garde art project. McLaren professed the art philosophy of the 'International Situationists,' an (anti-) art concept which grew up in France in the fifties in relation to Paris Dadaism and which experienced a renaissance in British Art Schools in the sixties, while McLaren himself was studying at St. Martin's School of Art" (Wicke, 135–36).

18. Greenblatt poses a similar argument regarding containment and subversion of power in the early modern state in his provocative essay "Invisible Bullets: Renaissance Authority and Its Subversion." The essay was included in Jonathan Dollimore and Alan Sinfield, eds, *Political Shakespeare: New Essays in Cultural Materialism* (Ithaca: Cornell University Press, 1985), pp. 18–47. In short, Greenblatt argues that the ability of the ruling order—personified by the monarch—to initiate subversion so as to apply it for the ruling order's own purposes marks "the very condition of power" (45). Such a notion, of course, frighteningly limits the possibilities for personal or communal agency in the face of dominant governmental or cultural powers.

19. John Fuller, *Are the Kids All Right?: The Rock Generation and Its Hidden Death Wish* (New York: Times Books, 1981), p. 66. Fuller's book studies rock music's "death wish" throughout drunkenness and drugs, to these self-destructive performances on stage, to the scene of perhaps rock's greatest tragedy: the suffocation of eleven people, crushed by the press of the crowd, waiting for a concert by The Who at Cincinnati's Riverfront Coliseum, 3 December 1979.

20. Ibid., 86.

21. Jean-Paul Sartre, *What Is Literature* (Cambridge: Harvard University Press, 1988), p. 71.

22. Lotman, 299.

Chapter Eight

1. Ludwig Wittgenstein, *Tractatus Logico-Philosophicus,* trans. D. F. Pears and B. F. McGuinness, introduction by Bertrand Russell (London: Routledge and Kegan Paul, 1961), p. 147.

2. Ibid., 151.

3. Bertrand Russell, introduction to *Tractatus,* p. xxi.

4. Ludwig Wittgenstein, "Lecture on Ethics," *The Philosophical Review* 74 (January 1965): 11–12.

5. In Ray Monk's biography of Wittgenstein, Fania Pascal is quoted as saying that, in this regard, Wittgenstein always "conjured up a vision of a better you" (339). See *Ludwig Wittgenstein: The Duty of Genius* (New York: The Free Press, 1990).

6. Carolyn Forché, as quoted in Paul Rea, "An Interview with Carolyn Forché," *High Plains Literary Review* 2 (fall 1987): 155.

7. Carolyn Forché, "El Salvador: An Aide Memoire," *The American Poetry Review* (July/August 1981): 6.

8. In his *Poetry and the World* (New York: Ecco Press, 1988), Robert Pinsky calls Forché's *APR* piece "a remarkable essay," largely because it maps out one of what he sees as the two primary responsibilities of a poet. The first is to carry forward an art learned, at least partly, from the dead, to gift it to a future generation. The second duty Pinsky connects to Forché's notion of a "poetry of witness" that uses "the art to behold the actual evidence before us" and thus answers "for what we see" (87). In essence, Pinsky envisions Forché's task as embodying the fundamental poetic responsibility to refuse "the received idea of what poetry is" and to offer up one's own revision, which itself will be "resisted, violated, and renewed" (89). Holden, on the other hand, makes compelling argument in *Style and Authenticity in Postmodern Poetry* (Columbia: University of Missouri Press, 1986) against Forché's contention that no distinction exists between political and non-political poetry, asserting that her argument is unnecessarily reductive: "Virtually *any* act could be seen as having political significance, if construed as implying all the possible political actions which the actor could have taken but did not. To buy a steak dinner (instead of eating more cheaply and devoting the savings in money to the cause of the oppressed) could be construed, from a radical perspective, as a de facto form of oppression" (80). It is refreshing, not to mention instructive, to see two good minds differ so fundamentally and yet so eloquently on a single issue.

9. Forché, "El Salvaor: An Aide Memoire," 6.

10 Ibid.

11. Hans Magnus Enzenberger, *The Consciousness Industry: On Literature, Politics and the Media* (New York: Seabury Press, 1974), p. 75.

12. Forché, "A Lesson in Commitment," *TriQuarterly* 65 (winter 1986): 33.

13. Sharon Doubiago, "Towards an American Criticism: A Reading of Carolyn Forché's *The Country Between Us*," *The American Poetry Review* (January/February 1983): 37.

14. Ibid., 39.

15. Michael Greer, "Politicizing the Modern: Carolyn Forché in El Salvador and America," *The Centennial Review* 30 (spring 1986): 160.

16. Larry Levis, "War as Parable and War as Fact: Herbert and Forché," *The American Poetry Review* (January/February 1983): 10.

17. Ibid.

18. Carolyn Forché, introduction to *Against Forgetting: Twentieth-Century Poetry of Witness* (New York: Norton, 1993), p. 31.

19. Forché's "A Lesson in Commitment" provides an explicit description of how she came to go to El Salvador. Briefly, her working, in Spain, with Salvadoran poet Claribel Alegria to translate Alegria's poetry, began to open her eyes to the state of affairs in El Salvador. She was later approached in San Diego by Alegria's nephew, Leonel Gomez, to come to see why El Salvador might be the United States' next "Vietnam" (31–33).

20. Forché, "A Lesson in Commitment," 36.

21. M. M. Bakhtin, *The Dialogic Imagination,* ed. Michael Holquist, trans. Caryl Emerson and Michael Holquist (Austin: University of Texas Press, 1981), p. 282.

22. Ibid.

23. Ludwig Wittgenstein, as quoted in Friedrich Waismann, "Notes on Talks with Wittgenstein," *The Philosophical Review* 74 (January 1965): 12–13. This

text is a transcript of shorthand notes made by the late Friedrich Waismann during and after conversations with Wittgenstein and Moritz Schlick in 1929 and 1930. Here Wittgenstein is shown expanding on the issue of the inexpressibility of ethics and the nature of good and evil.

24. Carolyn Forché, *The Country Between Us* (New York: Harper and Row, 1981), p. 9. All further references to the book are to this edition.

25. Levis, 10.

26. Forché, "El Salvador: An Aide Memoire," 3.

27. Bakhtin, 281.

28. Forché, "A Lesson in Commitment," 36.

29. Carolyn Forché, *The Angel of History* (New York: Harper and Row, 1993). This quotation from Forché's extensive notes to the collection appears on page 81.

30. Walter Benjamin, *Illuminations,* ed. and intro. by Hannah Arendt, trans. Harry Zohn (New York: Harcourt, Brace, and World, Inc., 1968), p. 259.

31. Hannah Arendt, introduction to *Illuminations,* pp. 17–18.

32. Forché, *The Angel of History,* 3. Because Forché often extends these poems across the page from margin to margin, any effort to reproduce their lineation exactly is severely limited both by the page and by printing conventions. To clarify matters somewhat, I've indicated carry-over lines with an indention of two spaces.

33. George Steiner, *Real Presences* (Chicago: University of Chicago Press, 1989), p. 3.

34. For a thorough discussion of ethics in literature, see Alan Shapiro, *In Praise of the Impure: Poetry and the Ethical Imagination* (Evanston: TriQuarterly Books [Northwestern University Press], 1993). Shapiro envisions a reader's ethical imagination as a "supple ruler, bending round to fit the shape of each experience, keeping our certitudes attentive to that penumbral area where judgment stands in tension with sympathy, and principle with circumstance, bringing our certitudes to bear upon the most compelling and difficult occasions so as to test their limits and resiliencies" (10). Shapiro ascribes this same agency to authors, in fact to independent individuals operating within a cultural context. As a result, he quite rightly states that such a view is "radically at variance with, on the one hand, some current theories (structuralist/poststructuralist/Marxist) which emphasize the sociolinguistic construction of and constraints upon our individual lives and deny the kind of empathetic, creative, and volitional independence I am ascribing to them; and, on the other, with the cult of 'openness' which dominates the practice and teaching of creative writing" (11). See also Martha Nussbaum's sensitive and intelligent ruminations in *Love's Knowledge* (New York: Oxford University Press, 1990).

35. Jean-Paul Sartre, *What Is Literature,* intro. Steven Ungar (Cambridge: Harvard University Press, 1988), p. 71.

36. These fragments are widely culled from Wittgenstein's writings. For an example useful to our discussion, it's worth noting that the phrase "the visual field has not a form like this" is taken from *Tractatus,* 5.6331, page 117 in the edition I've cited. The line is removed from a fascinating discussion of how the limits of language provide the boundaries of our world. Wittgenstein argues that the metaphysical subject does not belong to the world but rather is "a limit of the world." Wittgenstein asks, "Where *in* the world is the metaphysical subject to be found? You will say that this is exactly like the case of the eye and the visual field. But really you do *not* see the eye. And nothing *in the visual field* allows you to infer that it is seen by an eye. For the form of the visual field is surely not like this."

Forché's efforts to extend her language make good sense in this light, for Wittgenstein suggests "the limits of language (of that language which alone I understand) mean the limits of *my* world" (115). He continues with a statement from which Forché also excerpts in "Book Codes: I," that the "philosophical self is not the human being, not the human body, or the human soul, with which psychology deals, but rather the metaphysical subject, the limit of the world—not part of it" (119).

Index

A NOTE ABOUT THE AUTHOR

Kevin Stein is poet, critic, and professor of English at Bradley University. He is the author of *James Wright: The Poetry of a Grown Man,* published by Ohio University Press in 1988. He lives in Dunlap, Illinois, with his wife Deb and their two children.